p. xiii

p. 3

p. 6

p. 15

~~[crossed out]~~

p. 17

p.~~[crossed out]~~

p. 20

~~[crossed out]~~

p. 36

p. 37

~~[crossed out]~~

(p. 47)

pp. 47-48) faces express internal character — the
soul — so did bldg. ?

(p. 53) soul — so did bldg. ?
p. 50

pp. 52-57 Schlegel and Schelling on art as an
   expression of the artist

p. 63 How Ruskin advanced beyond Rio

p. 67

p. 68

Is the account of the marriage necessary? See
the east PP. for its effect on his work.

75

89  Q. insisted on handwork because
it was necessary if [for his theory of] human personality

~~[crossed out]~~

91

93

p. 97 — adoring theory of the debt to Democracy!

# SAVAGE RUSKIN

# SAVAGE RUSKIN

Patrick Conner

Wayne State University Press
Detroit 1979

For Edwina

*First published 1979 by*
THE MACMILLAN PRESS LTD
*London and Basingstoke*
*Associated companies in Delhi*
*Dublin Hong Kong Johannesburg Lagos*
*Melbourne New York Singapore Tokyo*

Published in the United States and Canada by
Wayne State University Press, Detroit, Michigan 48202

*Printed in Great Britain*

**Library of Congress Cataloging in Publication Data**

Conner, Patrick, 1947–
  Savage Ruskin.

  Bibliography: p.
  Includes index.
  1.  Ruskin, John, 1819–1900—Aesthetics.  2.  Authors,
English—19th century—Biography.  3.  Art critics—
Great Britain—Biography.  I.  Title.
PR5267.A35C65        709.2′4 [B]         78–17051
ISBN 0–8143–1619–0

"I takes and paints
Hears no complaints
And sells before I'm dry;
Till savage Ruskin
He sticks his tusk in
Then nobody will buy."

'Poem by a Perfectly Furious Academician',
*Punch*, 1855

# Contents

# List of Plates

# Acknowledgements

Of the many people who have helped in the preparation of this book, I owe a particular debt to Quentin Bell, who initially aroused my interest in Ruskin and whose small book *Ruskin* remains the best introduction to the man and his writing. I am indebted also to James Dearden for reading the manuscript and making many useful suggestions, and to John Burrow, Edwina Conner, Jules Lubbock and Susan Sloman for a number of other corrections and ideas. For permission to quote from unpublished material I am grateful to the Trustees of the National Gallery and the Bodleian Library.

P.R.M.C.

# Introduction

Nearly three yards of shelf-space are needed to house the 39 volumes of Ruskin's *Works* in the 'Library Edition'; a little more if you have the *de luxe* binding, and a good deal more again if you add the letters and diaries published since volume 39 appeared in 1912. Elderly second-hand booksellers declare that in their younger days the shelves devoted to Ruskin's 'Library Edition' comprised three of the least profitable yards in the shop.

Today Ruskin has many followers, but still not half as many as he deserves, and I hope that the present book may prompt a few more people to read what Ruskin wrote. Or at least, some of what he wrote; much of his writing is now from many points of view only just worth reading, and to approach him incautiously is to risk being repelled for ever.

This book, I venture to suggest, is the first to investigate Britain's most influential art critic as a *critic* — not as a theorist, but as a judge of paintings, architecture and society. What did Ruskin admire, what did he hate, and why? How did his taste differ from the tastes of fellow-critics? What made his writing so much more persuasive than theirs? How, indeed, could a man whom the art 'establishment' did not take seriously, whose prejudices were so blatant, and whose marriage ended in such a public and humiliating way, gain an influence in matters of taste that (in England at least) no one has come near to rivalling?

Many of the answers to these questions are to be found in Ruskin's own books, but some answers are to be found also in his personal life. So I have included, alongside an interpretation of what he wrote, a brief survey of Ruskin's friends and loves, his hopes and disappointments. His writings were deeply affected by his individual circumstances, whether directly or indirectly, and I have tried to bring out one aspect of this in particular. Ruskin's personal relationships brought his most painful failures: and yet in his writing he went to great lengths in investing paintings and buildings with human, personal qualities. It is as if he poured into his mental world of humanised art all those emotions which he could not experience in his dealings with other men and women.

Still other answers are to be found in the writing of Ruskin's contemporaries and immediate predecessors. Theirs were the years in which 'the Public goes to bed with a Periodical in her hand and falls asleep with it beneath her pillow', and the articles, reviews, guide-books, lectures and historical sketches of the period can fairly indicate how far Ruskin's attitudes were untypical, and how far they were simply those in fashion at the time. These sources are not necessarily obscure or anonymous, for early Victorian Britain was a time of renewed enthusiasm for the arts, and the late 1830s and 1840s saw an unmistakable renaissance in art criticism. The literary periodicals took a sudden interest in artistic debates, other periodicals were set up to deal exclusively with the visual arts, and Continental critics were translated and read in cheap editions. The *genre* of art criticism quickly acquired fresh principles, in which the notions of 'expression' and 'character' played a leading part; Ruskin was soon to seize upon these ideas, and dramatically exploit them. Moreover he grew up in a period of widespread excitement and controversy about the arts, and many assumptions scarcely questioned since the *Discourses* of Sir Joshua Reynolds came under fierce attack.

This brings us to 'Savage Ruskin'. Ruskin did not, of course, entirely deserve this epithet, bestowed on him in 1855 by *Punch's* 'Perfectly Furious Academician', and he was remembered by many as a good-natured youth or as a gentle and benevolent old man. But it is 'savage Ruskin' with whom this book is concerned: the man who was not only the most widely-read interpreter of art of his century, but also the most outspoken, the most extravagant in his praise, and the most brutal in his criticism. We may decide that this outspokenness was an ineradicable part of his character, that he could not help overlooking the faults of his heroes and the virtues of his *bêtes noires*, and it may also be that his lack of human contact made him less accommodating, and less temperate in his judgements. But – and this will be a recurring theme – there is another possible reason, more accessible but hitherto unexplored, for Ruskin's extremes of taste. This lies in the remarkable method which he evolved (initially inspired by other writers) for interpreting pictures and buildings themselves as 'personalities', with a whole range of human attributes, which could then be praised or denounced almost as if they were actually people. By means of enormous ingenuity and a set of highly dubious assumptions, Ruskin took this process to bewitchingly plausible lengths.

To me this is the most fascinating aspect of Ruskin's writings: not his elaborate and largely outdated theories of sublime and picturesque, 'theoria' and 'aesthesis', beauty and imagination, but rather his skill in making his readers see pictures and places through his eyes, thereby bringing about radical changes in British taste. Against a formidable body of traditional opinion, he managed to get away with the most hyperbolic accolades and sweepingly damning judgements – that Dutch painting was worthless, that Michelangelo was second-rate, or that the Renaissance in architecture had all been a great mistake.

The influence of Ruskin and the profound changes in his own taste demonstrate how flimsy and easily overturned are our own preferences for certain artists and styles over others. It seems that a single individual, provided he believes in and promotes his own tastes strongly and skilfully enough, can affect the opinions and surroundings of millions of people. The more we consider the phenomenon of Ruskin, the more we distrust all arbiters of taste, and the more it appears that, given the appropriate propaganda, we can be made to appreciate anything. Ironically, Ruskin himself regarded good taste as a kind of state of grace, connected with admirable qualities of character and not easily achieved; yet a study of his life and writings can only make us doubt it.

Fairly suddenly, in the middle of his life, Ruskin became a vociferous critic of the prevailing opinions about money, value, work and competition – in short a critic of Victorian capitalism. The causes of this change of direction have never been adequately explored, nor will the present book attempt an explanation, but it does offer a pointer. It has often been suggested that, after an upbringing which cushioned him from the realities of most people's lives, he was inspired to social criticism by seeing the plight of working people, belatedly, at first hand. But this is not entirely plausible: there was no blinding light for Ruskin on the road to Venice, no sudden realisation of the injustices and miseries of contemporary life. An alternative possibility is that it was the extraordinary, relentless logic of his art criticism, and in particular his belief that each society could be analysed into detailed collective character-traits, which by its own momentum led him to explore the fundamentals of his own society.

But this is speculative and, ultimately, it does not matter much. What remains indisputable is that Ruskin was full of brilliant, one-sided ideas that will always be worth considering. He could be witty, and outrageous, and (in later life) quite uninhibited, as if he wrote his lectures and chapters late at night and forgot to cross out all the wilder notions next morning. When he did labour over a passage, the result is often tedious, in contrast to much of the rest which has the virtues and vices of effortless self-indulgence. Henry James had it only half right when he imagined an innocent visitor to Ruskin's 'world of art':

> Instead of a garden of delight, he finds a sort of assize court, in perpetual session. Instead of a place in which human re-sponsibilities are lightened and suspended, he finds a region governed by a kind of Draconic legislation.

James might have added that those laws could be altered or reversed at very short notice, and moreover that the court proceedings were never dull, since the judge presiding was an irresponsible, intemperate genius.

# 1 Cottages and Villas

1819 is a year notable, in retrospect, for its literary births. It marks the first appearance of George Eliot, Arthur Hugh Clough, Charles Kingsley, and – on 8 February, in Hunter Street, London – John Ruskin. Other celebrated fellow-infants of 1819 were Princess Victoria and Prince Albert; John Ruskin went up to Oxford in the year of Victoria's accession to the throne.

Like the prospective Queen, Ruskin had a firmly Evangelical upbringing. He had few friends of his own age, or toys: 'as I grew older, I had a cart, and a ball; and when I was five or six years old, two boxes of well-cut wooden bricks.' A dazzling Punch and Judy, brought by his pitying Croydon aunt, was put away for ever by his mother after the aunt had gone. He had to find his own pleasures, in the patterns of the carpet, or, through the window, in 'a marvellous iron post, out of which the water-carts were filled through beautiful little trap-doors, by pipes like boa-constrictors; and I was never weary of contemplating that mystery, and the delicious dripping consequent'.[1]

At the age of three, John Ruskin was taken to have his portrait painted by James Northcote, a venerable R.A. Ruskin proved such a patient subject that Northcote used him (or at least his face) as a model for another composition, a classical scene in which a small nude figure on a leopard-skin has a thorn plucked from his foot by a grimacing satyr. Two years later, however, a dog bit his lip, marring the cherubic features, and the scar remained in evidence for the rest of his life.

In 1823 the Ruskins moved from their small Bloomsbury home to a three-storeyed semi-detached house at the top of Herne Hill, in the southern suburbs of London. There was a pleasant garden: like the Garden of Eden, Ruskin observed, except that in the Ruskin garden 'all the fruit was forbidden; and there were no companionable beasts'. Sunday was the day he most disliked, for fiction was not allowed (a more liberal regime than Princess Victoria's,

however, under which fiction was prohibited all week), and
church-going seemed so dull that Monday became his favourite
day of the week. But he did learn to preach an eleven-word sermon
at home, 'over the red sofa cushions', to the delight of his mother
and her friends. Ruskin remembered that it began, 'People, be
good'. [2]

He naturally saw a great deal of his parents, both of whom
exerted a deep and lasting influence on him. They had married in
January 1818, under rather inauspicious circumstances. Ruskin's
father, John James, had by this time established himself as a
'merchant' in the sherry trade, but he had spent most of the
previous nine years paying off the debts incurred by the failure of
his own father (John Thomas)'s grocery business. All this time, if
Ruskin is to be believed, John James was engaged to his cousin
Margaret, who had been living in the Ruskin household, but his
parents were opposed to the marriage. Then in September 1817
Margaret's mother died; in the following month John James's
mother died; and John Thomas, who had suffered spells of severe
mental imbalance, killed himself the day after that. Three months
later, John James and Margaret were married.

Margaret had always been made to feel the poor relation, and so
it continued after her marriage. She had been born Margaret Cock,
daughter of William Cock, who kept a tavern in Croydon. John
James wrote on his son's birth certificate that William Cock had
been a 'master mariner', which is hardly likely; Ruskin described
him as a sailor, which he possibly might have been at one time,
although there is no evidence to support it. What is clear is that
John James was ashamed of his wife's relatives, who were not made
welcome at Herne Hill.

John James's mother evidently instilled a sense of religious
responsibility firmly into each of Ruskin's parents-to-be, but
especially into Margaret (for as she wrote to her son in 1808,
'freethinking Men are shocking to nature, but from an infidel
Woman the good Lord deliver us' [3]). She confirmed in Margaret
the evangelical doctrine to which her early upbringing may
already have predisposed her. From the start, Margaret's ambitions
for John were primarily religious; she told her son later that she had
solemnly 'devoted him to God' before he was born, and her
heartfelt desire (Ruskin recalled) was to make an evangelical
clergyman out of him. Left in charge of his early education, she set

him to learn long passages from the Scriptures, and to read the Bible through from Genesis to Revelation, an exercise which would take him about a year; then he began again at the Beginning.

When Ruskin was eight his mother started to teach him latin, but her classical knowledge soon ran out, and tutors were engaged: Dr Andrews, a local evangelical minister, and a Mr Rowbotham who trudged up the hill each week to teach French and mathematics. The classical scholarship of the Rev. Andrews was in its turn exhausted, and for a while Ruskin spent his mornings at the Rev. Thomas Dale's private school in Camberwell, together with a handful of other pupils.

Ruskin gives a grim and credible account of his South London childhood, but there was one great compensation: it occupied only ten months of each year. For the remaining two months, John James took his wife and son with him on long tours of the countryside, calling at country houses to arrange sales of his sherry and often managing to look at the paintings inside. Ruskin evidently loved these tours, which took his family through some of the most spectacular scenery in Britain; he composed poems about the places they visited, and studied mountains, rocks and plants. For his thirteenth birthday Ruskin was given a copy of Samuel Rogers's *Italy* – the lavish edition illustrated with steel engravings largely after Turner, which Ruskin began at once to copy. Next year was added *Sketches in Flanders and Germany*, whose engravings by Samuel Prout delighted both Ruskin and his father, and the upshot was a family tour of the Continent in 1833, taking in France, Germany, Switzerland and Italy.

Ruskin had by now begun to take drawing lessons, and in 1835 John James engaged an established watercolour artist, Copley Fielding, to communicate to Ruskin the subtle technique of successive tinted washes at which he was so adept. Fielding's lessons confirmed Ruskin's enthusiasm, although Ruskin was more inclined to follow Prout's detailed rendering of architectural detail than Fielding's suggestive art. That summer the Ruskins set off on a second tour abroad, with Ruskin himself sketching, observing buildings and countryside, and again making scholarly studies of the local geology. For he was already the author of papers on the colour of the water of the Rhine and on the strata of Mont Blanc, both published (comprising Ruskin's first serious work in print) in

J. C. Loudon's *Magazine of Natural History* of 1834.

It was these tours of England and Europe which gave rise to Ruskin's first major publication, *An Introduction to the Poetry of Architecture*, subtitled *The Architecture of the Nations of Europe considered in its Association with Natural Scenery and National Character*. It is little read today, which is a pity; and it was not much read in Ruskin's lifetime either, since it appeared in monthly instalments in the short-lived *Architectural Magazine* (November 1837 to December 1838) and was not published in book form in England until 1893. It was printed under the pseudonym of Kata Phusin ('according to nature'), moreover, whom few people can have connected with the 'Graduate of Oxford' who was stated to be the author of Ruskin's next work.

On the merits of *The Poetry of Architecture* such little critical opinion as exists is divided. John Claudius Loudon, editor of the magazine and no mean judge, thought it unmistakably the work of a man destined for literary fame, and told John James Ruskin that his son was 'certainly the greatest natural genius that ever it has been my fortune to become acquainted with'[4] – although Ruskin had not quite reached the age of 19; and *The Times*, praising the magazine, found his articles the most noteworthy aspect of it. A twentieth-century biographer, on the other hand, calls the series 'windy and pretentious . . . a knowledge of pure architecture seems wholly absent'.[5] Perhaps so, but it is a delightful work nevertheless, full of acute and provocative observations on the combinations of roofs and trees, on reflections in green lakes and in blue lakes, on eaves and gables, hills and flowers ('all dahlias and tulips . . . should be avoided like garlic') and innumerable other aspects of the relationship between buildings and their environment. In one chapter Ruskin parodies a wealthy patron's instructions to his architect: '. . . door supports by sphinxes, holding scrapers in their fore paws, and having their tails prolonged into warm-water pipes . . .' In another he illustrates and discusses eighteen varieties of European chimney, pointing out their attractions and their degrees of 'humbug'.

The book is worth reading for its own sake, but it also contains a key to much of Ruskin's writing. As he later remarked of it, 'I could not have put in fewer, or more inclusive words, the definition of what half my future life was to be spent in discoursing of'.[6] The theme is that the architecture of any country reflects its national character. The topic of national character was a familiar one at the time, but unlike Goethe and many others who dwelt upon it, Ruskin shows little patriotic bias, portraying the English and their buildings as good-humoured but rather pedestrian.

We can see the beginnings of the tactic later exploited in *The Stones of Venice*, in which Ruskin assimilated the qualities of the old Venetians to the qualities of their architecture. In *The Poetry of Architecture*, too, parallels are drawn between the villas and cottages of various European countries and their inhabitants; but here there is a third factor, natural scenery, to be matched up in addition – not an easy task. For example, Ruskin decides that 'melancholy' is the essential character of Italian lowland cottages, and also of Italian lowland scenery; but this would seem to require him to call the Italian lowlanders themselves 'melancholy', which would be obviously untrue, and instead he declares their poverty-stricken state 'melancholy to the mind'. Ruskin was to find this sort of contrived operation necessary again and again: first the colossal generalisation, and later the attempt to rescue it by brazen sleight of pen.

Typically, Ruskin escapes the most obvious difficulties in his self-imposed task by making two qualifications: firstly, that the private villa (his main topic) is a less reliable guide to national character than the cottage (about which he says relatively little), since the former is likely to be designed according to the whim of an individual; secondly, that although cottages should harmonise with the surrounding scenery, villas need not, and indeed should preferably contrast with it, thus enhancing the view in a different way.

So *The Poetry of Architecture* set the pattern for much of Ruskin's writing – perceptive in specific points but shaky in generalisations. It can be seen that Ruskin had already begun to apply human qualities to buildings – a device which he was to take to astonishingly ingenious extremes – but at this stage he did so only in a vague and unspecific way, regarding the general effect of a style as one of mood, be it 'melancholy', 'veneration' or 'non-chalance'. He remarked also that English architecture reflects the fact that the English mind lacks the extremes of passion and sensation, a view shared by another distinguished analyst of 'Englishness'.[7] Most interestingly he introduced the idea of 'pride' in architecture, the concept central to his portrayal fifteen years later of Renaissance Venice, with its 'pride of science', 'pride of state' and 'pride of system'. In *The Poetry of Architecture*, pride is found evident in the Swiss cottage, which dares to look so neat in the midst of the mighty Alps, so that 'the feelings are irritated at the imagined audacity of the inanimate object, with the self-conceit of its impotence'.[8]

Ruskin was by no means the first to describe buildings or scenery in such personal terms. It is sometimes supposed that his evangelical upbringing or his preoccupation with religion in general led to his 'moralistic' criticism; there is much more to it than that, however, for similar personal epithets were used a generation before Ruskin by a diverse group of writers: the theorists of the Picturesque. In a sense Ruskin was from first to last himself a Picturesque critic of architecture (although this is only distantly related to his *theories* of picturesque, sublime and beautiful, and must be distinguished in particular from his low opinion of the conventionally Picturesque in painting, which he condemned as superficial). In fact *The Poetry of Architecture* demonstrates that he learned to look at buildings, and even to describe them, in the manner of William Gilpin, Archibald Alison, Uvedale Price, Richard Payne Knight and their followers, and we can see that many of Ruskin's later and more famous attitudes to architecture grew out of this particular visual code.

To take first the question of 'pride'. When the landscape garden was conceived in England in the early eighteenth century, it was defended as being more 'natural' than the formal garden, and sometimes also for its supposed implications of 'liberty'; but as the movement was extended, particularly to architecture, Picturesque theorists began to justify their tastes on the additional grounds of being less 'pretentious' and 'affected' than those of their adversaries. 'So let th' approach and entrance to your place /Display no glitter, and affect no grace', advised Richard Payne Knight, adding that the stately mansion should be shown 'mix'd and blended', rather than 'in solitary pride'.[9] The Victorian age had no monopoly on moral undertones, which are often to be sensed in the writings of Giplin, Knight and Price. It is no accident that Mr Willoughby, the hero of Gilpin's *Moral Contrasts*, preferred the simplicities of nature to 'pompous trifles': indeed he 'had a great dislike for affectation in every shape'.[10]

Connoisseurs of the Picturesque, moreover, became increasingly interested in architecture. 'Among all the objects of art', wrote William Gilpin, 'the Picturesque eye is perhaps most inquisitive after the elegant relics of architecture; the ruined tower, the Gothic arch, the remains of Castles and abbeys. These are the richest legacies of art. They are consecrated by time; and almost deserve the veneration we pay to the works of nature itself'. The Picturesque, he continued, should appeal to the emotions rather than to the intellect, so that the traveller must 'let the imagination loose'.[11]

Ruskin's 'Lamp of Memory' was later to celebrate the effects of age on a building, in similar fashion. But in a more general sense, too, his attitude to architecture was essentially Picturesque. All the major writers in this genre (including Wordsworth, whose *Guide through the District of the Lakes* Ruskin may have read) insisted that a building could not be appreciated in isolation; it must be seen in its surroundings, as a part of the scenery. Hence their emphasis upon the colour and texture of building materials, and on the silhouette of roof and chimneys. But although the works of Vanbrugh were sometimes praised in this context, and several writers had alluded to the Picturesque nature of Gothic, there was nothing approaching a systematic study of the visual qualities of various styles of architecture – until Ruskin's *Poetry of Architecture*. The qualities which interested Ruskin here are the very ones which embodied the Picturesque for Gilpin and Uvedale Price: roughness, variety, irregularity, contrast, and effects of light and shade.

By Ruskin's time, this enthusiasm had spread to practising architects, and especially to designers of cottages and villas. In the early nineteenth century a stream of pattern-books poured out, with designs for asymmetrical elevations and rough or varied surfaces for country houses and cottages. If Ruskin disliked the more fanciful *cottages ornés*, just as his disciple Philip Webb was to despise the 'dilettante-picturesque' of Norman Shaw, he must at any rate have been well aware of the prevailing fashions.

Ruskin was further qualified as a Picturesque critic by his training in drawing and painting. Payne Knight had observed that only 'persons conversant with the art of painting' could gain pleasure from the objects and circumstances called Picturesque,[12] and Ruskin certainly viewed buildings with a painter's eye. In this he was encouraged by Samuel Prout, a family friend and neighbour at Herne Hill: Ruskin was imitating Prout in his

drawings as early as 1835, and a Prout painting which hung in
Ruskin's childhood home had taught him, he later wrote, to
admire ruggedness. Ruskin numbered Prout 'among the true
masters of the nobler Picturesque', and found especial merit in
Prout's depiction of architecture. [13] In the first volume of *Modern
Painters*, Ruskin took the view that although other artists had
made contributions to the painting of architecture, Prout was the
first to represent the particular *feeling* of old buildings that Ruskin
felt so strongly. Before Prout's time, he thought, buildings had
been made to appear too neat and antiseptic; 'bricks fell out
methodically, windows opened and shut by rule: stones were
clipped at regular intervals'. What Ruskin admired in Prout's
buildings is very much what Gilpin would have admired — 'the
rent and the rust, the fissure, the lichen and the weed'. [14] For the
lack of these he condemned the neatness of the Swiss cottages in
*The Poetry of Architecture*.

   Another theme of the Picturesque theorists of the later
eighteenth and early nineteenth centuries, and one of especial
relevance to Ruskin, was that a building or location should possess
or express its own particular 'character', or as Knight and Repton
put it, 'characteristicness'. 'Doctor Syntax', the hero of William
Combe's satire on Picturesque touring, knew the value of this
quality:

> For I most solemnly aver
> That he from genuine taste must err
> Who flouts at grace or character. [15]

   Now the demand for character in architecture was not restricted
to the literature of the Picturesque, and it took more than one
form. Among architects and writers on architecture pure and
simple, it often meant that a building should fall into some
distinctive stylistic or functional category, such as 'Grecian',
'castellated' or 'cowshed'. Thus Sir John Soane claimed that every
building 'should express clearly its Destination and Character,
marked in the most decided and indisputed manner', [16] and C.R.
Cockerell praised Wren by saying that for him 'character was the
basis of art'. [17] But more often, and especially in the 1840s, such
writers were simply concerned that the nineteenth century should
produce some characteristic style of its own, or in the case of
churches, consistently adopt a particular style of the past. [18]

Among the theorists of the Picturesque, however, 'character' meant something else again. The term was first applied to gardens and natural scenery: in this sense Payne Knight wrote of the separate characters of scenery (such as 'classical', 'romantic' and 'grotesque'), and the famous trinity of the sublime, the beautiful and the picturesque were sometimes described as 'characters'. But such categories are not so self-evident as 'Grecian', 'castellated' or 'cowshed', and it was therefore necessary to explore the emotional overtones and human associations of a location in order to decide whether it possessed the required 'character'. Beautiful spots in a landscape, wrote Archibald Alison, 'are always distinguished by some prominent character; the character of Greatness, Wildness, Gaiety, Tranquillity or Melancholy . . . In the laying out of grounds, therefore, some character is necessary, to which we may refer the relation of the different parts.' Sometimes this approach led to fine discriminations and acute perceptions, such as are contained in Alison's discussion of the effects of combining certain forms with certain materials, or in the passage which suggests that 'winding Forms are (thus) expressive to us of Volition and Ease, and angular Forms of the operation of Force or Constraint'.[19]

Over architecture Alison was less subtle, but here too he was alive to the emotional connotations of various forms. He discerned a peculiar character in each order of classical architecture: 'The Tuscan is distinguished by its Severity; the Doric by its Simplicity; the Ionic by its Elegance; the Corinthian and Composite by their Lightness and Gaiety.' Furthermore, the various rooms in a house should exhibit 'distinct characters, as those of Gaiety, Simplicity, Solemnity, Grandeur, Magnificence &c.'[20]

Half a century later, Ruskin was to attack 'Alison the metaphysician' for his contradictions and vague classifications. But he might also have recognised that Alson had begun to use the tactic which Ruskin was himself to exploit, of attributing human qualities and emotions to buildings. This is especially clear in Alison's second edition, in which he added a chapter 'Of the Beauty of the Human Countenance and Form' listing facial qualities of the same kind as those he had previously noted in architecture—'the pale complexion is expressive of Gentleness, Tenderness and Debility; when blooming of Gaiety and Vigour and Animation', and so on.[1] There were other writers preceding Ruskin who more explicitly likened architecture to a human face.

For W.H. Leeds, 'the charm of physiognomy' predominated in
Gothic buildings, and according to J.C. Loudon, 'Character in
architecture, as in physiognomy, is produced by the prevalence of
certain distinctive features, by which a countenance, or a building,
is at once distinguished from every other of the same kind'. Some
buildings, for example, might 'exhibit what is analogous to
nobleness of character', while others 'will appear to possess a
character of extravagance or caprice'.[22] This is the point at
which Ruskin intervened in 1837. Like many of his predecessors,
he complained that in a large number of modern buildings 'there is
no character whatever'; and, like some of these predecessors, he
meant by character more than distinctive style, for in the same
breath he mocked at the practice of 'mimicking Swiss chalets'
(referring no doubt to Robinson's Swiss Cottage in Hampstead of
1829).[23] But whereas Alison or Loudon thought of a building as
expressing a single human trait, to Ruskin character could involve
a whole complex of qualities. And in Ruskin's book there is the
added implication that these qualities are somehow communicated
from the native builders through their unconscious but deep-
rooted feelings and temperament. When Ruskin stated, then, that
people do not yet 'have any idea of a fixed character, stamped on
a class of national edifices',[24] he already had in mind something
more than the associations of Alison or the analogues of Loudon.

This is made clear in the second part of *The Poetry of
Architecture* – Ruskin's ambitious treatment of 'The Villa'. Since
national idiosyncracies are more marked here than in 'The
Cottage', Ruskin could attempt a correspondingly more detailed
comparison with the character of the race. He begins by discussing
the lines, proportions, ornaments, colouring and materials of the
Italian villa of the region of Como, and after briefly mentioning
the rest of Italy, concludes that:

> The mind of the Italian, sweet and smiling in its operations, deep
> and silent in its emotions, was thus, in some degree, typified by
> those abodes in which he was wont to retire.[25]

Ruskin had visited Northern Italy twice, and did not yet know
much of the Italian people (whom he was later to dislike). One might
suspect this from his calling them 'silent in [their] emotions'. His
image of the typical Italian seems to owe something to Shelley,
whose *Cenci* he quotes in likening the dark places of the villa to the

deep-laid passions of 'the ancient system of Italian life'; and something to Claude and Poussin, to whom he also refers in the same chapter.[26] But when he comes to deal with the English and their villas, he cannot get away with such a simplistic stereotype. Fortunately he has a wide choice of styles, from which he selects Elizabethan as 'the only style of villa architecture which can be called English'. Though 'utterly barbarous as architecture', it is authentic because (Ruskin argues questionably) it was originally intended for a land of forests, to which it is suited by its irregularity, variety of form, and 'rich and entangled ornament'. Next, he lists its characteristics – Ruskin's first fully-fledged passage of that peculiarly Ruskinian criticism which describes a work of art in terms of a cluster of human attributes:

... It is a humourist, an odd, twisted, independent being, with a great deal of mixed, obstinate, and occasionally absurd, originality. It is . . .exactly typical of the mind of its inhabitant: not noble in its taste, not haughty in its recreation, not pure in its preception of beauty; but domestic in its pleasures, fond of matter of fact rather than of imagination, yet sparkling with odd wit and grotesque association . . .But the Englishman's villa is full of effort: It is a business with him to be playful, an infinite labour to be ornamental: he forces his amusement with fits of contrasted thought, with mingling of minor touches of humour, with a good deal of sulkiness, but with no melancholy . . .[27]

The personality described here is the recognisable ancestor of the character Ruskin later discovered in Venetian Gothic. The essential traits are here, 'independent', 'original' and 'not haughty'. Ruskin had not yet quite reached the point of attributing all these qualities to the builders, though he had introduced the idea that they could be motivated by 'deep-rooted feeling', and he had promised a series of essays on the habitations of the most distinguished men of Europe, 'showing how the alterations which they directed, and the expression which they bestowed, cor-responded with the turn of their emotions, and leading in-tellectual faculties'.[28] This project was never fulfilled: Ruskin's subsequent writing tended to regard painting as an expression of the individual creator, but architecture as an expression of the community. In this early work, however, his manipulations of

national character and architecture were not intended to demonstrate the *expression* of one in the other so much as a
*correspondence* between the two.

Ruskin was already sensitive to the social and political overtones
of architecture. He saw the villa as a type of building appropriate to
Italy, 'where the Roman power secured tranquillity', and where
power was distributed among a large number of individuals.
Palaces, on the other hand, suited monarchical Austria; and 'in
perfect republics, as in Switzerland, the power is so split among the
multitude, that nobody can build himself anything'.[29] Later he
suggested that a villa should not be situated in a district where the
land 'reminds us of the necessity of labour' and of 'the continuous
struggle of suffering existence.'[30] In subsequent books, Ruskin
moved two steps forward in his analysis. He sensed these overtones
in the details of architecture, not simply in the general effect; and
after at first considering whether a building was merely *reminiscent*
of rewarding work, he came to ask the famous question of *Seven
Lamps*, 'was the carver happy while he was about it?'[31]

The list of characteristics attributed to the Elizabethan villa is
worth examining. Like his seven lamps of architecture, they fall
into various logical categories. Some are qualities which can be
applied objectively and literally to a building, such as 'twisted' and
'mixed'. Others are less objective, though still applicable
literally — 'odd', 'absurd', 'sparkling'. Others apparently refer in
the first instance to the builders — 'original', 'matter-of-fact', 'with
odd wit', 'full of effort'; and there are others again which, though
human qualities, do not seem to refer to the builders — 'humourist', 'independent', 'obstinate', 'with a good deal of sulkiness'. The
magical persuasiveness of Ruskin's descriptions is due in considerable measure to his conflating all these, so that the reader, borne
along by balanced phrases and rhythmic cadences, accepts the
metaphorical with the literal, and the personal associations with
the undoubted fact. In *The Stones of Venice* Ruskin went further,
seeking to justify his epithets — even those in the last of the
categories above — by pointing to external conditions: to the lack
of supervision enjoyed by Venetian masons, for instance, which
lent authority to his description of Venetian buildings as 'independent' in appearance.

Superficially similar examples of 'personal' description often
crop up in the novels of the time; no doubt the Victorian public

enjoyed passages and paintings which bestowed human characteristics on non-human participants, whether these were buildings,
birds, animals or trees. Dickens was a notable exponent. Consider
his well-known description of the Maypole inn at the beginning of
*Barnaby Rudge* (1841):

> With its overhanging stories, drowsy little panes of glass, and
> front bulging out and projecting over the pathway, the old house
> looked as if it were nodding in its sleep. Indeed it needed no very
> great strength of fancy to detect it in other resemblances to
> humanity. The bricks of which it was built had originally been a
> deep dark red, but had grown yellow and discoloured like an old
> man's skin; the sturdy timbers had decayed like teeth; and here
> and there the ivy, like a warm garment to comfort in its age,
> wrapped its green leaves closely round the time-worn walls.

But notice that the human attributes here are purely physical
ones. The Maypole does not become a person in any sense other
than in that its features are those of an old, fat, dozing man; we
learn nothing of any mental traits or emotions that he may possess.
And this perhaps marks a difference between an imaginative simile
and an attempt at artistic appreciation.

Ruskin does sometimes operate at Dickens's level: he writes of
the 'nod' and 'frown' of a wall, and refers to the 'good-humoured
red faces' of bricks.[32] But there is something jarring and blatant in
Ruskin's use of such methods, and one feels that he is forsaking his
subtly insidious suggestiveness for a novelistic short-cut. Even
Ruskin's description of the English villa – his most Dickensian
character – he is principally concerned not with the most obvious
aspects of its physique, but with the emotional and intellectual aura
which its style suggests, and suggests, furthermore, to the observer
who has a reasonable knowledge of architectural forms. His
catalogue of the characteristics of the Elizabethan villa already
betrays a tendency to find great significance in the smallest details
of sculpture and ornament. It is aimed at the aesthete, the
connoisseur of the picturesque, who is expected to consider it with
a degree of seriousness.

A closer parallel to Dickens might be the architect George
Wightwick, whose book *The Palace of Architecture* (1840) is clearly
an attempt to exploit the growing amateur interest by appealing to

the imagination of 'the general reader'. This expensively produced
volume was in fact addressed to 'readers of either sex' – in other
words, to women – and it aspired to 'that station in regard to
Architecture, which the Novels of Scott occupy in relation to
History'. It might have been designed as the counterpart of *The
Poetry of Architecture*, which was published shortly before, and
which dealt only with cottages and villages; Wightwick's book
deals mainly with temples and cathedrals. Like Ruskin's work,
*The Palace of Architecture* contains some Dickensian simile: the
rounded Norman arch is likened to 'the bending from of the self-
humiliated Pilgrim', and the pointed Gothic arch to 'the erect
figure of the robed and mitred Bishop'. Wightwick also indulges
in a little religious symbolism, but this is imaginative rather than
strictly ecclesiological, so that a spire is held to represent 'the ever-
expanding capacity of God's love' and the pinnacles around its base
are 'the congregation of penitents at the foot of mercy'.[33]

Occasionally Wightwick takes the Ruskinian course of divining
a mentality in a building, such as 'an expression of service' in the
Corinthian portico, or 'firm resolve' in St Paul's. But fact is clearly
distinguished from fancy, and there are no examples to suggest to
us that the temperament of a race can somehow be transmitted in
detail into its buildings.

In summary, Ruskin's *Poetry of Architecture* gave a more precise
meaning to the current notion of 'character' in architecture. The
next chapters will suggest that attitudes to painting were developing in a similar way, and that the search for 'character' in building,
initiated by the followers of the Picturesque, bears striking
resemblances to a contemporary striving after 'expression' in
painting. Both seem to represent the same urge to find human
significance in art. Abstract beauty was not enough for the critics of
the early nineteenth century, and in both arts a demand for
'expression' or 'character' of *some* kind, no matter what, preceded
an enthusiasm for certain particular types.

Indeed, 'expression' was often used as a synonym for 'character'
by Picturesque theories. Alison wrote of 'Character or Expression',
seeming to use the two interchangeably,[34] and Loudon made
little distinction between the two in practice, although he hazarded
a Lockean classification of 'character' as residing in objects and
'expression' as being an idea in the mind.[35]

It was Loudon again who most clearly and prophetically

enunciated the principle that could be called dominating aesthetic of the Victorian age:

> (But) intricacy, harmony, variety or any other merely pleasing combination of the qualities or modifications of matter, are far inferior to such as are expressive of sentiment or character.[36]

I believe that Ruskin's ability to exploit this preference had a great deal to do with the eventual influence of his writing. Where other critics could only repeat the catch-phases of 'character' and 'expression', he was able to develop his Picturesque perceptions into something more. Even in the earliest years of his career, Ruskin was hypersensitive to every nuance of architecture and landscape, every emotional overtone, every subtlety of context and propriety. But we shall see how, in trying to give more substance to his hints and metaphors, he developed a technique of personalising architecture, and found ever greater significance in its personal and social implications; until he beguiled himself (and others) into seeing in a building a complete manifestation of a society's human qualities.

# 2 The Graduate of Oxford

Ruskin's own account of his upbringing, contained in the autobiographical *Praeterita*, leaves the impression that his mother was the dominant influence in forming his character. But *Praeterita*, written when Ruskin was in his sixties, is not always to be trusted; and his early correspondence with his father suggests that John James Ruskin may have had an equal effect on his young son. John James's prime concern was with this world rather than the next. When Ruskin reached the age of twelve, his father allowed him a taste of wine, Byron at dessert, and visits to the theatre; on these last occasions Margaret's principles forced her to stay at home.

John James was concerned above all with his son's social status. If Ruskin had indeed become a bishop, it is hard to imagine which of his parents would have been the more gratified. John James was conscious that he was a merchant and a grocer's son, whom no amount of wealth could turn into a gentleman; and that his wife, an innkeeper's daughter, was still further removed from the gentry. He determined that his son should suffer no such disadvantages, and had him enrolled at that bastion of the aristocracy, Christ Church, Oxford. He entered him, moreover, as a 'gentleman-commoner', although gentlemen-commoners were generally moneyed, well-born and uninterested in study, and Ruskin had the first qualification only. He later gave a very credible account of his college days, describing how 'I had been received as a good-humoured and inoffensive cur, contemptuously, yet kindly, among the dogs of race at the gentlemen-commoners' table'. After the small front parlour in Herne Hill, Ruskin could never feel at home as he dined in the great hall. And he amazed his fellow gentlemen by taking trouble over an essay; he was soon made to feel 'the impropriety of writing an essay with any meaning in it, like vulgar students'.[1]

But his friends were gentlemen indeed, for although they might sometimes ride round the quad on Ruskin's back, they never let slip a sarcastic remark about Ruskin's habit of spending his evenings with his mother. She had installed herself conveniently in the High Street — anxious, no doubt, lest Oxford life lead her hitherto sheltered son astray.

Her fears were justified. Ruskin did not learn to hunt, gamble or set fire to the college, but he did come into contact at Oxford with influences which in the long run were to disappoint his mother much more. Firstly, the Oxford Movement was at its height: most of the 'Tracts for the Times', controversial in their attempts to bring the Church of England nearer Rome, were published while Ruskin was an undergraduate. His evangelical upbringing had been too strong for there to be any question of instant conversion, but Ruskin's diaries and letters now and again betray a certain regard for the 'high taste and intellect' of Newman, Keble and Pusey. Both the Ruskin parents were violently anti-Catholic, and opposed to the recent Catholic Emancipation Act; in Ruskin's second year at Oxford, his father claimed in a newspaper article (later republished by Ruskin) that the very proximity of Roman Catholics to the British Constitution placed the nation in jeopardy. Ruskin's own publications of the 1840s are full of aggressively anti-Catholic allusions. Yet all the while there were nagging doubts. In 1850 Ruskin confided to his college friend, Henry Acland, that the 'blinking Puseyisms' and the 'dreadful Hammers' of geology were between them shredding his faith into rags.

Oxford cannot be blamed for Ruskin's passion for geology, which was long-standing — he had begun a 'Mineralogical Dictionary' at the age of twelve, and published a geological paper at fifteen. At Christ Church he soon came into contact with one of the most prominent and controversial geologists of the time, the Rev. William Buckland. Buckland was a flamboyant eccentric: exotic animals were often to be found in his rooms, either roaming freely about or served up at the dinner-table. At Buckland's table Ruskin 'met the leading scientific men of the day',[2] he remembered, and others who were not yet conspicuous, such as Charles Darwin.

The great geological controversies of the early nineteenth

century had implications far beyond purely scientific circles. For there had been a disturbing number of geological findings which did not seem, on the face of it, to confirm the Biblical account of the Earth's creation. If, as several geologists suggested, the Creation took longer than a week, did not this mean that Genesis was false — although God had revealed it directly to Moses? And if Genesis was false, might not all of Holy Scripture be subject to doubt? It was a devastating possibility. Buckland tried nobly to reconcile Genesis and geology: his inaugural *Vindiciae Geologicae* (1820) affirmed the moral authority of the Bible, but had to admit that there might be 'occasional differences touching minute details of historical events'. He suggested that the Genesis text was ambiguous, and should be taken to mean that heaven and earth were created not 'on the first day' but 'in the beginning', which expresses 'an undefined period of time' sufficient for geological changes.[3]

In 1823 Buckland won approval by putting forward geological evidence for the existence of the Flood, but it did not escape the critics' notice that he asserted that all species were extinguished by the waters, whereas the Bible keeps two of each. Furthermore, he took the 'days' of the Genesis account as a metaphorical description of indefinite lengths of time.[4]

Then in 1836, the year before Ruskin's arrival at Oxford, Buckland's 'Bridgewater Treatise' was published, its purpose being to show how geology provided evidence of God's 'stupendous Intelligence and Power'. The book satisfied neither side. It allowed the possibility of 'the direct agency of Creative Interference', which was welcome to those who wanted to believe in miracles, but not to those (such as Sir Charles Lyell) who found sufficient explanation in uniform natural forces. On the other hand Buckland dropped his claim that the Biblical Flood had actually happened, and made it clear that Genesis could not be taken literally. This pill was sugared with continual declarations of piety, but these were not enough to prevent Dean Cockburn of York from publicly denouncing the book as tending to atheism.

Such was the conflict of ideas in which Ruskin could not fail to become involved. In 1840 he was made a Fellow of the Geological Society, of which, he said, it was his ambition to be President. In the next few years he seems often to have acted as Buckland's assistant, and associated with other leading geologists. Did this weaken the Bible-based evangelical faith in which he had been brought up? One would not believe it if one judged merely from the confidently orthodox tone of his published writings in the 1840s. But his private correspondence tells a very different story. In 1842, when he had only recently come down from Oxford, he confessed to a college friend (the Rev. Edward Clayton): 'I should almost be glad to be what you call me – a private judgement man – rather than the nothing I am; but I feel it so intolerably difficult to come to any conclusion on the matter, that I remain neither one thing nor the other.'[5] Next year he sent Clayton a little essay arguing in effect that there was death before Adam in Eden, and probably elsewhere too – a trivial point, it might seem today, but a very significant one for the doubt-racked Ruskin, who came down against the literal Biblical version accepted by his parents in favour of the heretical viewpoint based on geological evidence. The Biblical account was not exactly mistaken, wrote Ruskin, but 'very much like an Eastern allegory'.[6]

More than once in the ensuing years Ruskin confessed in letters to his friends how strongly he felt 'the geological difficulty', which also troubled many of his contemporaries. In addition he experienced moral doubts (again in common with many others) about aspects of Biblical and Christian teaching, such as the doctrine of eternal punishment. Sincere doubting of this kind played a major part in the intellectual life of the 1840s, often tormenting those concerned; sometimes it was also associated with a certain sense of adventure and danger – a sense caught by J. A. Froude (later a friend of Ruskin's) in his melodramatic, ambiguous novel on doubt, *The Nemesis of Faith*, which was ritually burnt by Professor Sewell in 1849. Moreover doubters were expected to keep their doubts to themselves, for the general good, and Ruskin duly maintained a firmly orthodox attitude in print throughout the 1840s and 50s, although year by year his faith was disappearing.

The varieties of Victorian doubt make a fascinating study; Ruskin underwent many of them, geological and moral, Tractarian and Liberal. And Ruskin's doubts have an added interest, in that as his religious opinions changed, so did his attitudes to art and artists. We can see later how his final 'unconversion' in the late 1850s involved a shift in allegiance away from the 'Christian' art of the early Italian masters towards paintings which he described, with relish, as 'frankly animal'.

Meanwhile, Ruskin had suffered a disappointment of another kind. Early in 1836 the four daughters of his father's partner in the sherry business, Pedro Domecq, came to stay at Herne Hill: they were Roman Catholics but lively and pretty, and Ruskin, who had had little experience of girls of any kind, quickly fell in love with the eldest, Adèle Clotilde, aged fifteen. It was a serious matter for Ruskin, though his parents realised this too late. She continued to visit Herne Hill, and Ruskin wrote for her a short story about Neapolitan bandits, a Venetian tragedy, and a series of love poems. Adèle was flattered and amused, but no more than that. In 1839 a marriage was arranged between Adèle and a young French Baron, whom she duly married the next year. Ruskin, agonised, commemorated the final parting with a long poem in the manner of Shelley:

> Farewell! that glance so swift, so bright,
> Was lightly given, but not in vain;
> For, day by day, its visioned light
> Must burn within my brain. . . .[7]

In an effort to forget Adèle he plunged himself into his studies, but even here he was unlucky. While working desperately for his final examinations, Ruskin experienced a tickling cough and a taste of blood. His mother, on hand as always, took him home, and his degree was postponed. The three Ruskins went on a long tour of Italy, with John sketching and versifying; he was ill again, but in Switzerland he finally recovered.

At this stage of his life, most of Ruskin's literary efforts were directed to poetry, encouraged all the while by his father. His first work of any kind to be published was a poem ('Skiddaw! upon thy cliffs the sun shines bright . . .'), written at the age of nine. Two years later, when the family holidayed in the Lake District, Ruskin recorded the event in a detailed 'Iteriad'. A number of pieces in various idioms followed, and were published in the fashionable annuals alongside contributions from such figures as Coleridge, Southey and the young Tennyson. At Oxford, Ruskin interspersed his lyrical offerings to Adèle with Byronic poems on themes from Herodotus. His Alpine poems of the early 1840s are sometimes regarded as his best; but personally I prefer three macabre poems about the Scythians. *The Scythian Grave*, pub-

lished in 1838, refers to that tribe's custom of setting up a guard of
fifty fully-armed corpses over the tombs of their kings:

> The foul hyenas howl and haunt
> About their charnel lair;
> The flickering rags of flesh they flaunt
> Within the plague-struck air:
> But still the skulls do gaze and grin,
> Though the worms have gnawed the nerves within;
> And the jointed toes, and the fleshless heel,
> Clatter and clank in their stirrup of steel.[8]

Perhaps Ruskin's verses came too easily to him. Some lapse into
melodrama, others avoid it, but all are uninspired. It has been said
before that Ruskin's prose can be far more poetic than his verse.
Luckily, he realised it himself, and in 1845 gave up verse-writing as
a serious occupation, to the great disappointment of John James
Ruskin. Had not his son won the coveted Newdigate Prize, recited
the prize poem to an audience of two thousand, and been
introduced to Wordsworth as a result? But the Newdigate Prize
for Poetry has so often been won by people whose true talents have
turned out to lie elsewhere.

Ruskin continued to write in verse, occasionally, throughout
his life. One of his last productions was an edition of the nursery
rhyme, 'Dame Wiggins of Lee and her Seven Wonderful Cats', to
which he added four verses (illustrated by Kate Greenaway) on
'what the cats did when they went to school'. The verses are
charming enough, but they are a sad finale to a poetic career of
which so much had been expected.

However, Ruskin did not decide to abandon verse until he had
made his mark in prose. In 1843 the first volume of *Modern Painters*
(by 'A Graduate of Oxford') was published and generally well
reviewed. It was expensive and sold slowly, but had some notable
admirers, Sydney Smith and Wordsworth among them. Tennyson saw the book lying on Samuel Rogers's library table, and
asked a friend to borrow a copy for him. Its theme, as Tennyson
put it, was 'the superiority of the modern painters to the old ones';
Claude, Gaspar Poussin, Salvator Rosa and Canaletto were all
compared unfavourably to Turner, and Dutch and Flemish artists
(apart from Rubens) came off especially badly. It is hard to forget

Ruskin's contemptuous reference to 'the various Van somethings and Back somethings' of Holland.

It is not always an easy book to read; Holman Hunt may have stayed up all night engrossed in it, but he was a man of exceptional enthusiasm and persistence. A more typical reaction was that of the Rev. F. W. Robertson of Brighton, who advised a correspondent 'to resolve not to finish more than a few pages each day . . . Do not read it, however, with slavish acquiescence; with deference, for it deserves it, but no more'.[9]

The book lends itself well to digestion by stages, for Ruskin passes methodically through chapters on tone, colour, chiaroscuro, space, skies, cloud, earth, mountains, foreground, water and vegetation, in each case comparing the achievements of former painters (especially of the seventeenth century) with modern (especially Turner). These are not simply comparisons between artists: Ruskin matches the paintings he considers against his own observations of natural phenomena under various conditions.

He had deen devoted to the painting of J. M. W. Turner for some years, and in 1836 (the year in which he lost his heart to Adèle) he had first tried to declare his allegiance publicly. The occasion was the annual exhibition of the Royal Academy, to which Turner had contributed three pictures, 'Juliet and her Nurse', 'Mercury and Argus' and 'Rome from Mount Aventine' (plate 1a), which provoked a wide range of critical comment. Some reviewers were dazzled; others were contemptuous, including John Eagles of *Blackwood's:* '. . . white gamboge and raw sienna are, with childish execution, daubed together.'[10] Ruskin wrote an indignant reply, abusing these critics as they had abused Turner. On the artist's own suggestion the letter was sent to the purchaser of 'Juliet and her Nurse' instead of *Blackwood's*, but in Ruskin the seeds of *Modern Painters* were sown.

Ruskin's praise of Turner was not, in itself, as controversial as his denigration of 'the old ones'. After all, Turner had been a full member of the Royal Academy for forty years, and for much of that time had been widely recognised as one of England's leading artists. But there existed a considerable body of opinion wich rated Turner's *earlier* work – his epic scenes in the manner of Claude, say, or his Venetian paintings – more highly than his later experiments with light and colour. Here Ruskin disagreed entirely. Turner had been a great painter from the time when he could first hold a brush, Ruskin believed. Nothing could equal his current paintings (such as those which had recently been exhibited at the Royal Academy), whose grand atmospheric effects exactly matched Ruskin's own literary talents. One was 'Snowstorm' (1842), in which sea and sky are mingled in a choking explosion of snow and spray. Another was 'The Slave Ship' (1840) (plate 1b), which the *Spectator* called a freak of 'chromomania'; Thackeray could not decide whether the picture was sublime or ridiculous. But Ruskin thought it Turner's greatest work, and if any prose can do justice to the painting, it is Ruskin's:

> The waves do not rise everywhere, but three or four together in wild groups, fitfully and furiously, as the understrength of the swell compels or permits them; leaving between them trea-cherous spaces of level and whirling water, now lighted with green and lamp-like fire, now flashing back the gold of the declining sun, now fearfully dyed from above with the undistinguishable images of the burning clouds, which fall upon them in flakes of crimson and scarlet, and give to the reckless waves the added motion of their own fiery flying. Purple and blue, the lurid shadows of the hollow breakers are cast upon the mist of night, which gathers cold and low; advancing like the shadow of death upon the guilty ship . . .[11]

Before the reader reaches this purple prose, however, or the equally remarkable but more subdued observations of nature, he is presented with a showy analysis of 'general principles', rather in the manner of Locke, which betrays the lingering influence of Oxford; and this section makes great play with the notion of 'truth'. Truth is a term fundamental to Ruskin's art criticism, but unfortunately he uses it in a hopelessly inconsistent way, both in this volume and in his later writing. Sometimes Ruskin's 'truth' means the faithful representation of natural detail: 'Go to Nature in all singleness of heart, and walk with her laboriously and trustingly',[12] was his famous advice, and he later praised the Pre-Raphaelites for adopting this policy. But frequently Ruskin calls for a different kind of truth — one which he often, and justly, spells with a capital 'T'. This is a Truth 'of emotions, impressions and thoughts', something far more important than mere material truth or imitation. This Truth may be conveyed by signs and symbols which are not themselves imitative of anything; a pencil outline can contain more Truth than a detailed painting which is far more deceptive as an imitation of nature.

This second sense enables Ruskin to argue that Turner was supremely Truthful. Even without the capital letter, the meaning is often made clear by an added epithet, as in 'real truth', 'moral truth', 'essential truth', 'Divine Truth', 'deep final truth', or (the ultimate distillation) 'deep Alpine truth'. Ruskin adds that only a deeply penetrative imagination, like Turner's, can achieve such truth, an imagination which he describes in the second volume of *Modern Painters* with a Roget-like battery of metaphors:

> It never stops at crusts or ashes, or outward images of any kind; it ploughs them all aside, and plunges into the very central fiery heart . . . it gets within all fence, cuts down to the root, and drinks the very vital sap of that it deals with. [13]

The Truth of Tintoretto is similarly attributed to that artist's imagination; his 'Massacre of the Innocents' is 'the only Imaginative, that is , the only true, real, heartfelt representation of the being and actuality of the subject'. [14] However Ruskin was never entirely happy under the banner of Imagination. In general he preferred to campaign for Truth – whatever the ambiguities.

The confusion stems from the fact that Ruskin was opposed to two different orthodoxies, sometimes simultaneously. One was the set of conventions of landscape painting which insisted on brown-dominated colour schemes, generalised forms and stylised lighting effects; this tradition, Ruskin felt, ignored the simple truth of nature. The other was the idea that a painter was to be judged merely according to his skill in transcribing the external world or in selecting and combining certain aspects of it; to Ruskin, this attitude underrated the artist's own individual contribution to his art. In each respect, Ruskin was attacking a tradition sanctioned by Sir Joshua Reynolds and still strong. A fellow-opponent of these traditions was William Blake, who also attacked Reynolds on both counts: there *was* a place for 'servile copying' of particulars, wrote Blake in his copy of Reynolds's *Discourses*, yet when on the next page Reynolds advised that 'you cannot do better than to have recourse to nature herself', Blake added 'Nonsense! Every Eye sees differently. As the Eye, Such the Object'. [15] Similarly James Duffield Harding, Ruskin's drawing instructor, tried to teach his readers to produce an 'accurate' representation of the details of nature, but insisted at the same time that he who aspired to the title of Artist must do much more: he must address the mind through the expression of sentiment; his work should be 'less felt as a copy of nature, than as an embodiment of feelings which nature has inspired'.[16]

Like Blake and Harding, then, Ruskin offered a double theme, and his exhortations to 'go to nature' were not intended to deny the value of the artist's personal vision. Moreover, he attached more importance than most of his English predecessors to art which revealed (to him) great feelings and sympathies on the part of the artist; and one indication of this lies in the fact that Ruskin abandoned the traditional terminology of 'imitation' and 'copy-ing'. In the previous hundred years, each writer on artistic matters had tended to use the word 'imitation' to describe whatever method he happened to admire, be it following earlier painters, following nature directly, selecting from nature or following a mental abstraction from nature.[17] 'Copyism' on the other hand was used to describe whatever fell short of 'imitation' in the relevant respect, and was scorned as a pastime for learners and plagiarists. Ruskin took the line that imitation could not by any definition (and he considered several) be regarded as a genuinely artistic occupation. A skilful imitation might yield pleasure, he allowed, but it was a paltry pleasure – 'we feel a kind of pleasurable surprise, an agreeable excitement of mind, exactly the same in its nature as that which we receive from juggling'. And we must not be completely deceived, he observed, since in that case even the sensation of trickery and deception is lost.[18]

But one might still ask what these principles amounted to in practice; and some of the most revealing answers are to be found in Ruskin's own drawings.

As a boy, he had shown an aptitude for accurate copying, which was further encouraged by his lessons in the gentlemanly arts of sketching and watercolour. The family travels provided Ruskin with the picturesque subject-matter which young tourists were accustomed to record, and the work of Samuel Prout influenced his style. But Ruskin had discovered Turner too, and by the age of fourteen could also produce a fair imitation of Turner's engraved views of Italy. Meanwhile John James had bought a watercolour by the capable Copley Fielding, who became Ruskin's next teacher. Ruskin soon added several of Fielding's skills and mannerisms to his repertoire; before long he was adept in the fine drawing and spacious effects of David Roberts; and by the time he went up to Oxford, his sizeable folio of varied work was sufficient to earn him a useful reputation.

But Ruskin's growing admiration for Turner prevented him from remaining complacent about his accomplishments. If the standards of the Society of Painters in Water-Colours were all, he could have regarded himself as a promising artist; but what was Ruskin, or even the Society's President Fielding, compared with the astonishing Turner, who could break every rule of composition and colour and yet produce a masterpiece? And how could Ruskin, after seeing the work of that towering imagination, be content to aim at more and more faithful approximations to nature? In September 1840 he advised a correspondent that to capture the overall 'character' of a scene might involve 'lies' for the sake of a greater truth; he should not 'compose a scene' at all, but rather 'imbue your mind with the peculiar spirit of the place'. 'You are to give this spirit, at all risks, by any means . . . and you wll soon emancipate yourself from any idea that artists' sketches are to be mere *camera-lucidas*, mere transcripts of mechanism and measurement.'[19]

This seems to have been Ruskin's own policy during his winter convalescence of 1840 to 1841, and to judge by his free, unfussy drawing of the Trevi fountain, he absorbed the atmosphere of Rome to good effect. Some of his drawings done at this time are over-finished, but he also brought off some rapid and delicate effects which show that Ruskin was not simply a keen and thorough observer, but also an artist already.

Although he continued to be influenced by the leading lights of the Society of Painters in Water-Colours (such as J. D. Harding, who succeeded Copley Fielding as Ruskin's instructor), Ruskin's attitude to painting diverged increasingly from theirs. He cared less for abstract principles of composition, and became more impressed by the intrinsic beauties of nature – a process which he later summarised in an incident at Fontainebleau, one of several revelatory experiences with which Ruskin dramatised his autobiography. As he was lying by the roadside, sketching an aspen tree, its outlines seemed to grow more and more beautiful, making it unnecessary for him to impose any arrangement; 'they "composed" themselves, by finer laws than any known of men'.[20] As nature itself took on a more exalted role in Ruskin's mind, so did the value of transcribing nature. Yet this was not to be the highest purpose for an artist; Ruskin always felt that Turner could achieve a kind of imaginative penetration of a subject, and there were occasions when Ruskin was inspired to try for the same effect. So both truth and Truth are to be found in his own art. He could record with pleasure the natural lines of the aspen, and only a few months later create the bold, dramatically exciting sketches of 'The Falls at Schaffhausen' (plate 2a).

But perhaps Ruskin made too much of his distinction between imaginative works of art and the more prosaic recording of appearances. Even his drawings of details of Venetian architecture in 1845 (plate 2b) are not the simple 'facts' that he would sometimes have us believe. They are 'literal' in a sense, but they are subtle and individual, as recognisably Ruskin's as the swaying pines and sharply-contrasted foliage which he was painting at the same period. And in the last analysis they are no less imaginative; they embody his ideal of intricate, colourful, ever-varied architecture, elaborate and yet light and elegant, and they are much more than 'factual' representations of buildings, even supposing that such a thing were possible. In some cases the buildings themselves scarcely live up to Ruskin's image of them. Ruskin was over-conscious of his inferiority to Turner, and certainly his pastiches of Turner's grand manner are feeble by comparison with his supposedly 'factual' sketches.

By this time the painter had another problem to contend with: the camera. By 1841 it was possible for amateurs to take respectable daguerreotypes or calotypes without any great knowledge of chemistry or powers of endurance. Since Louis Daguerre (himself a painter) had published his techniques two years before, the exposure time required by his method had been reduced from 15-20 minutes to two minutes or less – in midsummer, as little as ten seconds. In principle any traveller could bring home clear, sharp images of the sights he had appreciated. But in practice the era of the holiday snapshot was still several decades away. For one thing, the leisured traveller needed a porter to carry about the cumbersome equipment; which may explain why as late as 1849, Ruskin (aided by his valet-porter) could photograph the Matterhorn and believe – probably rightly – that he was the first to do so.

It is notable that the new invention did not greatly affect
Ruskin's drawing or painting. One of the first to use photography
as an architectural record and even to use photographs as the basis
of some of his drawings, he was also quick to realise that the
photograph was not a threat even to detailed drawings of
buildings. Even the 'historical topographer', he wrote, had to make
omissions, or use signs, as his 'instinctive affection' directed — 'the
only inspiration he is capable of, but a kind of inspiration still'.[21]
This applies to Ruskin's drawings, many of which do display his
'kind of inspiration' in a way that his daguerreotypes do not.

Away from the streets of the cities and towns of Europe, Ruskin
was meanwhile developing his own distinctive style of drawing
rocks and mountains, inspired but not restricted by his passion for
geology. Chunky masses and swirling contours are the hallmarks
of this style, with particular attention given to the vegetation
creeping and twisting in the crevices. Ruskin the geologist was
now considering mountain forms as the product of enormous
natural pressures, compressing and disintegrating, continually
forming and reforming on a huge scale. 'It is not so much what
these forms of the earth actually are, as what they are continually
becoming, that we have to observe.'[22] For example, a photograph
would be unlikely to pick out the 'governing lines' of a mountain:

> In Nature, or in a photograph, a careless observer will by no
> means be struck by them, any more than he would by the curves
> of the tree; and an ordinary artist would draw rather the
> cragginess and granulation of the surfaces, just as he would
> rather draw the bark and moss of the trunk.[23]

This quotation lists four norms which, Ruskin believed, the true
artist must exceed: Nature, the photograph, the careless observer,
and the ordinary artist. They were exceeded by Turner, as Ruskin
claimed; and although he did not claim it, they were often
exceeded in the drawings of Ruskin himself.

# 3 Critics and Faces

> Regular features, do you like regular features? Or is it
> expression that interests you?
>
> Expression; I think I like expression . . .
>
> *Coningsby*, 1844

The later 1830s saw a sudden burst of activity in the visual arts in
England. Not that the art produced was much greater in quantity
or quality than that of previous years; but there was certainly more
public debate, more controversy, and more excitement generated
over artistic questions. In the first place a number of institutional
events coincided. The rebuilding of the Houses of Parliament,
which had burned down in 1834, gave publicity not only to 'the
battle of the styles' but also to the relative merits of oil and fresco.
Meanwhile the National Gallery was under construction, despite
heavy criticism of its design; the Institute of British Architects and
the first government School of Design were established in 1837;
and the Royal Academy, probed by the Select Committee of
1835–6, moved into Trafalgar Square in 1838, together with the
national collection of paintings.

At much the same time patrons of art began to organise
themselves. The 'Society for the Encouragement of British Art'
was established in 1835, followed in 1836 by 'The Art-Union of
London', modelled on a Scottish society set up shortly before.
Annual 'Exhibitions' – an idea still novel enough to warrant
inverted commas – were now no longer restricted to the capital,
but held in the chief provincial cities, where they were associated
with newly-founded 'Institutions for the promotion of the Fine
Arts'. To cater for the growing interest, the *Art-Union Monthly*

*Journal* was founded in 1839: though it did not pay its way for nine years, it gained in its first year an average monthly circulation of nearly three thousand, and survived Dickens's caricature of it as the 'Pecksniffery'. [1]

Collectors of contemporary painting now became a considerable force. Among them were self-made industrialists who were not over-impressed by traditional connoisseurship, and such men provided a valuable stimulus for artists who – like the Pre-Raphaelites in their early years – were not regarded as respectable by the artistic establishment; on the other hand, some of the new patrons may have associated themselves with the old in the hope of acquiring the social grace of 'taste'. The infant *Art-Union Journal* described the situation delicately:

> There are two classes of persons on whose support such associations as these have strong and especial claims; the first consists of those who, although possessed of taste, are not wealthy; the other of those who have ample means, but who, from various causes, and especially from the want of having their attention drawn directly and frequently to the subject, have hitherto evinced little interest in the progress of the arts, and little taste for their productions. [2]

For the needs of serious students, early Victorian England supplied a number of critics and chroniclers of art – but, on the whole, it was not their writings on art that made them notable. Charles Eastlake was known as a painter, as President of the Royal Academy, and then as the first Director of the National Gallery; Edmund Head edited a history of German, Flemish and Dutch painting while relaxing from his duties as a Poor Law Commissioner; and Anna Jameson turned to art after establishing herself as a writer on Shakespeare and travel. Maria Graham (later Lady Callcott) also entered the literary world as a travel writer, and for every individual who knew her as an interpreter of painting, there must have been ten more who knew only her *Little Arthur's History of England*. Two other contributors to the literature of art, Charles Bell and Alexander Walker, owed their fame to publications on the human nervous system. Bell and Head were both knighted for their accomplishments in fields other than art.

On the Continent, meanwhile, the 'history of art' was developing as a scholarly discipline, based on a study of original documents and contemporary sources. Eastlake, writing in 1840, recognised that England lagged behind in this department: he believed that 'the credit of instituting a new kind of research in the history of art, as opposed to the habit of copying Vasari, is perhaps due in the first instance to Pungileoni'[3] (whose biographies, however, were hardly known in England). Second came Baron von Rumohr, who (wrote Eastlake) added criticisms derived immediately from the works of art concerned, instead of depending on hearsay, recollection or engravings. The third pioneer art historian mentioned by Eastlake was another German, Passavant, the tourist and biographer of Raphael.

Not surprisingly, German names appear increasingly often in the English footnotes of the first third of the century: the Schlegels, Kugler, Waagen, Passavant, Rumohr, Müller. Englishmen who failed to learn German were at a disadvantage, and Ruskin was one of them. In many English minds Sir Joshua Reynolds remained the supreme authority half a century after the last of his *Discourses* was delivered, for want of an adequate British successor. The most useful history of Italian art was Luigi Lanzi's, but when an English translation was finally published, eighteen years after Lanzi's death, the *Edinburgh Review* criticised it for failing to provide any good stories, and by way of example offered a feeble anecdote of its own.[4] Continental scholarship and enthusiasm were to have impact on English attitudes, but it took time.

Some of the liveliest commentaries appeared in the periodicals, whose sudden concern with art was unmistakable. The first architectural journal (as distinct from pattern-book) was published in 1834 – the *Architectural Magazine* – closely followed by three others in the next eight years. The literary periodicals began to devote more space to artistic topics: in July 1836 John Eagles's 'Hints to Amateurs' formed the first of his many articles on art for *Blackwood's*, and Nicholas Wiseman and John Steinmetz began their tenancy as art critics in the newly-founded *Dublin Review*, to which Pugin himself contributed not long after. In August 1834, W. H. Leeds began to write for the *Foreign Quarterly*, having already written for the early numbers of *Fraser's*. Leeds wrote on every department of the visual arts, but he specialised in architecture, and was among the first to make a serious effort to view architecture from an artistic – rather than a functional, archaeological or symbolic – point of view. Anyone, he urged, could become proficient in 'the aesthetic part of architecture'.[5]

Leeds's hopes were amply fulfilled in the next ten years, during which art criticism flourished as never before. Its potential was enlarged by the growing taste for 'expressive' art, which enabled an imaginative critic to give lyrical accounts of whatever he felt to be 'expressed' by a particular building or painting. J. A. Symonds, looking back on the 1840s, thought that 'weary of symmetry and the Greek ideal, one and unchangeable, Art sought variety, and the wider field of expression'.[6] In architecture, the triumph of Gothic over Grecian in the 1840s is partly attributable to skilful propaganda about the superior 'expressiveness' of Gothic. 'Grecian architecture is beginning to lose our favour', Leeds reported in 1839, pointing to its lack of variety and (especially in its nineteenth-century versions) its stereotyped colours and capitals. 'We have also rendered it quite cold and bare by dispensing with those embellishments and sculptures which . . . gave not richness alone, but variety, meaning and expression to the individual building.'[7]

'Expression', in fact, was a focus of the quickening interest in the arts at this time, no less in painting than in architecture. Art criticism has always been bedevilled by such infinitely flexible terms as 'expression', 'imitation' and 'nature'; as the cult of 'expression' gathered momentum in the early nineteenth century, so the meaning of the word became clearer, and it is worth giving a brief account of this development.

At its broadest, 'expression' may refer to the overall emotional tone of painting. To give the correct 'expression' to a Nativity scene, wrote Jonathan Richardson the Elder in 1715, the colours should be 'chearful' – but for a Crucifixion, sombre colours were necessary. Another of Richardson's examples is the depiction of the Raising of Lazarus. If a painter of this subject chooses to show some of the spectators holding 'something before their noses', this appropriate as an expression of the length of time Lazarus has been dead, but it would be out of place in a painting of the laying of Christ in the sepulchre ('however, Pordenone has done it').[8]

A little less generally, 'expression' referred to the emotions (or 'passions') conveyed by the *figures* in a painting, by means of their poses, gestures and faces: it was 'the soul made visible'. And when a painter was praised, in the eighteenth century, for his powers of expression, it was very often his portrayal of *faces* that was alluded to. As the influential Roger de Piles wrote in 1708, 'above all it is the eyes that act as the windows of the soul'.[9]

If an aspiring artist wanted to become proficient in 'expression', he could study the series of faces published by Charles Le Brun, dictator of the artistic establishment under Louis XIV. Le Brun's engravings, which showed the facial dispositions appropriate to every kind of human emotion, remained influential longer after their first appearance at the end of the seventeenth century; an English edition of 'Lebrun's Passions' in 1863 still declared itself 'admirably adopted for students, and all who wish to read the various expressions of the human face'.

But in the second half of the eighteenth century, doubts were voiced (notably in neo-classical circles) as to whether this kind of dramatic expression, indicating agony for example by convulsed face and limbs, was admissible in the higher reaches of art; for it militated against beauty, by which was meant orderliness, balance, purity and restraint. On these grounds Gotthold Ephraim Lessing claimed that intense emotion should not be depicted. He praised the sculptor of the struggling 'Laocoon' (plate 3a) for showing the chief figure's mouth as only slightly open (although his plight would have made a full-scale grimace more appropriate); here was an example of beauty justifiably promoted at the expense of expression.

Several of Lessing's contemporaries shared this attitude. Anton Raphael Mengs admired the art of the ancients because 'amongst all the parts of expression, none were so powerful as to predominate over Beauty'.[10] Mengs's publisher, the Chevalier D'Azara, in his chapter on 'Expression' advised painters to 'choose those lines which do not destroy Beauty';[11] and the same principle was asserted by Winckelmann, the later Goethe, and Sir Joshua Reynolds.

But critics came gradually to pay greater respect to 'expression', which (they began to suggest) might in itself be a worthy end of art, so that even 'beauty' should sometimes be sacrificed to it. There are signs of this view in Wickelmann's *Reflections on the Painting and Sculpture of the Greeks* (1754), although his subsequent *History of Ancient Art* retracted somewhat. In England 'expression' found an early champion in Henry Fuseli, who blamed Winckelmann (a little unfairly) for leading German artists to subordinate 'expression and mind' to what they called beauty.[12] One of the

earliest English histories of Italian painting, written by the Rev.
John Thomas James (later Bishop of Calcutta), was more explicit,
and attacked 'the modern sculptors', especially Canova and
Thorvaldsen, for having 'followed the beautiful as their chief aim'.
This was not what art was all about, in the view of James; what he
preferred is made clear by an earlier passage. In the days of Guido,
he wrote disapprovingly,

> Beauty first began to be made the leading principle of
> art . . . Pure beauty may be used as contrast, or as ornament;
> but the want of expression of sentiment, essentially belonging to
> it, must convince us that it is, as a general principle, totally
> inadequate to the common objects of historical painting.[13]

The change in outlook is well illustrated by early nineteenth-
century opinions of Reynolds's *Discourses*: for while the writings of
Reynolds dominated English art criticism for half a century, they
became a natural focus of attack for the vocal minority of
dissenters. 'Reynolds cannot bear Expression', wrote William
Blake in his copy of Sir Joshua's *Works*, and although that was
untrue (Reynolds adopted a position of compromise on the
subject), Reynolds's course was still too close to neo-classical
orthodoxy for Blake's liking: 'If you mean to preserve the most
perfect beauty *in its most perfect state*, you cannot express the
passions.' 'What Nonsense!' commented Blake. 'Passion & Expression is Beauty Itself. The Face that is Incapable of Passion and
Expression is deformity Itself.'[14]

Hazlitt, too, objected to Reynolds's view that expression was
hostile to beauty (though he observed that Reynolds was not
always consistent in following his principle), and he was worried
by Reynolds's desire for 'universal' expression as opposed to
'particular'. Hazlitt hoped to see portrayed feelings of every kind,
and not just the noble restraint and stiff upper lips which the fourth
*Discourse* seemed literally to demand.

So 'expression' gained favour in England, either as being
beautiful in itself (the opinion of Blake and Hazlitt) or as being
more valuable than 'mere' beauty (the opinion of the Rev. James
and of the artist John Opie, who warned that the pursuit of beauty
could lead to 'the namby-pamby style'[15]). A third development
was the recognition that expression might be profound without
involving ugly contortions of limbs and features. Winckelmann

and Mengs were aware of this possibility: 'a simple figure without action has perhaps an expression appertaining to the inward man, that is the soul; and the other of much action, ought to represent only an external motion'.[16] However it was the subsequent taste for the Italian painters *before* Raphael, and for Raphael's more subdued work, that finally won approval for restrained and apparently deep expression. The rather blank faces depicted in early Renaissance painting were thought to be full of subtle spirituality; this was the sort of expression which the German Romantic critics of the late eighteenth century could wholeheartedly admire, often at the expense of the 'lifeless beauty' of Greek art. Friedrich Schlegel extended this analysis to the art of painting as a whole, believing that whereas sculpture could best represent the actual forms of material beauty, the fittest aim for painting was 'imparting a glorified expression to individual figures, or diffusing a divine and holy sentiment throughout a composition'.[17]

Where Germany had led, England gradually followed, and English critical opinion in the early decades of the nineteenth century inclined towards more gentle or subtle facial expression, and away from the dramatic displays of Le Brun, Johann Kaspar Lavater and his fellow-physiognomists of the eighteenth century. By 1839, pictures which were felt to exhibit religious feeling were receiving particularly fervent applause. In the Royal Academy exhibition of that year, the painting which the *Art-Union* found 'perhaps the most faultless picture in the exhibition' was not Turner's 'Fighting Temeraire', though that was greatly appreciated, but Charles Eastlake's 'Christ Blessing Little Children'.[18] For the next four years, until Eastlake turned his attention to literary work, it was his portrayals of heartfelt emotion that, to the *Art-Union*, stole the show from Wilkie, Turner and the Landseers. The *Art-Union* evidently believed that such feeling could only be rendered by a character of unusual goodness: 'it is the emanation of a mind nobly, gracefully, and beautifully constructed.'[19] Its account of Eastlake's 'The Prophecy for Jerusalem' begins, 'we cannot find words to express our admiration of this work', and then proceeds to give it what must be the most ecstatic review in the history of the journal.[20] In the following year, Eastlake is said to have achieved 'the level of the greatest masters of expression who have ever lived'.[21] It seems that the crowds were drawn not only by Frith's 'Derby Day' and John Martin's biblical spectaculars: John Eagles, commenting for *Blackwood's* on Eastlake's painting 'The Prophecy for Jerusalem', found 'it was so difficult of access that we fairly confess we are not qualified to speak of it as we should'.[22]

What lay behind this enthusiasm for a painter now largely forgotten? The answer may well be found in Eastlake's formula of emotional appeal together with calm restraint of expression. His version of 'The Sisters' (1844) and 'The Visit to the Nun' (1845), both painted for the young Queen Victoria, are sentimental in subject-matter but cool in facial expression; one might say of them, as did one critic of Eastlake's once-famous 'Haidée' (plate 3b), that there is 'less of sentiment than of that classic immobility of feature, that intentional negation of expression'.[23] The new masters of 'expression' were not the most diligent followers of Le Brun, but those who could exploit the steady gaze.

Eastlake could also 'touch the heart', as critics increasingly demanded in the 1830s and 40s. Usually (through not always) it was the painters renowned for 'expression' who were considered to pluck at the heartstrings most satisfyingly. Raphael was held to score over Michelangelo in this respect – Michelangelo 'who overwhelms our imaginations, but never touches our hearts'.[24] In general it was felt the moderns were here superior to the ancients. The *Art-Union* voiced a widely-held opinion on the first page of its inaugural issue:

> We take it as indisputable that the Artists of Great Britain greatly surpass the existing Artists of any other nation; and if, in some respects, they fall short of the power for which the Old Masters are so renowned, at least they paint from the heart, and with greater certainty excite those sympathies, to produce and foster which is the noblest privilege of Art.[25]

*nos?*

It is no surprise to find Eastlake likened, by both *Blackwood's* and the *Art-Union*, to Raphael;[26] not to find him, and others regarded as masters of expression, praised as much for their personality as for their skill. On the other hand there were some who condemned subdued facial expressions and restrained actions as 'dry' or 'stiff', and attributed them to the pernicious study of early Italian painters. But these hostile critics, with their taste for dramatic and demonstrative expression, were fighting a losing battle against the coming fashion; the German tourist Johann Passavant dismissed those English who failed to appreciate Eastlake's art as 'perverted by the extravagant style of their artists'.[27] The new taste favoured subtlety and moderation, as presented by Eastlake and the early Italians.

Raphael, too, had never enjoyed a higher reputation. For several decades critics had debated whether he or Michelangelo was the greater artist. By Ruskin's day the contest was over: in England – although not in France – Raphael had won, and was placed in the seat of honour among the painters who occupy a frieze of the Albert Memorial.

However, the early Victorian was not necessarily expected to revere Raphael at first acquaintance; a little cultivation might be required. It was widely known that even Reynolds had failed to admire Raphael's work in Rome, until his judgement had matured. Similarly the youthful Anna Jameson, when confronted by Raphael's 'Marriage of the Virgin' in Milan, found that 'it disappointed me at the first glance, but charmed me at the second, and enchanted me at the third. The unobtrusive grace and simplicity of Raphael do not immediately strike an eye so unpractised, and a taste so unformed as mine now is'.[28] Eastlake, whose paintings were so often compared to Raphael's, took several years to achieve a full appreciation of the Italian master, [29] and so it seems did Ruskin.[30] *Check Diaries*

It is interesting that the fashion for restrained expression in painting, as exemplified by Raphael, should have been in the ascendant in the 1830s and 40s, decades which are often supposed to have seen the rise of ostentatious decoration to satisfy the base commercial instincts of the *nouveaux riches*. Yet at this very time Raphael and his predecessors were gaining favour for their calm and undemonstrative qualities. Thomas Phillips, in his lectures as Professor of Painting at the Royal Academy, prefaced his long and enthusiastic account of Giotto's art with a remark of Reynolds's to the effect that uncultivated men enjoy a strong display of passion, but cultivated men prefer 'deep and clear but moderated tokens of feeling'.[31] If so, many writers of the time were very cultivated indeed.

One factor which helped to establish Raphael's work as fit to be admired by the discerning was the moral undertone attached to his subjects and faces. The Rev. Richard Cattermole, brother of the watercolourist, published a *Book of the Cartoons* in 1837 to demonstrate that 'Raphael has nowhere sought more beauty; he has aimed at the higher qualities of expression and character, employing these with a view to make art the means of exalting the human mind, by its connexion with morality and religion'.[32] The feeling was that since these higher qualities could only be portrayed by a man of exceptional character, one was communing with a source of moral strength in studying his pictures. In fact, the spectator could imagine that he was communicating indirectly with the New Testament characters themselves, since Raphael was judged to have had a certain *rapport* with the figures he painted — 'the power of imbibing their spirits', as another clerical admirer put it, 'that blending of his spirit with theirs'.[33] Furthermore, 'expression' represented true worth as opposed to superficial charm. A character in Mrs Jameson's *Diary of a Désennuyée* is made to say, 'I am not easily infatuated by a woman merely beautiful',[34] and there is something of this high-mindedness in her and her contemporaries' enthusiasm for Raphael's Madonnas.

Raphael's 'expression' was admired for a further reason. An ability to render the required expression in a face, accurately and recognisably, was as highly valued as ever in painters, but depicting a single passion was no longer the supreme test of skill. An ingenious artist might succeed in presenting two or three emotions mingled, and for those who aspired to this, Raphael's faces provided valuable models. In 1819, for example, a student's guide was published containing drawings — mostly of heads — after Raphael's *Cartoons*, together with an 'Index of Passions' comprising some fifty entries from Affection and Agony to Wonder and Zeal. Several of these are combinations — so that the face of Elymas, the sorcerer struck blind, is said to show 'Arrogance, dejected', while that of the healed cripple at the Beautiful Gate exhibits a fine balance of joy, gratitude, doubt and astonishment.[35] Another writer praised the 'wonderfully mixed expression' of Christ in Raphael's *Transfiguration*.[36]

Of course, remarks of this kind were open to ridicule; in particular, there was often precariously little difference between a 'deeply expressive' face and a face which was totally expressionless, as was neatly observed in the short-lived *Artist and Amateur's Magazine* of 1843. Here 'Palette' and 'Chatworthy' are made to discuss the Nazarene painter Overbeck, whom Schlegel and others had praised for the pious expressions of his figures.

It has not not been the object of this Artist to produce Expression [says Palette ] but to avoid it, and in its place to offer a blank; which if it does not convey an idea of the sentiment looked for, does not militate against it . . . Every person who has handled and scrawled with a pencil will have observed that in making an attempt at drawing, the human head in particular, a kind of spurious character and expression will be accidentally produced.[37]

Subdued facial expressions were also admired at a less exalted level – in the flourishing school of genre-painting, whose leader was David Wilkie. The importance of 'expression' in such paintings is obvious: the faces of the characters depicted must not only help to 'tell the story', but also in many cases signal the dramatic moment that the artist is trying to capture. But even in this sphere, the more perceptive critics demanded a certain degree of restraint. For example, the *forte* of Charles Leslie, a prominent *genre* painter, was thought to be his subtle renderings of character and expression (such was 'the general verdict',[38] we are told); moreover, his characters were 'free from all mawkishness. There is no trading in the "deep domestic" as a good saleable article for the market'.[39] It was the moderation of Leslie's expressions that the best judges commended: after Leslie's death, Ruskin praised his 'delicate expression', and Tom Taylor (dramatist and art critic of *The Times*) typically admired in a character in one of Leslie's 'Don Quixote' pictures of 1824, 'the sweetest half-smile – a triumph of subtle expression'.[40] In another Don Quixote painting (of 1849), Taylor admired the Duchess's face 'eradiated with one of those latent half-smiles', while 'the puzzled but well-disciplined attendants stand around, doing their best to suppress all expression in their looks'.[41] 'Palette's' ironical praise of blank expression was evidently applicable to genre as well as to religious art: what in a statue of Apollo might be interpreted as noble stoicism could be seen as Christian piety in a Madonna, or as diplomatic tact in a figure of popular fiction.

Not much has been said so far of the dwindling group of English disciples of classical art. These champions of the antique did not, on the whole, dispute that in 'modern' art there was more scope for 'expression'. They might declare, in the manner of Winckelmann, that Greek statues exhibited calm and dignified expression;[42] yet

there were several English admirers of classical art who not only
appreciated strong and violent facial expression but tried to
introduce it into their own work, and often to combine it with
classically-inspired forms. Fuseli and Blake are well-known
examples; another was Benjamin Haydon, who although a
passionate Graecophile – to the point of hoping that his dying
words would be 'Elgin Marbles! Elgin Marbles!' – was also a
worshipper of Raphael. He dressed as Raphael had dressed,
likened himself to Raphael in print, and was said to sleep with a
picture of Raphael hanging at the head of his bed. Haydon seems
to have admired Raphael's more dramatic displays of facial
expression: his students learnt that the brows must be lifted to give
an appearance of fright, but knit for an effect of terror or horror,
and 'in insanity, the brows are vacantly raised'. Moreover Haydon
subscribed to the notion that special personal qualities are needed
to depict such 'expression' successfully.

> It cannot be explained [he declared in his seventh lecture], it
> was visible in the first dawn of Raffaelle's early works, it was
> seen with the slightest line of his pen. No principle can be laid
> down: you must muse on the characters and stories introduced,
> and at the time of execution you see the very face agitated by the
> very look you want, in the innermost depths of your brain, and
> there the vision remains till you have put it on your canvas.[43]

Haydon's interest in expression was aroused to a considerable
extent by Charles Bell, who was later to become eminent as an
anatomist. In 1806 Wilkie arranged for Bell to deliver a course of
lectures on 'The Anatomy of Expression in Painting'. Haydon
attended the lectures and enrolled at Bell's school of anatomy, as
did Charles Eastlake, Haydon's first pupil, three years later.
Haydon's most successful pupils – Eastlake, William Bewick and
the Landseers – were all taught 'expression' on Bell's principles,
and it is surely no coincidence that all (except the unfortunate
Haydon himself) gained a reputation for skill in that department.
Haydon's own paintings included a number which laid special
emphasis on facial expression: the catalogue for his exhibition at
the Egyptian Hall includes such unheroic titles as 'The First Child
of a Young Couple – very like Papa about the Nose and Mama
about the Eyes'.[44]

Bell's *Essays on the Anatomy and Philosophy of Expression* (1806) eventually ran to seven editions, and the book was praised by authorities as diverse as Fuseli, Flaxman, Darwin and Queen Charlotte.[45] In search of expression, Bell visited Bedlam, bull-baitings and the House of Commons; he was also well versed in the literature of art. Much of the book is devoted to the physiological and anatomical bases of expressions, with examples (in the later editions) from Italian painting – an enterprise of which Le Brun might have been proud. But Bell was also concerned to show that there is something particularly exalted about human facial expression. We read in the first chapter of how beauty lies largely in expression; the book closes with a declaration that 'the noblest aim of painting is unquestionably to affect the mind, which can only be done by the representation of sentiment and passion'; and there is an ingenious chapter in which Bell claims that in human beings, 'there is added a peculiar set of muscles to which no other office can be assigned than to serve for expression'. Expression, he believed, is an essentially human characteristic; there is no expression in the 'lower creatures', and though the horse does exhibit expression 'in his eye and nostril', this is only a misleading product of coincidence.

Haydon frequently quoted Bell's work, and Haydon's pupil John Landseer took it as his text in the essay that accompanied his *Twenty Engravings of Lions* in 1823. In his catalogue of pictures from the National Gallery, Landseer also provided an early example of the lyrical rapture with which Victorian critics were to greet faces which caught their imagination:

> As regards the human face divine, the essence of character is a sort of electric fluid, which – playing through the atmosphere of human affections – excites, thrills, and sparkles, as it unites material loveliness with immateriality; or mind with matter. Eyes cannot "rain influence", or hope to be appointed to judge "the prize of wit or arms", without partaking of this ethereal essence.[47]

Another student of Sir Charles Bell's *Essays* was John Ruskin. Ruskin found the book 'often to my notions wrong', and therefore refused the *Quarterly*'s request that he write a favourable review as a tribute to Bell, who had recently died.[48] However Ruskin made careful notes on the *Essays* during his Italian tour of 1845, and in the second volume of *Modern Painters* several

respectful references to that work and to Bell's Bridgewater
Treatise, *The Hand*, appeared. On one occasion, Ruskin endorsed
Bell's attitude to the expression of the Laocoon group, an attitude
which typified the new generarion of critics who wanted to see
great emotions portrayed with restraint and delicacy, and who
regarded the Laocoon as too blatant. Winckelmann, Schiller and
Payne Knight had praised the mental fortitude represented in the
figure of Laocoon, and his appearance of suffering in noble silence.
Bell, however, denied that the sculptor intended Laocoon to
express this or any mental state; he aimed only 'to represent
corporeal exertion'; and Laocoon's mouth, Bell thought, was
made slightly open largely for the sake of consistency with other
anatomical features.[49] Ruskin observed that Bell 'has most wisely
and incontrovertibly deprived the statue of all claim to expression
of energy and fortitude of mind',[50] and went on to offer his own
account of true mental expression in art.

I think Ruskin was always fascinated by facial expression,
although this aspect of his art criticism is seldom mentioned by
commentators. At the age of sixteen he described a (ficititious) St
Bernard dog, at least half seriously:

> . . . his dark eye, with a singular expression – marvellous sad, I
> thought; it was not exactly philosophical, it was not a reasoning
> light, but a kind of calm melancholy – as if the animal was in the
> habit of feeling deeply. – It might be fancy.[51]

Soon after came his *Poetry of Architecture* with its comparisons of
buildings to human faces. At this time also, Ruskin greatly
admired Thomas Landseer's animal engravings 'as portraits of the
minds of animals'.[52] The first volume of Ruskin's *Modern Painters*
deals mainly with natural phenomena, though it has a much-
quoted passage of praise for Edwin Landseer's painting 'The Old
Shepherd's Chief-mourner', giving full credit to 'the fixed and
tearful fall' of the dog's eye. In the next two years his reading
included Charles Bell's volume on expression and Archibald
Alison's *Essays on Taste*, which in the edition read by Ruskin
contains a long chapter on the human face. He also read a book
which was to influence him profoundly, *De la Poésie Chrétienne* by
Alexis-François Rio: more will be said presently of Rio's work,
which was instrumental in making Ruskin decide to revisit Italy
early in 1845.

On 2 April 1845 Ruskin set off on a tour that was to have far-reaching effects on British taste. It was his first journey abroad without his parents, although he was still accompanied by his manservant and (from Geneva onwards) his guide. Ruskin was taking an independent path in another sense too, for he went to Italy principally to study the Italian painters of the fourteenth and fifteenth centuries — painters whom Rio had greatly admired, but whom his parents, and the great majority of those with opinions on the subject, regarded as barbaric and unworthy of serious attention.

Ruskin paused *en route* to experience the towns, the countryside and the food. He wrote home nearly every day. 'Ordered dinner at $\frac{1}{4}$ to 7', runs a typical letter, 'and ran out & made a sketch in the market place, and then down to the river side (Yonne) to see Sun set. Such an avenue. Every tree a new perfection. Turners and better than Turner at every step.'[53]

He spent a week in Lucca, drawing the frescoes and admiring the medieval architecture; then a fortnight in Pisa, furious at the deterioration and destructive 'restorations' of its works of art, but copying the fourteenth-century frescoes with desperate interest. As he sketched Benozzo Gozzoli's 'Abraham parting from the Angels' (plate 3c), he found 'such a quivering distress about the lips and appeal for pity in the eye, that I have had the tears in mine over and over again while I was drawing it'. But there was no time to be lost. 'The plaster on which is this passage has already risen in a blister from the wall, & will be blown into the Arno before the year is out'.[54]

In Florence Ruskin's devotion to the early Italian masters became even more fervent. He ignored most of the traditionally acclaimed masterpieces in the Uffizi and the Pitti Palace, preferring to sit in the dark churches and study the early followers and successors of Giotto. All the while he took careful notes, which have never been published; they clearly show Ruskin's pre-occupation with facial expression. The greater part of the two notebooks is devoted to the paintings of the fourteenth and fifteenth centuries on the Campo Santo and in the churches and galleries of Florence. Ruskin described their colours, drapery and overall composition, but he paid far more attention to the figures' faces than to any other single aspect, noting mouths, lips, eyebrows and (especially) eyes, and the emotions which the

combination of these expressed. He disliked faces which he found
'expressionless' – these were alternatively called 'insipid' or
'apathetic' – yet the faces he found most expressive and admirable
were 'tranquil' and 'passionless'. The finest fresco of the Campo
Santo, in his opinion, was the one (now attributed to Taddeo
Gaddi) which depicted Satan accusing Job before God: 'The
principal figure is most perfect in serenity of power; no expression
of indignation or passion of any kind in the look given to the evil
spirit.'[55]

Highest of all in Ruskin's esteem was Fra Angelico, whose work
Ruskin contrasted (in his notebook) with Raphael's 'contemptible
domesticity'. And the painting which was 'as near heaven as
human hand or mind will ever, or can ever go' was Angelico's
panel with the 'Annunciation' and 'Adoration of the Magi', now
in the Museo di San Marco (plate 3d). This is not one of those
Annunciations of Angelico's in which Gabriel steps gracefully into
a spacious colonnaded loggia. It consists rather of two scenes very
much in the Gothic idiom, showing stilted, attenuated figures
against a gold-diapered background. Ruskin paid particular
attention to the faces; he observed that those of Angelico's
common men were often disagreeable, but his saints' were
magnificent, and his angels' were heavenly.

Ruskin ascribed to these early painters considerable subtlety in
portraying complicated states of mind. There is a monk in the
'Trionfa della Morte' said to be:

> abandoned to a fixed, quiet, tearful despair, seemingly rather
> reviewing his past life, than intent on what is around him . . .
> But this monk's head is rendered doubly fine by its opposition I
> hope intentional to a nun's face beside it in a frantic parozysm
> [*sic* ].[56]

In Fra Angelico's 'Annunciation', 'The Virgin's face is absolutely luminous with love'; another face had 'a kind of thus far
shalt thou go and no farther expression that in some degree checks
and chills me'; a head of Christ revealed 'the ineffable expression of
divinity'; and the 'singularly fine expression' on the face of Ham is
one of 'stupid, half surprised, utterly hardened apathy'.[57] And
there is repeated praise for examples of either 'sweet' or 'intense'
expression.

These studies bore fruit in the second volume of *Modern*

*Painters*, which was written in the winter of 1845 to 1846 and published the following April. This volume contains Ruskin's most detailed examination of expression in both men and animals. According to Ruskin, all living things exhibit 'vital beauty' insofar as they are 'illustrative or expressive of certain moral dispositions or principles'. In the case of plants, the range of such dispositions is limited, and we can only judge their vital beauty according to their appearance of energy or happiness. Animals, however, can display various sorts of moral characteristic, and are vitally beautiful in as much as they exhibit any of several desirable kinds of 'moral honour', such as majesty, earnestness or gentleness. Conversely, ugliness is related to manifestations of vice: 'there is no high beauty in any slothful animal'.[58]

But the ugliest animals, we learn, are those which express nothing at all, those in which 'the eye seems rather an external optical instrument, than a bodily member through which emotion and virtue of soul may be expressed'. So in ascending order of vital beauty, we begin with owls and cats, who have a 'corpse-like stare'; then come examples of reptiles and birds, and then the gazelle, camel (wholly deceptive in its gentle expression, Ruskin later noted), ox, horse, dog and man. The same is true of the mouth, whose expressiveness increases as we progress from the fish and alligator through the carnivores up to the Negro and finally to Raphael's St Catherine. In conclusion, when considerations of 'typical beauty' do not complicate the issue, 'the beauty of animal form is in exact proportion to the amount of moral or intellectual virtue expressed by it', and the moral virtues are the fairest of all.[59]

In man, similarly, both intellectual powers and moral feelings are said by Ruskin to be reflected in the body and especially in the face – a commonplace of the literature of painting. Ruskin added here an original third possibility: that the body may be emaciated by extreme 'moral enthusiasm' or 'soul culture'. The human race is peculiar in that many different traits are expressed within the same species, but once again (wrote Ruskin) vital beauty lies in faces which express noble characters, and ugliness in those which exhibit 'signs of sin'. Of these last Ruskin proved himself a connoisseur, dividing them into four categories of pride, sensuality, fear, and cruelty, and explaining the features of each.

A generation earlier, this sort of interpretation would not have been received so tolerantly. In 1809, Martin Archer Shee had ridiculed the flights of fancy of Winckelmann and Daniel Webb, both by then dead. Winckelmann's celebrated description of the Laocoon was a prime target for Shee's sarcasm:

> The tortures produced by the serpents, are nothing compared with those which Laocoon suffers from the Connoisseur. Every feature is put to the rack of Expression . . . languor depresses one lip, and by the help of a painful sensation, draws up the other, while agony and indignation take possession of the nose: no ordinary common-place indignation, but an intelligent explanatory passion that announces the cause while it exhibits the effect.[60]

Shee also attacked Webb, who had repeated Pliny's story that Aristides managed to depict 'an infant creeping to the breast of its mother; who, though expiring from her wounds, yet expresses an apprehension and fear, lest the course of her milk being stopt, the child should suck her blood'.[61] Shee was less confident than his predecessors that intricate mental states could be portrayed in a painting if the painter possessed enough skill and physiognomical knowledge. He mockingly expected that he might read of 'muscles making metaphysical distinctions, delicate emotions dimpling in all directions'.[62] But in the 1840s, Shee's prophecy began to be fulfilled, and delicate emotions dimpled again in interpretations of painting, so that Ruskin's inferences from facial features to details of character represent to some extent a return to the critical style of the later eighteenth century – with the difference that the new school was not emboldened (or hampered) by physiognomists and their scientific pretensions.

This renewal of interest in the human face in art is partly attributable to the increasing popularity of anecdotic painting, but it was also associated with the mounting enthusiasm for early Italian art. In 1847 Lord Lindsay's *History of Christian Art* was published, and both Lindsay and Ruskin, who reviewed the work for the *Quarterly*, assumed that for many of the paintings discussed, the facial expression of the figures was a vital element. The two men did not always agree in their assessments: comparing Michelangelo's souls at Judgement Day with those of the *Trionfa della Morte* at Pisa (then attributed to Orcagna), Lindsay felt that Michelangelo's faces betrayed doubt and despair, while 'Orcagna' had represented every diversity of human character; Ruskin disagreed with Lindsay's analysis in both cases, but he did agree that 'Orcagna trusted for all his expression to the countenance', and that Michelangelo was capable of great effect 'by expression of countenance alone'.[63]

As in the previous year's volume of *Modern Painters*, Ruskin related the painting of faces to the artist's character, for 'devotion could be told by the countenance only'; and while other painters' less exalted thoughts set limits on their portrayal of the countenance, Ruskin wrote,

> . . . with Fra Angelico the glory of the countenance reaches to actual transfiguration; eyes that see no more darkly, incapable of all tears . . . lips tremulous with love, and crimson with the light of the coals of the altar . . .[64]

Now this description of lips crimson and tremulous with love has a parallel in an unfinished ghost story, *Velasquez the Novice*, written by Ruskin at the age of seventeen. Here there is a character called Ada, whose 'lip quivered redly',[65] and Ada unquestionably represents Adèle Domecq, with whom Ruskin was in love at the time. By 1847, however, he was a suitor of Charlotte Lockhart, daughter of the *Quarterly's* editor, and it was for her (Ruskin said later) that he wrote the review.[66] Whether or not Angelico's figures actually stood for Charlotte in Ruskin's fantasies, it seems likely that his enthusiasm for expression on canvas was partly affected by his hopeless loves in flesh and blood.

Still, it was more than a transient phase. Ruskin is so well known for his devotion to the beauties of landscape, sky and sea that it is easy to overlook his lifelong sensitivity to anything evocative of human emotions or character. It seems that he almost resented any artefact which offered him no 'expression' to interpret. Thus the animals he most despised were those he found the least expressive, and he wrote of Greek statuary without enthusiasm, because he could not think of an 'ancient statue which expresses by the countenance any one elevated character of soul, or any single enthusiastic self-abandoning affection'.[67] In *The Seven Lamps of Architecture*, Ruskin scorned machine-finished surfaces on the grounds that they could not communicate the feelings of the workman; and in *The Stones of Venice* he attacked the buildings of the Renaissance as 'cold' and not expressive of human qualities.

When we read Ruskin's explanations of Venetian façades, it soon becomes clear that he saw them as yet more faces — faces to be scrutinised for every superficial clue to their supposed inner character.

# 4 Personalities

Ruskin's tour of 1845 did not end with the early masters of Florence.In July he moved up to the mountains, then on, slowly, through Italy, with J. D. Harding as his sketching companion for some of the journey. He spent five weeks in Venice, where he embarked on what was to be one of the major undertakings of his life, the study of Venetian architecture. Again he was horrified at the state of the city – 'monuments torn down and pavements up, the cloisters everywhere turned into barracks or repainted . . .'[1] St Mark's captivated him, even though the carving of the capitals, each different from the others, had been blurred by an acid used to clear them. He spent a frustrating day in a gondola drawing the intricate details of the Ca'd'Oro palace (plate 4a) while workmen were hammering away the mouldings; and when he managed to obtain some daguerreotypes of the palaces he had been trying to draw, he was delighted. Unlike many of his fellow artists, who regarded the new invention as a threatening rival to their efforts, Ruskin saw it as a welcome ally. 'Daguerreotypes taken by this vivid sunlight are glorious things. It is very nearly the same thing as carrying off the palace itself.'[2]

A potential rival of a different kind was Mrs Anna Jameson, whose book *Sacred and Legendary Art* had begun to appear that year in the *Athenaeum*. She was staying in Venice, and here Ruskin met her for the first time. 'Knows as much of art as the cat', he reported, no doubt with relief, and more maliciously he passed on the landlady's comment about her: 'E vecchia – rossa.'[3]

There was one more great and unexpected revelation on this tour: the paintings of Tintoretto. The delicate charms of Fra Angelico had not closed Ruskin's mind to turbulent, monumental visions, and he was overwhelmed by the Venetian artist's flying figures and storm-tossed trees, achieved with a few majestic brush-strokes. Tintoretto's 'Flight into Egypt' (plate 4b) made him feel a bigger man, Ruskin wrote – even the donkey was stupendous.

Ruskin was nearly sold a 'Tintoret' as he was leaving, but in the daylight of his final morning he rejected it as a copy, and set off home, regretfully.

The book which contained the fruits of this tour, the second volume (1846) of *Modern Painters*, was kindly received by the periodicals, except for Ruskin's old enemy, the *Athenaeum*. Ruskin's praise of Tintoretto attracted great interest, since the Venetian artist was little known in Britain, and so did his favourable treatment of the early Italians, who were just beginning to be recognised as something more than 'primitive'. The volume is less contentious than the first, but also less interesting: one can still feel the dead hand of the Oxford Graduate in Ruskin's laborious distinctions between Typical and Vital beauty, between Theoria and Aesthesis. However it is clear that, besides his freshly-awakened fascination with facial expression, he had undergone a significant change in attitude during the three years that separated the volumes. In the latter, he began to assess a painting not simply as a representation of its subject, but as a revelation of the character of the man or woman who painted it. In other words, a painter's vanity, his cowardice, his noble-mindedness or his powers of intellect might all (so Ruskin came to believe) be evident in his art; and a work of art must therefore be judged as one would judge the personality it reflects.

Ruskin at first applied this principle in a rather crude form: the character of an artist might be known, he suggested, 'by the kinds of face he chose to depict'. Expressions of fear and ferocity, for instance, had a 'sympathetic attractiveness for minds cowardly and base, as the vulgar of most nations'. Also

> There is not a greater test of grandeur or meanness of mind than the expressions it will seek for and develop in the features and forms of men in fierce strife; whether determination and devotion . . . or brutal ferocity and butchered agony, of which the lowest and least palliated examples are those battles of Salvator Rosa which none but a man base-born, and thief-bred, could have conceived without sickening.[4]

By a similar test, Correggio and Guido betrayed 'marked sensuality and impurity', while Salvator, Caravaggio and 'the lower Dutch schools' showed 'signs of evil desire ill repressed'.[5] Ruskin admitted that the context of the painting must be taken into account in deciding whether an expression of grief or fear represents a noble or a shallow mind; nevertheless, few painters emerge from Ruskin's test with unsullied repute. He discovered failings even in Raphael's treatment of faces. As for Perugino, 'there is about his noblest faces a short-coming, indefinable; an absence of the full outpouring of the sacred spirit that there is in Angelico; traceable, I doubt not, to some deficiencies and avaricious flaws of his heart . . .' But Ruskin deduced that Perugino was in the main a devout man, as could be seen 'in every line that the hand of Perugino drew'.[6]

This is surely an alarming point of view, and it is worth considering how Ruskin came by it. The notion that an artist's character is related to his output was not entirely new to English (or European) art criticism. The connoisseur Richard Payne Knight, for example, maintained that virtue in life accompanied greatness in art, and felt that the converse was true as well: Jacques-Louis David painted 'with as little feeling for the real beauties of liberal art as he showed for the sufferings of his fellow-creatures, when a member of Robespierre's committee'.[7] Benjamin Haydon likewise believed 'that a downright vicious man could not be a great painter', an opinion which provoked conversation at Elizabeth Rigby's (later Eastlake) dinner-table in 1844.[8] Allan Cunningham, author of the popular *Cabinet Gallery of Pictures*, was surprised that a man as dissipated as Morland could have portrayed 'images of country simplicity and rustic modesty'. And William Etty's paintings of the female nude led to repeated accusations of his being an immoral man; his early Victorian biographer found it necessary to construct a long and elaborate defence of Etty's character, claiming that only a man whose heart was as pure as Etty's could paint beautiful women with such innocent enthusiasm.[9]

The principle that great art (and in particular noble expression) must issue from a good man was often illustrated by reference to Raphael. Raphael was not quite as satisfactory in this respect as Fra Angelico, for there was some doubt over his diligence, not to mention his death, which Vasari had attributed to an over-active session with his mistress. Still, his fine character was praised by all. According to Vasari, nature was vanquished by art in the person of Michelangelo, but 'subjugated in that of Raphael, not by art only, but by goodness also'.[10] Jonathan Richardson described Raphael in terms likely to endear him to the potential connoisseurs of 1719, as 'one of the politest, best-natured gentlemen that ever was'.[11] By the nineteenth century, this tradition was well established and often amplified; the Rev. W. Gunn declared that 'Raphael never condescended to represent vice; his mind was too much that of an angel to bear the sting attendant on its conception'.[12]

By the middle of the nineteenth century, it had become almost second nature for critics to attribute Raphael's art to his character, or at least to speak of the two in the same breath. Even the hard-headed Leslie, opponent of Ruskin and debunker of explanations which invoked religious inspiration, wrote of Raphael's pure and gentle heart, and his 'knowledge of human nature'[13] — the quality which Ruskin rather implausibly attributed to Turner. And Lord Lindsay overcame the difficulty of Raphael's mistress by connecting the 'decline' of the painter's art with 'his intimacy with the Fornarina'.[14] In view of such remarks, we should consider Ruskin's judgements about the personalities of semi-legendary painters and builders not simply as a quirk of his own arrogant, bombastic temperament but also as the culmination of a gradual process in which ever smaller details of paintings and their painters' lives were scrutinised for their moral significance.

The earliest examples of this 'artist-oriented' approach are to be found in art criticism, as in literary criticism, in late eighteenth-century Germany. The importance of the painter's feelings, as distinct from his abilities or intellect, had been stressed as never before by Wilhelm Wackenroder, whose *Outpourings from the Heart of an Art-Loving Friar* of 1797 inspired amongst others the critic Friedrich Schlegel. In the early years of the nineteenth century, Schlegel often affirmed the principle that great art could issue only from an exalted character — that is, a sincerely Christian character, for merely playing with Catholic symbols would not do. And so the painter should cultivate the inward life, since his task was to paint not what he saw before him, but what he saw within himself. If he could not see anything within himself, Schlegel maintained, he should not try to paint at all.[15] Moreover there were certain artists of the time — notably the Nazarenes, Otto Runge, and Caspar David Friedrich — who shared Schlegel's belief in art as a revelation of the inward soul.

But then, it might be asked, how is one to judge whether a painting reveals true spiritual emotion, given that religious symbols may be no more than the superficial, *ersatz* product of a pagan in disguise? A simple solution was to look at the faces depicted and to assess their expression, placing particular value on any signs of devotion, repose or faith.

Schlegel himself would no doubt have denied that he was doing anything so unsubtle. He declared himself opposed to the traditional critiques of a painting in terms of separate aspects such as composition, drawing and colour, and required instead that a great picture should 'form an harmonious and indivisible whole'. The fittest aim of painting was 'the imparting of a glorious expression to individual figures, or diffusing a divine and holy sentiment throughout a composition'.[16] But his comments on particular artists suggest that for Schlegel even the sentiment of the whole was determined to a large extent by the facial expression of the figures, and he found it especially in the blank or subdued faces drawn by the contemporary artists Cornelius and Overbeck on the one hand, and by Raphael and his predecessors on the other. Schlegel's view of the early Italian masters is that of Ruskin and the next generation of English critics:

> But in the countenance − there where the light of the painter's genius most gloriously reveals itself − every variety of expression or complete individuality of features, yet everywhere that childlike tenderness and simplicity which I tend to consider as the original characteristic of the human race.[17]

A similar attitude was suggested by Schelling: 'The artist's soul shows itself − in his work − in his originality, and in his treatment of the passions.' Schelling's example was a sculpture of Niobe which represented 'peaceful power in the storm of the passions'.[18] He and Schlegel may be said to have established the notion that art reveals the artist's soul, but it was the religious and philosophical 'soul' that they had in mind, much as Pugin did thirty years later; they did not find specific character-traits reflected in a work of art, as Rio and Ruskin were to do. At this early stage, an artist's soul was deduced from his choice of subject or theme, his originality or lack of it, his use of religious and other symbolism, and his ability to present a movingly calm figure.

English writers were slow to adopt the critical outlook of Schelling and Schlegel, despite two stimulating German visitors, J. D. Passavant and G. F. Waagen, who published (in 1836 and 1838 respectively) entertaining accounts of their tours of English art collections, and added a degree of scholarship to the familiar format of the cultural tourist's diary. Both books contained occasional comments more reminiscent of the Schlegels than of any contemporary English critic, but these were merely dropped in passing, and did not add up to a critical principle. Passavant, who had been a close associate of the Nazarene painters Pforr and Overbeck, wrote of the medieval painters of Italy and Germany that 'the influence of Christianity led them rather to aim at portraying the emotions of the soul, and thus it was that they devoted their powers more generally to painting, as offering a larger sphere for the representation of the feelings'.[19] Waagen was especially interested in such art of the earlier period as England could offer, since, as he said, 'the richness of *our* [Berlin] Museum in pictures of the Italian school of the fourteenth and fifteenth centuries, has led me particularly to study them'; and he remarked of Overbeck's 'Christ on the Mount of Olives' that 'we find in it all that depth and purity of religious feeling which makes Overbeck the first painter of our times of subjects for churches. Such a picture is an emanation of the artist's soul, not, like most church pictures of these days, coldly put together in the established common-place forms'.[20]

One book above all others seems to have freed English critics from their inhibitions about interpreting art in personal terms. This was Alexis-François Rio's *De la Poésie Chrétienne*, published in Paris in 1836. Rio was an admirer of Friedrich Schlegel, and shared many of his attitudes on artistic questions; but as far as most of his English readers were concerned, he presented a number of fresh ideas.

In the first place, his tastes were diametrically opposed to the orthodox English connoisseur's: for Rio the early sixteenth century saw not the perfection of painting, but its corruption, and the start of the fatal decline was set by Rio at an even earlier time, the beginning of the fifteenth century. The book was written in praise of the painters of the fourteenth and fifteenth centuries, or at least of those who resisted the temptations of this world and especially the dangerous lure of 'naturalism'.

Secondly, there was a new tone of intolerance towards those artists Rio did not admire. The same tone is to be found in the next decade in the writings of Pugin and Ruskin, but it had not been much in evidence in previous years, when amused disdain was more fashionable.

Thirdly, and related to the last point, Rio's criticism operated at a very personal level, in that he viewed painting often as a direct manifestation of the painter's character. Sometimes Rio envisaged an age-spirit, which he held responsible for the artistic products of its time; alternatively he found great significance in the personal life of the individual artist. In either case, Rio was not much concerned with developments in artistic technique and knowledge (such as the mastery of perspective or chiaroscuro, which had been of major interest to those few others who had studied this early period) but attached more weight to the state of each artist's soul or character, and these he deduced chiefly from biographies. Quoting Vasari's story of Filippo Lippi's abducting the novice Lucrezia Luti as she was on her way to the cathedral to see the girdle of the holy Virgin, Rio concluded that such a depraved character could never have achieved the elevated art of his predecessors.

Although the notion that only a virtuous man can be a great artist was not a new one, Rio used it with unprecedented gusto. He revelled in the familiar anecdotes of the lives of the painters – of how Piero di Cosimo's love of nature prevented him from allowing his trees to be pruned, or how Fra Angelico's tears flowed every time he painted Christ on the cross – and he linked these to the painters' subjects and styles. Rio added a few untraditional suggestions of his own: he implied that Benozzo Gozzoli was indebted to Angelico not so much for any stylistic qualities as for his piety, and suggested that Raphael's change in style might be due to changes 'in his own heart'.

A difficulty with this personal approach is that it could lead to a conflict of criteria: one might admire a painting for the qualities of soul it is thought to express, yet dislike it as a representation, or vice versa. Rio avoided such split judgements by playing down the importance of mimetic criteria: he condemned landscape painting as an inferior activity, and he repeatedly attacked the 'decadence' of naturalistic painting. But when he came to confront the issue squarely, he was not prepared to say that to aim at a precise imitation of nature was in itself undesirable. Instead he resolved the dilemma, just as Ruskin was to do, by deciding that it was only the by-products of 'naturalism' that were pernicious. When in the fifteenth century the imitation of nature became the supreme and avowed aim of art, wrote Rio, painters were led to neglect the spiritual for the material, and to substitute the prosaic portraits of living people for the traditional types of Christ, the Virgin and the Saints. [21] This interpretation of the Renaissance was taken up in essence by Ruskin, and rapidly gained a large following.

It is arguable that Ruskin was more deeply affected by Rio's *De la Poésie Chrétienne* than by any other work on the subject of art. According to E. T. Cook, Ruskin's biographer and editor, it was his reading of Rio that made him return to Italy in 1845 to study the early Italian masters; [22] once arrived in Pisa and Florence, Ruskin succumbed still further to Rio's spell, and its influence remained with him for many years. We have seen how, in the 1846 volume of *Modern Painters*, Ruskin began to derive the personality of individual artists from the expression which they portrayed in their figures. In doing so, he was surely adapting Rio's method to suit his own ends. For Rio had criticised paintings in terms of their authors' personalities, but his evidence seldom went beyond traditional anecdotes and what he could glean from the pages of Vasari; Ruskin, though prepared to utilise Vasari when convenient, went further, and based his evaluations of a painter's character upon the details and qualities of his art. This distinction is illustrated by the respective remarks of Rio and Ruskin on Perugino. Rio, anxious to vindicate Raphael's master, whom Vasari had implicitly accused of cupidity and irreligion, offered in reply the story that Perugino had decorated an oratory and asked only for an omelette in payment. [23] Ruskin's evidence, on the other hand, was 'internal' (though no less flimsy): he asked the reader to consider, as a demonstration of the painter's personal piety, 'what Rio has singularly missed observing, that Perugino, in his portrait of himself in the Florence Gallery [plate 5], has put a scroll into the hand with the words "Timete Deum": thus surely indicating what he considered his duty and message'. [24]

Rio was not particularly concerned with facial expression. On one occasion only did he make a major point of linking it with the artist's character, and this, as one might expect, occurs in his discussion of Angelico. [25] Ruskin, in his review of Lindsay's *History of Christian Art*, attached more significance to Angelico's faces. So saintly a character was Angelico that 'he could not by any exertion, even for a moment, conceive either agitation, doubt or fear': as a result, Ruskin declared, all his attempts to draw these

were a failure, and the only form of movement which the Blessed
Angelico could successfully portray was 'the spiritual speed of
Angels'.[26]

There is barely a whiff of such personal inference in the first
volume of *Modern Painters*, which Ruskin had written shortly
before his reading of Rio. (References to the mentalities of
painters – their 'restlessness', 'morbidity', lack of 'sacred sympathies' and so on – were all added in the third edition of the first
volume published in September 1846.) It was evidently in the
space of a couple of years that Ruskin became convinced that the
successes and failures of artists were attributable to their individual
personalities. The honesty of a work of art was always 'more or less
corrupted by the various weaknesses of the painter, by his vanity,
his idleness, or his cowardice',[27] claimed Ruskin in the 1846
edition of the first volume, and the 'failure' of the French school
was said to be due to the fact that vanity was their ruling motive.[28]
Ruskin now introduced a new means of detecting a painter's
character: as well as the faces he chose to depict, the degree of his
finishing could be revealing. But one must not jump to hasty
conclusions, since

> the fact is, that both finish and impetuosity, specific minuteness
> and large abstraction, may be the signs of passion, or of its
> reverse; may result from affection or indifference, intellect or
> dullness. Some men finish from intense love of the beautiful in
> the smallest parts of what they do; others in pure incapability of
> comprehending anything but parts; others to show their
> dexterity with the brush, and prove expenditure of time.[29]

Of course this is true. But far from being deterred by this
difficulty, Ruskin saw it as a challenge. He admitted that not all
paintings offer complete insight into their creator's personality,
but he had no doubt that some do – 'there are some pictures which
rank not under the head of failures, but of perpetrations or
commissions; some things which a man cannot do or say without
sealing for ever his character and capacity'. A case in point was the
heads painted by Domenichino. 'The man who painted the
Madonna del Rosario and Martyrdom of St Agnes in the gallery of
Bologna, is palpably incapable of doing anything good, great, or
right, in any field, or kind whatsoever.'[30]

In this edition Ruskin also began to draw inferences about the characters of contemporary artists – a more dangerous ploy. The mind of Constable (who had died in 1837) had a 'strange want of depth (though 'his works are to be deeply respected')[31]; and Turner, who was still alive, was said to fall short of perfection in his art because of his education, his impetuous character, and his lack of religious feeling. Even before reading Rio, Ruskin had relied on Turner's painting as a surer guide to his personality than the report of acquaintances. 'Everybody had described him to me as boorish, unintellectual, vulgar. This I knew to be impossible', wrote Ruskin, describing his first meeting with the artist.[32] However Turner must have remained something of a disappointment to Ruskin, and the fact that Ruskin continued to praise Turner's nobleness of character (even after looking through his erotic sketches) demonstrates how firmly the critic believed that art was ultimately a matter of personal qualities.

Before leaving the subject of Ruskin's debt to Rio, there is one further source of information worth considering: the manuscript notebooks of Ruskin's Italian tour of 1845. These include a dozen respectful references to Rio. (No other contemporary critics are named except for Kugler and Lanzi, who are each mentioned once.) It is here that Ruskin's first recorded attempts at Rio's mode of criticism appear. One passage is especially significant:

> Note the way in which Rio speaks. p. 453 of the Christ Mort. of Mantegna at Milan [plate 6a], which is one of the most fearfully disgusting pictures in the world. The two heads of the women crying on the left hand are of detestable and monotonous ugliness . . . [these and other features] make it to my mind perfectly conclusive as to the detestable and irredeemable character of Mantegna.[33]

On several occasions Ruskin's turn of phrase suggests the idea that painters communicate their own characters into the characters of their figures. Of the Pisan fresco depicting St Ranieri attacked by the devil, 'it is remarkable what a deep feeling of sanctity is generally imparted to St R's head . . .' The two leopards in the same fresco 'are themselves fine instances of great gentleness and intelligence being put into the brute face, without giving it any human attributes'.[34] And 'generally speaking, the larger a face is drawn, the more its expression evaporates. This is peculiarly true of Fra Angelico, and I believe of all painters whose feeling is greater than their knowledge'.[35]

A criterion which Ruskin was to use in his published work was the ability of a painter to depict certain types of character more successfully than others. 'Generally Orcagna seems not quite successful in representing piety or the good and joyous passions, as malignity and grief. There is more truth about his devils than angels.' Ruskin seems to have regarded this as indicative of the painter's own personality, for on the next page he wrote, 'he is a poet, but I should not suppose him religious nor of pure feeling'.[36]

Another clue which Ruskin seems to have used here for the first time is the face of a painter as depicted in a portrait or self-portrait. He hoped no doubt that this might confirm his already formed view of the painter's character. One can imagine the anxiety with which he studied the several portraits of painters in the Uffizi: 'Perugino's I thought at first too hard and cold in expression, but I found on long looking that it was merely the consistency and quietness of deep character, the sad, wise valour of George Herbert.'[37]

The part played by Rio in English art criticism as a whole has not been generally recognised, [38] although it seems likely that he, more than any other individual, was responsible for the infiltration of Continental notions of art criticism into England. He had the advantages of socially influential friends in England and an English wife, which may have made his fervent ultramontanist Catholicism more acceptable. One person who received Rio's ideas by personal impact was Anna Jameson; she had been an admirer of German culture since her two-year convalescence in Germany (1927–8), and in 1833 had struck up a dramatic friendship with A. W. Schlegel ('. . . they tell me it was a complete conquest. Pity I am married!'[39]). In 1841 she wrote from Paris to her sister that 'the great event of my life here has been the meeting with Rio'.[40] Rio escorted her round the Louvre, and when soon afterwards Anna Jameson began to write on artistic subjects in earnest, including reviews for the *Athenaeum*, many references to Rio's *De la Poésie Chrétienne* appeared; she dwelt on the styles and subjects dear to Rio, and declared that art is to be viewed as a revelation of the artist's personality. The introduction to her *Handbook to the Public Galleries of Art*, published the year after her meeting with Rio, made her policy clear: quoting Goethe's advice to readers that they should study the character and circumstances of a poet as well as his productions, she added that this was equally applicable to painters:

> Almost every picture (which is the production of mind) has an individual character reflecting the predominant temperament — nay, sometimes the occasional mood of the artist, its creator.

And as regards portraits, generally thought to be a lesser branch of the art:

> There is, besides the physiognomy of the individual represented, the physiognomy, if I may so express myself, of the picture; detected at once by the mere connoisseur as a distinction of manner, style, execution, but of which the reflecting and philosophical observer might discover the key in the mind or life of the individual painter.[41]

If there was to be such a close connection between life and art, the traditional fare of 'lives of the painters' had to be scrutinised afresh. Later in the same volume, Anna Jameson remarked with relief that the reputation of Raphael, supreme exponent of 'expression', had been cleared by Passavant's recent biography: Raphael was not, after all, 'idle and dissipated'.[42]

However Anna Jameson did not often put Rio's principle into practice. The idea that a work of art is to be seen as an emanation from its creator's character is made explicit in the introductions to several of her books, but it is seldom utilised in the criticism contained within the books themselves. In her best-known work, *Sacred and Legendary Art*, she applied this analysis only to the most amenable characters, such as Fra Angelico:

> His conception of the angelic nature remains unapproached, unapproachable; it is only his, for it was the gentle, passionless, refined nature of the recluse which stamped itself there.[43]

And of Filippo Lippi:

> As we might have expected from the character of the man, his angels want refinement . . .[44]

But on the great majority of artists whose characters were not so clearly described by Vasari, neither Mrs Jameson nor Rio himself were prepared to pass this kind of moral judgement. It was Ruskin who took the further step of criticising a work of art in terms of the personality which he inferred from the artist's work.

When the three volumes of Lord Lindsay's *Sketches of the History of Christian Art* were published in 1847, they comprised the most detailed treatment then available of European art in the fourteenth and fifteenth centuries. Lindsay went beyond Rio in dealing with architecture and the painting of northern Europe as well as of Italy, but one can hardly doubt the strong influence of the Frenchman in his method. A reviewer noted, 'It is pleasing to observe the testimony which Lord Lindsay bears to the devout character of many of the early painters. Giotto, he observes, was no less a Christian than a painter . . .'[45] Lindsay also emphasised the personal piety and dedication of several other Italian artists including (of course) Fra Angelico. Using one of Rio's favourite metaphors, he declared that in Angelico's case, 'the emotions of his heart animated his pencil' with such tenderness and repose that his delineations of the wicked were inevitably feeble. Lindsay did however dissociate himself gently from Rio in this chapter, saying that Angelico had recently been 'unduly extolled' and referring in a footnote to 'the Catholic estimate . . . by the eloquent and elegant Rio'.[46]

The *Athenaeum*, which took a strong interest in art and its literature, gave Rio's book a long and generally favourable review soon after its original publication in Paris.[47] The reviewer was George Darley, the poet and critic. Darley was a man of independent views – it was Leonardo's portraits, and not Raphael's, in which he found 'inward beauty' and 'deep metaphysical expression and character'[48] – and Rio's work confirmed his appreciation for the early masters. He attacked their detractors ungrammatically but savagely: 'Unable to discern the recondite beauties lying under the formality of these old-fashioned pictures, *wooden* is the epithet applied to them by those who have a vast deal more of the block about themselves.'[49]

Darley continued to promote the early Italians until his death in 1846. It is difficult to decide how much he owed to Rio. He was not inclined to ascribe their art to their personality or to their faith, and he found fault with Rio for insisting that Roman Catholicism inspired their painting. He was critical, furthermore, of Ruskin's very personal references (in the second volume of *Modern Painters*) to Salvator Rosa's 'brutality', Raphael's 'corruption', and

Caravaggio's 'signs of evil mind'.[50] Yet even though Darley did
not associate stylistic habits with specific traits in the artist, he did
believe that the work of his favourite painters, such as Leonardo
and Francesco Francia, expressed certain unspecified emotional
qualities. Of the first two Francias bought for the National Gallery
in 1841, Darley declared that 'they are most deeply expressive.
They make us tremble and thrill at the core by their very calmness';
and he was well aware of the importance of subdued facial
expression in creating this 'thrillingly calm atmosphere'.[51] He was
evidently ready to find subtleties of emotional tone in a picture, but
not prepared to follow the (questionable) policy of Rio and
Ruskin in claiming to derive these qualities from the character of
the artist or his age.

By the time *Blackwood's* came to review Rio's book (in its
English translation), Rio's style of criticism was no longer a
novelty. J. B. Atkinson, the reviewer, found Rio too intent on the
psychology of art, and neglectful of its physique; nevertheless,
Atkinson declared, 'the world, especially the community of art,
cannot be too frequently reminded that, to execute a great and
good work, a man must first make himself great and good'.[52] Yet
another admirer of Rio's book was Henry Drummond, the
Irvingite and parliamentarian, who tried in one of his pamphlets to
show that religion was the true source of all great art, 'availing
myself principally of the recent work of Monsieur Rio for that
purpose'.[53] Drummond emphasised that the decline of the arts was
not due to any lack of patronage, as the previous generation had
claimed; it was the inevitable result of the lack of religious feeling,
in artists and public alike.

Drummond clearly had in mind more than the subject-matter
which religious tradition provides: like Rio, he saw great art as
flowing directly from the brush of an inspired painter, and the
mark of great art was the ability to portray a pure and holy face.
Only a personally virtuous man could achieve this. So Drummond
condemned the work of Andrea del Sarto, 'for he was a dishonest,
irreligious man', and he used the story of Raphael's mistress, often
avoided by tactful commentators, in support of his thesis. Raphael
suceeded in his art 'so long as he was a pure and holy man himself;
but as soon as he ceased to be so, his inspiration left him . . .after he
became the slave of lust, and the baker's wife supplied in his
affections the place which sanctity had held before'.[54]

In view of the number of similar opinions expressed at this time, it is fair to say that the evaluation of art according to its supposed religious inspiration was one of the major innovations of early Victorian art criticism. Rio's book played a leading role in this, and so no doubt did the fear of working-class revolution – a fear widespread among the classes to which artists and critics belonged. But of the new group of art critics, only Ruskin found a means of identifying art and character which could catch the imagination of a popular audience. Rio's method was limited by a lack of knowledge about the spiritual or personal lives of the great painters, and it could hardly be applied to Gothic architecture and craftsmen, whose very identities – let alone characters – were then almost entirely unknown. Enterprising architectural critics therefore tended to resort to symbolism: Drummond was fairly typical in trying to derive the 'decline in architecture' in England from the relative significance of altar, font and pulpit in the Reformation. The most telling of Ruskin's innovations lay in his going beyond the restrictions of history and tradition, and making *assumptions* about the character of painter or builder – assumptions supported, it is true, by a careful selection (and distortion) of historical sources, but based primarily on the work of art and the personality he felt it represented.

*       *       *

For Ruskin 1846 was a year of uncertainty as well as triumph. Neither poetry nor the Church now held out the prospect of a career, and he had written enough for the time being – perhaps too much – on the beauties of nature and painting. The colour and delicacy of medieval Italian architecture had attracted him the year before, as his sketches made on tour indicate, but he had not yet discovered architecture as a vehicle for his ideas.

Ruskin tried to recapture the experiences of that year by taking his father back to Italy to see the treasures he had discovered there, but inevitably he failed. John James was not captivated by Fra Angelico, or the Campo Santo frescoes. Ruskin grew irritable, relations between father and son were strained, and both must have thought how satisfactory it would be if Ruskin were to settle down with a wife. Soon afterwards, a very eligible lady did come into Ruskin's orbit, Charlotte Lockhart, a grand-daughter of Sir

Walter Scott. Ruskin was quite taken with her. When her father, the editor of the prestigious *Quarterly Review*, asked Ruskin to review Lord Lindsay's *History of Christian Art* he accepted, saying later that he had done so to recommend himself to Charlotte. But wherever marriages are made, they are not made in the pages of the *Quarterly Review*. Charlotte was unimpressed, and Ruskin, in a mood of deep depression, was sent by his parents to recover in Leamington.

The Ruskin parents were even more anxious than Ruskin that Charlotte Lockhart should be married to their son. When another young and vivacious girl came to stay, Mrs Ruskin intimated that he was actually engaged to Charlotte. The young girl was Euphemia Gray, daughter of an old family friend, who had stayed with the Ruskins on four previous occasions. After the second of these, when John was 22 and she 13, he had written for her his subsequently successful fairy story, *King of the Golden River*. On her fourth visit, in March 1846, she was nearly 18; he fell in love with her, and she came to stay again the following April. She soon became suspicious about his supposed fiancée: indeed the episode remains mysterious to this day. Ruskin was possibly hedging his bets, and had proposed obliquely to Charlotte – his parents seem to have believed that some bond existed. 'I have not yet had the courage to ask John who his Lady-*love* is', Effie wrote home on her nineteenth birthday, 'of the last syllable I suspect there is little . . . I suspect from what is said that the lady has a fortune and that love must come after marriage.'[55]

When Charlotte was finally lost to him, Ruskin again became morbid and ill. Another spell at Leamington did not help much. He went to stay with a friend in Scotland, still in dark depression, consoled only by the thought of pretty, flirtatious Effie Gray. The possibility arose of his visiting the Grays' home at Bowerswell, Perth; now at last Margaret Ruskin, worried no doubt by her son's state of mind, encouraged him to pursue his suit with Effie. He proposed, and she accepted happily.

The omens attending Ruskin's wedding were of a kind which the most extravagant of Gothic novelists would blush to invent. The following spring, while the Chartists were on the march in England and all Europe was in a ferment of revolution, John Ruskin went up to Perth, which had been the scene of the suicide of Ruskin's grandfather shortly before he was born. Effie, indeed, was born in the very room in which John Thomas Ruskin had cut his throat. In 1842—4 the Grays had built a new Bowerswell a few yards from the old; and in this house, which the Ruskin parents could not even now bring themselves to enter, John and Effie were married on 10 April 1848.

Was this section about the marriage necessary in this book?

# 5 Marriage

Effie and John did not see each other for the first five months of their six-month engagement, but they exchanged letters nearly every day – more passionate on his part than on hers. Among endearments, he suggested how she might help him in his architectural studies, by taking notes and carrying out background research. He clearly visualised her role:

> . . . you will have often to wait for me while I am examining cathedrals, by the *hour* – you may do it at the Inn – but in most cases – when it is not cold, I imagine it will be in the church – that you may see what I am about . . .[1]

In this way she would come to share his enthusiasm, he hoped. His letters also expressed his dislike for the social life of fashionable London; and he looked forward above all to their trip to Chamonix, with his parents, which would take place a fortnight after the wedding. Not enough of Effie's correspondence survives to reveal her own views on these subjects.

A month before the wedding the Ruskins learnt that Mr Gray had lost heavily in railway shares, so that his daughter could contribute no money to the marriage. John James wrote angrily to Mr Gray, and although Effie's father was not quite the 'ruined man' that John James had supposed, the affair brought an element of resentment between the two families at the outset. More disappointing to John was the fact that the February revolution in France made the projected family expedition impossible.

John and Effie spent their honeymoon in Scotland and in the Lake District. They did not consummate the marriage. Later, each of them gave an account of why they did not do so, and the two accounts agree substantially. As Effie wrote to her father in March 1854,

> He alleged various reasons, hatred to children, religious moti-

Plate 1a. J. M. W. Turner, 'Rome from Mount Aventine', *Earl of Rosebery Collection.*

Plate 1b. J. M. W. Turner, 'Slavers throwing overboard the dead and dying' ('The Slave Ship'), *Museum of Fine Arts, Boston, U.S.A.*

Plate 2a. J. Ruskin, 'The Falls at Schaffhausen', *Fogg Art Museum, Harvard University, U.S.A.*

Plate 2b. J. Ruskin, 'Details of Venetian Architecture', *The Ruskin Galleries, Bembridge School, Isle of Wight.*

Plate 3a. 'Laocoon' (detail), *Vatican Museum* (*Anderson, Mansell Collection*).

Plate 3b. C. L. Eastlake, 'Haidée' (detail), *Tate Gallery, London.*

Plate 3c. J. Ruskin after Benozzo Gozzoli, 'Abraham parting from the Angels' (detail), *Ashmolean Museum, Oxford.*

Plate 3d. Fra Angelico, 'The Annunciation and Adoration of the Magi' (detail), *Museo di San Marco, Florence* (*Mansell Collection*).

Plate 4a. J.Ruskin,'Casa d'Oro, Venice', *The Ruskin Galleries, Bembridge School, Isle of Wight.*

Plate 4b. Tintoretto, 'The Flight into Egypt', *Scuola di San Rocco, Venice (Anderson, Mansell Collection).*

Plate 5.   Perugino, 'Portrait of Francesco delle Opere' (believed by
Ruskin to be a self-portrait), *Uffizi Galleries, Florence*
(*Mansell Collection*).

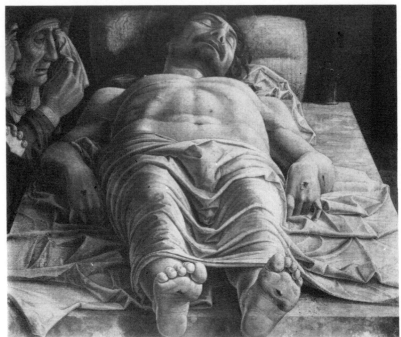

Plate 6a. Mantegna, 'The Dead Christ', *Pinacoteca di Brera, Milan* (*Mansell Collection*).

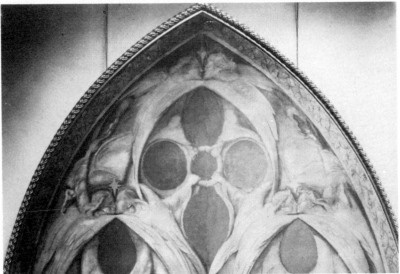

Plate 6b. J. E. Millais, 'Design for a Gothic Window' *Courtesy Mary Lutyens.*

Plate 7a. Arthur Hughes, 'April Love' (detail), *Tate Gallery, London.*

Plate 7b. D. G. Rossetti, 'Ecce Ancilla Domini' (detail), *Tate Gallery, London.*

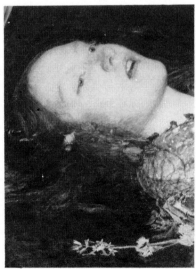

Plate 7c. J. E. Millais, 'Ophelia' (detail), *Tate Gallery, London.*

Plate 7d. J. E. Millais, 'The Huguenot' (detail), *Huntingdon Hartford Collection, New York (Mansell Collection).*

Plate 8b. Ruskin in old age (photograph), *Mansell Collection.*

Plate 8a. Michelangelo, 'Head of a Man Shouting', *Ashmolean Museum, Oxford.*

*motives*

ves, a desire to preserve my beauty, and finally this last year told me his true reason (and this to me is as villainous as all the rest), that he had imagined that women were quite different to what he saw I was, and that the reason he did not make me his wife was because he was disgusted with my person the first evening, 10 April. [2]

Ruskin's statement mentions Effie's fragile nervous state at the time, and his own anxiety; and

It may be thought strange that I could abstrain from a woman who to most people was so attractive. But though her face was beautiful, her person was not formed to excite passion. On the contrary there were certain circumstances in her person which completely checked it. [3]

Exactly what Ruskin meant is a matter for speculation. The traditional interpretation is that he was referring to Effie's pubic hair; that he had seen only smooth-skinned nudes in sculpture and painting, and had expected his wife to be like them. At any rate, the initial postponement grew into a permanent state of married celibacy. This was not such a uncommon state — nor is it today — but the subsequent ordeals of lawsuit, medical examination and (above all) publicity were exceptionally humiliating for both of them.

The first months of their marriage were not made easier by the fact that the Ruskin parents had no intention of seeing any less of their son after his marriage than before. In July the two couples were staying at Salisbury, where John had a cold and Effie grew irritated at her mother-in-law's endless fussing over him. Effie was deeply worried too by her father's plight. In August it was judged safe for them to go to France, and John was back in his element, spending his days examining the Gothic churches of Normandy. But Effie was not the research assistant that he required. At Salisbury she had tried to sketch, but her husband's concentrated studies in France left no place for her. 'Poor Effie would be far better off with Papa and you than with me', wrote John to his mother. [4] The news from home was bad: railway shares were still falling, John James Ruskin was reluctant to find a position for Effie's brother George, and in September her aunt died. Effie was often in tears and her hair was falling out.

*true? I don't recall it.*

Soon after their return to England, the young Ruskins moved into their own (leased) home at 31 Park Street. John still worked hard at *The Seven Lamps of Architecture*, but Effie was happier and healthier here in the heart of fashionable London. Railway shares picked up, moreover. But at Christmas Effie became ill; her mother came down to stay with her, and when she returned to Perth in February, Effie went too. There another of her brothers died, of whooping-cough, and Effie remained with her family; John remained with his, and as of old the three Ruskins set off for Switzerland in April 1849. John James, who took Effie's departure as an insult, wrote to Mr Gray suggesting that she had deserted her husband, and Mr Gray replied that the Ruskin parents should stop interfering in the lives of John and Effie.

After a separation of eight months, Ruskin returned to his wife at Perth. She made the happy suggestion that the two of them should go to Venice, where the architecture and the social life were equally brilliant. On 3 October 1949, they left England together.

They travelled in two carriages, one for John and his man-servant, the other for Effie and her companion, Charlotte Ker. They took more than a month to reach Venice, pausing often *en route* and putting their carriage on to the train where a railway existed. In Venice they stayed in the Albergo Danieli, a former *palazzo* standing next to the Ducal Palace and overlooking the lagoon. In the evenings the crowds would gather in the Piazza San Marco, where the Austrian military band played and the ladies and gentlemen refreshed themselves beneath the gaslit arcades — 'The place is like a vast drawing-room', wrote Effie.[5] However Venice was an occupied city at that time, and the Italians naturally refused to attend the social occasions arranged by their Austrian conquerors. At first Effie had taken the Italian side ('I am a thorough Italian here and hate oppression', she had declared in Milan[6]), but her play-politics were no match for the dashing moustaches of the Austrian officers. She was soon being escorted by the captain who a few months before had bombarded Venice with explosive balloons; and while the homeless Italians spent their nights huddled beside the bridges, she was in great demand at the military balls. 'Prince Troubetzkoi danced the galope with me twice as fast as Lord Charles . . .'[7]

Ruskin himself was hard at work, a conspicuous figure taking daguerreotypes with a black cloth over his head, or climbing about the columns of the Ducal Palace. He, too, found the Austrians more congenial than the Italians, and he seems to have objected less to the intrusion of Austria into Venice than to the guns and powder magazines which marred the beauty of the city.

The couple returned from their hectic winter in time for the London summer season of 1850. Effie was presented at court and repeated her social successes, while John was engaged in writing up the first volume of *The Stones of Venice* (published in March the following year), in theological controversy (the misleadingly-named *Notes on the Construction of Sheepfolds* was published at the same time) and in his first contacts with the Pre-Raphaelites. By September 1851 they were back in Venice, in whose cosmopolitan society Effie shone still more brightly than before. The pages of her letters home are packed with Princes, Dukes and Archdukes, dancing with her or calling for tea. A certain Baron Diller, one of Marshal Radetsky's *aides*, quarrelled with another officer over some question of dancing with Effie, and received a severe sabre wound in the resulting duel. Meanwhile her husband remained at their hotel: 'John never speaks to any body', Effie wrote, 'or troubles himself to speak at all unless it happens to amuse him at the moment and fortunately for him he is not expected by any etiquette here from going out at all which agrees perfectly with his taste although not with mine'.[8]

Ruskin's own daily letters to his father are less vivid, their most frequent topics being Turner, the Bible and his writing. There are hints of an awakening interest in political and social matters: he writes of 'desperate abuses going on in governments, and real ground for movement among the lower classes, which of course they are little likely to guide by any very just or rational principle'. After illustrating this point at length from the 62nd Psalm, he remarks

> However I must mind and not get too sympathising with the Radicals – Effie says, with some justice – that I am a great conservative in France, because there everybody is radical – and a great radical in Austria, because there everybody is con-servative. I suppose that one reason why I am so fond of fish – (as creatures I mean, not as eating) is that they always swim with their heads against the stream. I find it for me, the healthiest position.[9]

As they were packing to leave for England, Effie's jewels were stolen from her hotel room, and there was nearly another duel. Suspicion of theft fell on an English officer, whose friend Count Thun challenged Ruskin to name the weapons with which they would meet; but Ruskin, whose sword was probably a good deal less mighty than his pen, wisely declined.

They travelled home with Lord and Lady Feilding, recent converts (or 'perverts', in the usage then current) to Roman Catholicism. The Feildings tried hard to persuade John and Effie, with a succession of stories (as Effie reported) about miraculously bleeding roses and blushing stones. At church in Paris the Ruskins were surprised to hear the Abbé calling on the congregation to pray for their conversion. Old Mrs Ruskin was full of anxiety on her son's behalf, especially when she heard soon after his return that he was lunching with the recently seceded Archdeacon Manning. Ruskin was certainly interested in Catholic faith and doctrine, and was less ready than Effie, let alone his parents, to dismiss Catholic miracles as impostures. But his mother need not have worried, for Ruskin was in little danger of conversion, less even than he had been ten years before. He may well have been conscious that his published attacks on the Roman Church had been founded on ignorance, and that his interest in the subject was intellectual rather than emotional. He was not inclined to fasting or flagellation, he wrote (to his mother-in-law, who was also anxious); he was past the age of Romance.[10]

Back in England in July 1852, they moved into 30 Herne Hill, which adjoined the old Ruskin home. John James had leased this house for them, and made expensive arrangements to furnish it — 'in the worst possible taste', as Effie observed.[11] John James was concerned lest suburban life might prove too dull for Effie and her husband, but he had now also to consider the possibility that the couple would not make each other happy under any circumstances.

Ruskin worked hard at the second and third volumes of *The Stones of Venice*, while Effie grew bored and depressed, refusing invitations because her husband could not accompany her. The great event of the winter was the Duke of Wellington's state funeral in November, which she managed to attend with her father who had come up to London. She naturally saw a good deal of the Ruskin parents, who were patronising and critical by turns, and her letters show her increasing resentment at their influence over her life; but her mother was sympathetic, and so was her friend and confidante Elizabeth Eastlake.

That winter she agreed to sit as model for the twenty-three-year-old John Everett Millais, who by now was a good friend of both the Ruskins. He had first intended her for 'The Proscribed Royalist', but in the event she sat in March for 'The Order of Release' – ironically titled, in view of later events, although in the picture it is the lady who releases her husband. Even at this stage, John James Ruskin remarked meaningfully on the attention Millais was paying to Effie, as if to suggest a degree of guilt on her part. In May 'The Order of Release' appeared in the Academy Summer Exhibition, where it was a great success with critics (except for *Blackwood's*, which found the woman's face plain and hard, defiant instead of tender) and public: 'It is hardly possible to approach it for the rows of bonnets', wrote the delighted Effie. [12]

Next month Effie and John Ruskin set off for a tour of the Highlands, taking with them Millais and his brother William. The journey was interrupted in Stirlingshire, however, where Millais chose a rocky stream at Glenfinlas as the location for a portrait of Ruskin. The party put up at the small village of Brig o'Turk for nearly four months. They spent many days down by the stream: Millais painting, his brother and Ruskin's man-servant fishing, Effie sewing or taking lessons in drawing from Millais. Ruskin did some drawing and paddling, but was largely occupied in preparing an index to *The Stones of Venice* and lectures for the autumn. When it rained Millais and Ruskin had violent bouts of battledore and shuttlecock indoors. One morning Millais went swimming and bruised his nose on the bottom of the stream; that afternoon he crushed his thumb while building a bridge by which Effie could cross. Luckily Effie was on hand to tend his wounds. '. . . I led him home as best I could', she wrote in her diary. 'He lent on me all the way and it was dreadful pain between his nose and thumb'. [13]

At the end of July Millais started on Ruskin's portrait, painting an inch or so a day, in the sharp meticulous manner of his earlier 'P.R.B.' work. Effie was his deepest concern. He was miserably in love with her. He sketched her constantly, supervised her drawing, and escorted her home down the lonely, muddy road, and yet she was inaccessible to him. His state of gloom was not lightened by the news that his close friend Holman Hunt was intending to leave for the Middle East, and Ruskin, believing that this prospect was the chief cause of Millais's wretchedness, wrote asking Hunt to change his mind.

Far from resenting Millais's attentions to Effie, Ruskin was glad to have somebody to amuse and occupy her; he would not have imagined that his marriage was threatened any more by the young artist than by the hussars of the Austrian army in Venice. It was later gossiped that Ruskin (or even the elder Ruskins) contrived the whole trip as a means of transferring Effie to Millais from her husband, who in the circumstances would thus appear the injured party. But as Mary Lutyens has observed, even if Ruskin did want to be rid of his wife, he had no desire to lose his principal protégé as well. His enthusiasm for Millais's work was at its peak that crucial summer; the rocky background of the Ruskin portrait was painted in with minute fidelity, and moreover Millais had shown an unexpected talent for highly inventive architectural designs. One of these, an arrangement of flowing figures that seems to belong to the 1890s rather than to 1853, is for a window consisting of three pointed arches, each formed by the wings of a pair of kissing angels (plate 6b). Millais recorded that it represented eternal happiness and the struggle for life, but that sounds like Ruskin's idea; to judge by the angels' profiles, the painting is a multiple beatification of Effie – Millais's equivalent of Rossetti's 'Beata Beatrix'.

In October the party left Brig o'Turk and split up. Ruskin went to Edinburgh to give his first public lectures, a series of four, which were a success: each was attended by over a thousand people, including Effie's parents. But by the new year relations were more strained than ever. Millais 'knew all' about John and Effie's marriage, and was writing confidential letters to Mrs Gray, and yet Ruskin was still sitting for the unfinished portrait which John James had commissioned. Millais declared to Mrs Gray that once the portrait was done, he would 'begin a new life' with Holman Hunt in the East.[14] In South London Effie and the Ruskin parents were infuriating each other. Finally in March, Effie wrote to her parents explaining why 'I do not think I am John Ruskin's Wife at all . . .'[15] and begged them to help her escape. They pretended that she was going to Perth for another visit, and on 25 April 1854 John saw her off at the station, suspecting nothing. That evening he was served with a citation, and learned that Effie was suing for annulment of their marriage. For a fortnight Ruskin appeared in public as if nothing had happened, although the affair was the talk of London society; then to the rage of Effie's supporters, he wrote a long letter to *The Times* on the high moral value of Hunt's picture 'The Awakening Conscience'. He then went abroad with his parents, as they had previously planned. He did not contest his wife's suit; she was granted a decree of annulment while he was on the Continent, at his favourite Chamonix.

When Ruskin returned in the autumn, Millais had yet to complete the long-delayed portrait, but by December it was hanging at Denmark Hill. There is no record of Ruskin and Millais meeting subsequently. Millais and Effie were married the following summer at Bowerswell, and they lived together for forty years, in general happily, although Effie continued to suffer from ill-health and sleeplessness. The money that Ruskin had settled on Effie was returned to him at the annulment, so that Millais could not at first keep his wife in the manner to which she was accustomed. Within a year of the marriage there was also a child to provide for, and seven others followed. Millais had already begun to paint in a freeer, more rapid style; in 1853 he had been elected an Associate of the Royal Academy, and thenceforth his work moved closer to the mainstream of Victorian painting. By 1860 he had abandoned the overall precision and the intensity of his Pre-Raphaelite days. With the influence and support of Effie, the *enfant terrible* of the Academy finally became its President.

The tragic events of Ruskin's marriage were discreetly over-looked by the editors of Ruskin's *Works*, E. T. Cook and Alexander Wedderburn, although they treated most of his life and writings with staggering thoroughness. But their well-intentioned omission did no service to Ruskin in the long run: for anyone who hopes to understand the tone of his writing, its aggressiveness and its deliberate unconventionality, must keep in mind Ruskin's personal life. It is not simply that the failure of his marriage made him feel more than ever an outsider, a prophet crying in the wilderness; or that when he attacked the social and economic institutions of mid-Victorian England, he was also attacking the fashionable world which Effie represented. At a more profound level, Ruskin's critical orientation — the very personal approach to paintings and architecture with which the preceding chapters have been concerned — is surely linked to his aloofness from his wife and his contemporaries in general. Ruskin may have found it hard to form friendships with other human beings, but he had no difficulty in peopling his imagination with painters and civilizations, to which he responded with love, hate and the range of intermediate emotions which most people reserve for one another. Even the Effie whom he had loved was largely a figment of his ever-creative imagination; he was never so affectionate towards her as during their engagement, when they were several hundred miles apart, and (as he himself confessed) the more often he wrote to her, the more he loved her. 'May you not be in some degree surrounding her with imaginary charms — take care of this',[16] his mother had warned, too late. On the other hand, the characters with which he invested works of art could not disillusion him so easily. In Ruskin's mind, the paintings of Turner and the stones of Venice were more human than the men and women whom he had to meet face to face.

# 6 *Seven Lamps* and
its Rivals

It was once widely believed that Ruskin initiated the Gothic
Revival by both precept and example. When the French historian
Hippolyte Taine visited Oxford, he inspected the recently-built
'bâtiments de Ruskin', Keble College and the University
Museum, and concluded that Ruskin's books were worth more
than his buildings. The truth is that apart from the lodge at
Brantwood Ruskin never designed a building of any kind.
Moreover his studies of Gothic architecture came not at the
beginning but at the peak of a wave of enthusiasm for the subject. If
one examines a review of Ruskin's *Seven Lamps of Architecture* in
one of the periodicals of 1849—50, one may find half a dozen other
works of a similar kind noticed alongside it. And when Coventry
Patmore came to review *The Stones of Venice*, he had to deal also
with contemporary books by E. A. Freeman and Edmund Sharpe
on Gothic building — 'only two of a host of writers who have
lately written on this unaccountably popular subject of medieval
art'.[1]

If Ruskin had been writing on this topic thirty years before, he
would no doubt have contributed to the great antiquarian debate
of the time, which concerned the origin of the pointed Gothic arch.
Was it borrowed from the Saracens? Was it inspired by bent
willow-branches, by the intersection of overlapping round arches,
or by the upturned keel of Noah's ark? By the 1830s, when the
teenage Ruskin began to take a serious interest in architecture,
leading antiquarians regarded all such solutions as superficial, and
were trying instead to explain the superseding of round arch by
pointed in terms of the structural advantages of the latter. An
increasingly scholarly approach diverted attention from arches
alone to vaults, piers, windows and all the details of Gothic
buildings; the differences between Gothic styles received closer

75

scrutiny, and devotees began to express a preference for one Gothic period over another. They began also to search for ways of describing a style as a whole (whether this were Gothic in general or a subdivision such as 'Middle Pointed'), for some principle or significance which underlay the many component features.

Some, like Augustus Welby Pugin and the leaders of the Cambridge Camden Society, sought this significance in the religious connotations of the Gothic style, emphasising its historical and (later) its symbolic associations with Christianity. Others, like William Whewell, E. A. Freeman and Coventry Patmore, took what Patmore called the aesthetic view, and tried to discern some single physical quality which comprised the essence of each style. Ruskin took a third course, and sought it in the human qualities which he found revealed in buildings.

These enterprises were made possible, however, by the solid scholarship of the previous generation. Ruskin knew William Whewell's *Architectural Notes on German Churches* (1830 and 1845) and Robert Willis's *Remarks on the Architecture of the Middle Ages, especially of Italy* (1835); at a less technical level he was conversant with Thomas Hope's *An Historical Essay on Architecture* (1835) and Joseph Woods's *Letters of an Architect from France, Italy and Greece* (1828). Ruskin must have been interested by the latter's tentative recommendation of Italian Gothic as a style for English architects to consider: 'There is sometimes a simplicity and good proportion in the general design of a façade of an Italian Gothic, which is very pleasing . . . I would not recommend that they should be copied altogether, but they afford useful hints for design.'[2] However Italian Gothic did not really gain a following until the late thirties and forties. Willis described its characteristics but did not admire them, writing of 'the inferiority of the Italian to all the other Gothic styles'. He deplored its use of marble mosaics, panels and stripes, 'producing to English eyes the most disagreeable effect'.[3] Yet not long afterwards this very effect was achieved in T. H. Wyatt and David Brandon's new Italian Romanesque church of St Mary's, Wilton (1843), and then in the subtle polychrome of William Butterfield's designs. In the 1840s the fashion gathered momentum with Gally Knight's publications on Italian medieval architecture; in 1847 the *Ecclesiologist*, that severe arbiter of church design, at last gave its sanction to the use of Continental medieval models, including Italian; and in 1850 the first Italian Gothic public building in England was completed – James William Wild's Northern Schools of St. Martin-in-the-Fields.

But what of Venetian architecture? Here Ruskin was indeed the great influence on public taste, but he was not, as is often supposed, the first to proclaim its merits. Joseph Woods typified the early nineteenth-century view of the architecture of St Mark's and the Ducal Palace in calling it 'rich but not correct; and it bears perhaps the stamp of riches and power, more than that of good taste'.[4] Similarly Joseph Forsyth had found fault with the Ducal Palace, and faintly praised St Mark's as 'a very singular pile'.[5] In March 1835, however, W. H. Leeds in the *Architectural Magazine* wrote an article under the name of 'Candidus', extolling the charm and character of Venetian architecture, and was soon involved in a running debate with 'Verus' who admired Palladian architecture but disliked that of medieval Venice as being 'neither Greek nor Gothic'.[6]

Ruskin may have read this dialogue, since the *Architectural Magazine* was the scene of his own first major venture into print two years later. In its context, his *Introduction to the Poetry of Architecture* appears as something more than a youthful experiment: it formed the central feature of the last years of a very reputable periodical (and the first in England devoted exclusively to architecture). The *Architectural Magazine* also contained a year-long correspondence, heavy with geometrical detail, in which Ruskin took on all comers (including the resident pundit Candidus) on certain questions concerning the convergence of perpendiculars. He already appeared entirely self-assured and fluent in specialised architectural controversy, and few of his readers can have guessed that 'Kata Phusin', as he styled himself, was not yet out of his teens.

The magazine included many other articles of interest. It tried to cater for the amateur and the professional, mingling literary and theoretical pieces with designs for Norman-style villas, ovens and hot water systems. It reprinted James Anderson's innovatory defence of Gothic on both structural and psychological grounds, and included a series of articles by 'The Conductor', Loudon himself, on general issues such as the varieties of taste and their connection with moral qualities; translations from the French neo-classical critic Quatremère de Quincy; several articles on 'character' and 'expression' in architecture; and reviews of scholarly

works by Wolff, Möller, Pugin and Willis. Here was a rich nursery
for many of Ruskin's ideas on taste, expression, symbolism and
decoration – ideas which developed gradually, among the ever-
increasing number of enthusiasts, and which for the most part
originated no more with Ruskin than with Pugin or with any
other individual.

Between *The Poetry of Architecture* and *The Seven Lamps of
Architecture* Ruskin's architectural ideas underwent a ten-year
incubation, while he wrote and published the first two volumes of
*Modern Painters*. But his interest in Gothic architecture grew, and
he kept abreast of the latest building experiments as well as the
literature. (Staying at Salisbury soon after his marriage, he drove
with his wife and parents to see the new Italianate church at
Wilton. His wife admired it, but reported that 'John said the
church and everything about it made him feel quite sick, as bad as
Babies before breakfast . . .⁷). In *Seven Lamps* he joined in the
current debate over which pre-Renaissance style was most
appropriate for Victorian England, proposing three possible Italian
styles and one English.

But in the main *Seven Lamps* is a disappointing and confusing
book. Looking back in his old age, Ruskin thought highly of *The
Poetry of Architecture*, but he was less enthusiastic about *Seven
Lamps*: 'I never intended to have republished this book, which has
become the most useless I ever wrote.'⁸ Although in saying this he
was referring to the 'restorations' and demolitions of the buildings
he had then admired, his private remarks about 'the utterly useless
twaddle of it' show that his disgust with *Seven Lamps* was more
general. 'But I find the public still like the book', he continued.
They had always done so, although (or possibly because) unlike the
earlier work, it did not serve primarily to promote a 'visual'
appreciation of buildings. Digby Wyatt observed in the *Athenaeum*
that Ruskin's 'lamps' shone most brightly when they illuminated
any other subject than architecture; and Coventry Patmore knew
'a literary lady, who cannot tell a Doric shaft from a flying buttress,
who is nevertheless profound in the "Seven Lamps"'.⁹

The book is diffuse, even by Ruskin's standards, in style and
subject-matter. Only two of the lamps – 'Power' and 'Life' –
continue the tactic of the earlier work in attributing human
qualities to architecture, and neither 'power' nor 'liveliness' (which
are not exclusively human qualities anyway) were new to the

vocabulary of criticism. *Seven Lamps* is primarily a book of its time, in its emphasis on symbolism in church architecture, its discussion of the technical development of Gothic details, and its participation in current controversies of restoration, deception and styles appropriate to Victorian England.

Yet it is evident that an important ingredient had been added to Ruskin's architectural criticism, in that he had become interested in the mentality of those responsible for a building – the public, the architects and the craftsmen. In *The Poetry of Architecture* (1837–9) Ruskin had applied human qualities to architecture; in *Seven Lamps* (1849) he was concerned with the qualities required in the 'builders'; later in *The Stones of Venice* (1853–5) the two were synthesised, so that architecture was derived from the personality of the builders *through* its human characteristics. Largely hidden beneath the pompous sermonising of *Seven Lamps* is Ruskin's genuine and increasing concern for the attitudes of a society, a concern which was to act as the cement necessary to fasten the lightly-cast adjectives of the 1830s firmly on to the Venetian buildings described in 1853.

For *Seven Lamps* was written after Ruskin had returned to England in the winter of 1848, having travelled widely on the Continent at a time when most of Europe was in a state of political ferment. His correspondence shows how deeply he was affected by the suffering and injustice he witnessed in France, and reveals a new sympathy with the people's cause.[10] These signs of concern with social problems coincided in Ruskin with a more intense interest in Gothic architecture, largely aroused by his visit to Lucca in 1845: 'Absolutely for the first time I now saw what medieval buildings were, and what they meant.'[11]

However, Ruskin's motives are not yet quite clear. If one thinks only of the circumstances under which he wrote the book, it is easy to believe that the architectural criticism it contains was directly affected and guided by his concern for the state of society. But if one looks at the tendencies of contemporary art criticism, an alternative motive presents itself. Ruskin made use of many of the current styles of architectural judgement in the course of *Seven Lamps*, and only in the 'Lamp of Life' did he employ an entirely original method; even this last can be regarded as a synthesis of techniques which had already been adopted. To put the truly 'Ruskinian' mode of criticism into perspective, we may contrast it with two contemporary critical traditions, the 'artistical' and the 'ecclesiological'.

## 'ARTISTICAL'

It may seem rather artificial to distinguish a purely 'artistical' attitude among the jumble of architectural appreciation in the mid-nineteenth century, but this distinction was made at the time and is still useful. It was the poet Coventry Patmore who consciously set out to explain 'The Aesthetics of Gothic Architecture' and of other styles too.

Patmore's interest in the visual arts was lifelong. He had toyed with the idea of setting up as a painter before his first volume of poems was published; he then became associated with the Pre-Raphaelites (whose work he brought to Ruskin's attention in 1851), and furthermore wrote over twenty clear-minded articles on the subject of architecture. In the course of some of these he declared himself opposed to three prevailing types of explanation. In the first place, he held strong reservations about ecclesiological symbolism: ' . . . interesting as this kind of symbolism may be in itself, it has absolutely no part at all in the purely artistical character of the buildings.'[12] Secondly he attacked those who felt it necessary to justify all architectural detail in terms of 'constructional necessity'. Pugin was his principal target here, but he might also have mentioned Ruskin, and indeed the majority of contemporary theorists.[13] Thirdly Patmore disapproved of those who regarded architectural detail in isolation from the building as a whole, and he rightly named Ruskin as a prime offender. 'It will at once be observed that Mr Ruskin criticises the details of Greek architecture as if they were not architecture; as if they might be plucked from the building like flowers from the stalk, without any loss of significance.'[14]

Patmore's own 'artistical' approach consisted of describing the 'expressional character' of buildings or styles in terms of such qualities as weight, upbearing power, solidity, permanence or their opposites — more abstract and less human qualities than those which Ruskin ascribed. Most of the criticism contained in *Seven Lamps* was not 'artistical', Patmore observed, but rather an enquiry into 'the suggestive powers of forms in general'.[15] Only 'The

Lamp of Beauty', Ruskin's fourth chapter, seemed to offer an interpretation of architecture that was as 'artistical' as Patmore's own.

'The Lamp of Beauty' contains a brilliant and original attempt to analyse the visual merits of architecture without recourse to symbolism or structural constraints. It suggests, in essence, that our sense of beauty is dependent on our experience of natural forms: that we appreciate what unconsciously reminds us of forms which are often to be seen in nature. This is not quite to say that forms are beautiful because they are copied from nature, as Ruskin carefully points out; rather 'it is out of the power of man to conceive beauty without her aid'.[16] Nevertheless, Ruskin is led to some absurd conclusions, such as the implication that the appearance of King's College Chapel would be enhanced if it looked like an upturned animal instead of an upturned table.[17] Other instances are more persuasive. If we agree that the horizontal bands on a spire should occur at decreasing intervals rather than regular ones, might not our preference be ultimately derived (as Ruskin suggests) from the fact that this arrangement prevails in the stems of common plants? The younger Eastlake was evidently impressed, for he applied this rule convincingly to St Luke's, Chelsea, in his *History of the Gothic Revival.*[18]

The work which Patmore believed had furthest advanced an 'aesthetic' view of architecture was not *Seven Lamps* but the *History of Architecture* published in the same year.[19] It was the first book of the historian Edward Augustus Freeman, who not long afterwards passed scornful judgement on Ruskin's Edinburgh lectures.[20] Like Patmore, Freeman tried to isolate a single 'leading principle' for each style, but these amounted only to 'horizontality' in Grecian architecture, 'rest and immobility' in Romanesque, while Egyptian architecture, he concluded, hardly suggested any idea at all.[21] Not a very enlightening analysis, but — as we shall see — Freeman had more to contribute in other respects.

Yet another publication of 1849 was James Fergusson's ambitious treatise on Beauty, which suggested that works of art, and especially buildings, could be assessed in a fairly precise fashion. Fergusson proposed an ingenious scoring system in the manner of Roger de Piles but applicable to all the arts, each of which was to be judged according to its 'technic' beauty, its 'aesthetic' beauty (which scored double) and its 'phonetic' or 'intellectual' beauty, which scored treble. For example, the art of gardening scored four for technic beauty, six for aesthetic, and two for phonetic, and when the scores were appropriately weighted, they gave a total of 22. Architecture scored four in each category, totalling 24. When applied to specific buildings, the Parthenon was found to exhibit the most overall beauty, closely followed by Rheims Cathedral and the Hypostyle Hall at Karnac. (Like Freeman, Fergusson wrote of the ancient Egyptians as 'scarcely dreaming of the aesthetic form'.)[22]

Fergusson modestly admitted that his calculus did not claim 'anything like minute accuracy', but Ruskin devoted an appendix to a critique of the book, and it was also taken seriously by Edward Lacy Garbett, whose *Rudimentary Treatise* of 1850 was perhaps the sanest treatment of the subject that had yet been made. Garbett, more clearly than Ruskin, picked out a major flaw in Fergusson's system: − there were many artistic effects of architecture which could not be evaluated within either the 'aesthetic' category or the 'phonetic'. For 'aesthetic' referred only to 'mere gratification of sense', as Fergusson had put it, or in Garbett's terms, beauty without expression, whereas 'phonetic' beauty implied something more than architecture could supply, the possession of a detailed language of some kind.[23] Fergusson seems in practice to have given high 'phonetic' ratings only to buildings which were suitable for the display of sculpture or painting.[24] Garbett's solution was to insert between these two 'another class of art − a class possessing *expression but not speech*, − totally incapable indeed of telling a tale, yet perfectly capable of expressing various human emotions'.[25]

In granting 'human emotions' to architecture, Garbett allowed a wider range of qualities to be 'expressed' therein than Patmore had done, but his examples of expressive architecture show little advance on the clichés of the preceding century − 'the sublime majesty of the Doric', 'the heavenward aspiration of the Gothic temple', 'the mild repose of Palladio'. Another list of qualities, not connected to specific styles or buildings, is more promising: a building might be 'grave or festive, meek or ostentatious, awful or playful, majestic, reposing, agitated, or aspiring'. These attributes are reminiscent of Alison's *Essay*, which Garbett quoted at great length; but unlike Ruskin in 'The Lamp of Life', Garbett did not reach the point of deriving these qualities from the characteristics of the builders or their age.

'ECCLESIOLOGICAL'

The Cambridge Camden Society and its many sister societies were not concerned with architectural criticism, strictly speaking. They aimed above all to spread a knowledge of the various elements of a church, its furniture, and its ritual, and to encourage the building of new churches (and the restoration of old) in a truly 'Catholic', pre-Reformation spirit. However friends and foes of the movement agreed that ecclesiologists had their own particular way of judging and appreciating church architecture, and that this point of view could not be called aesthetic. 'It is essentially religious, and only incidentally artistical', observed the not wholly hostile E.A. Freeman.[26]

Ecclesiologists were chiefly interested in the religious propriety of the features of a church, and in their symbolism. An early paper by John Mason Neale examined a Norman moulding, whose limpet-like shape represented faith, he believed, because the shell-fish was a conventional symbol for Christian belief. The chevron pattern of the moulding, on the other hand, 'may well symbolise either impalement or exposure to the teeth of wild beasts'. And since there was a tripartite abacus beneath, the entire meaning was that 'by faith in the Holy Trinity the Blessed Martyrs underwent their torments'.[27]

Some attention had been paid to ecclesiastical symbolism in the previous decade. Readers of the *Architectural Magazine*, for instance, would have come across Friedrich Schlegel's interpretation of the Christian significance of medieval art, and not long after would have found Quatremère de Quincy's denunciation of 'those cold, insignificant, and misplaced allusions, which render edifical decoration an enigma to the generality of persons, and a puerile sport to the few that understand its meaning'.[28] But ecclesiologists in general do not seem to have taken much interest in the subject until the publication in 1842 of Ayliffe Poole's *The Appropriate Character of Church Architecture* and of G.R. Lewis's *Illustrations of Kilpeck Church*, both of which quoted (as the second edition of Pugin's *Contrasts* had done the year before) from the thirteenth-century treatise of Durandus on church symbolism. Symbolism was firmly identified with ecclesiology in the following year, when Neale and Webb brought out a new edition of 'Durandus', to which they added a hundred-page defence of the principle of 'sacramentality', which gives 'an esoterick signification' to church architecture.

The analogies of Durandus are in reality rather mundane. A weathercock heading into the wind, for example, is said to represent a preacher boldly facing the rebellious, and cement, being composed of lime, sand and water, stands for charity, good works and the spirit.[29] As several critics observed, this kind of symbolism is purely arbitrary, and it is difficult to believe that medieval church-builders were always aware of it. A character in Robert Kerr's satire is made to relate 'the legend of Friar Junyper', whose grotesque sculptures were not symbolic of higher things, but merely parodies of Junyper's enemy the abbot, whom (to the people's delight) he portrayed 'in many postures, and under many circumstances'.[30]

Occasionally, however, the leading ecclesiologists used a symbolism of a different kind, claiming that the styles and details of a building represented moral qualities, instead of (or as well as) doctrines and Biblical events. Neale and Webb suggested that Protestant churches were in this sense more symbolic than their worshippers realised: their roofs were held up by cast-iron pillars, 'typifying that the whole existence of the building depends on the good-will of the congregation', that is, rather than on God; and every decoration of such a church 'symbolises the spiritual pride, the luxury, the self-sufficiency, the bigotry of the congregations of too many a PUE-RENTED EPISCOPAL CHAPEL'.[31] This is very much in the style of Pugin, but as in Pugin's writing, the qualities said to be symbolised are chiefly sectarian.

Now Protestants could not hope to compete in the detailed symbolism explained by Durandus, for post-Reformation symbolism of this nature was generally admitted to be faint and scarce. They might scorn the whole system, like one of Kerr's characters who reported that 'all the vagaries of the Symbolists and Ecclesiologists came to be propounded to a world enraptured with laughter'.[32] Or they might make do with what little symbolism a low or broad churchman might legitimately adopt: George Wightwick's design for a Protestant Cathedral emphasised the significance of its cruciform plan and 'triplet features'.[33] Ruskin took a third course, and relied on the symbolism of moral qualities, as Neale and Webb had begun to do. For just as *Seven Lamps* as a whole can be seen as an attempt to 'win Gothic for Protestantism', so can the 'Lamp of Sacrifice' in particular be regarded as a demonstration that ecclesiastical symbolism was not under exclusive contract to Roman and English Catholics.

Ruskin's addiction to allegory has been studied in an enormous chapter by George P. Landow, who shows how it was largely derived from the Biblical and Christian typology central to the Evangelical belief of his mother. Ruskin was brought up on a diet of Evangelically approved literature, chiefly consisting of the Bible daily, Milton, Bunyan, Herbert and Wordsworth,[34] all of whom exploited the scriptural Type. He studied the sermons of the Evangelical preachers whom he heard, until he could predict from Henry Melvill's opening text the elaborate allegory that he would proceed to unfold. Landow justly observes that the 'Lamp of Sacrifice' is permeated with typology, but one might add that the very theme of self-sacrifice was a particularly Evangelical one. This Lamp of Ruskin's places emphasis on the opportunity given to builders to win God's favour by their own pious efforts – that same 'self-sufficiency' which Neale and Webb discerned and despised in Protestant chapels. It does not simply ask that churches be built in a spirit of sacrifice, but requires that their decoration should *represent* sacrifice, and that 'we should consider increase of *apparent* labour as an increase of beauty in the building'.[35]

But Ruskin adopts two conflicting roles in the space of a few pages. The attitude just mentioned is that of Ruskin the aesthete, who is chiefly concerned with appearances, and for whom 'the waste of actual workmanship is always painful, so soon as it is apparent'. But Ruskin the Evangelical moralist took a contrary view: 'it is not the church we want, but the sacrifice; not the emotion of admiration, but the act of adoration; not the gift, but the giving.' This other Ruskin believed that months of toil, whose product is almost invisible, are nevertheless valuable to God, and are also in the worker's own ultimate interests, since 'He will multiply and increase sevenfold'. To say that God might appreciate artistry would no doubt have been a concession to Romanism which Ruskin could not have allowed himself at that time; even the edition of 1880, purged of the most rabid sectarian taunts of 1849, insisted that heavenly dividends were won by psychological offerings and not by superficial show.[36]

Sometimes, however, Ruskin's artistic sensibility got the better of his Protestant logic, and on these occasions his argument was much more persuasive. He deplored, for example, the kind of intricate carving which 'looks as if it were only fit to be put in inlaid cabinets and velveted caskets, and as if it could not bear one drifting shower or gnawing frost. We are afraid for it, anxious about it, and tormented by it; and we feel that a massy shaft and a bold shadow would be worth it all'.[37] Of the two warring *personae*, the artist had here gained the upper hand.

This contradiction within the 'Lamp of Sacrifice' indicates how difficult it was to evaluate a style or building both as a work of art and as a system of symbols. Ecclesiologists tried to avoid this problem by minimising the aesthetic element in their judgements. When John Petit compared the artistic qualities of various medieval styles, Neale and Webb condemned him for making 'a kind of ideal picturesque', and worshipping a false idol.[38] After Webb's *Sketches of Continental Ecclesiology* (1848) their attitude seems to have become official policy; the hundredth issue of the *Ecclesiologist* believed that the study of church architecture was approaching the completeness of an exact science, for 'it is admitted to be a subject not so much of taste as of facts'.[39] Ruskin was never able to separate art and propriety so clearly. He would have sympathised with the fierce attack made by Neale and Webb on the decadence of the Perpendicular style, but he could not have added, as they did, that 'considered merely as specimens of art, King's College, and Henry the Seventh's Chapels, are matchless'.[40]

Despite the *Ecclesiologist*'s favourable review of *Seven Lamps*, and their occasional similarities of method, Ruskin was not regarded by his contemporaries as an ecclesiologist or as a sympathiser with the movement. He was a not very active member of the Camden's sister society at Oxford,[41] whose proceedings were reported by the *Ecclesiologist*, but which was often criticised for its apathy towards Catholic propriety and ritual. Robert Kerr, who called Ruskin 'the high priest of all latitudinarians', placed him and the ecclesiologists at opposite poles,[42] and Coventry Patmore thought that Ruskin had over-reacted to the ecclesiological movement. 'Mr Ruskin has probably been sickened, as we have been, by the sentimental ravings on the subject of Gothic symbols, put forth by Puseyite clergymen.'[43]

Pugin, on the other hand, was often classed as an ally of the *Ecclesiologist*. The *Christian Remembrancer* asserted that 'it is well

known . . . that writers of that journal are avowed disciples of
Pugin'.[44] (That journal itself implied that the influence ran in the
other direction: 'he [Pugin] seemed to value the more firm and
consistent line advocated by our Society.'[45]) Pugin reprinted a
controversial review from the *Ecclesiologist*, and strongly recom-
mended to Roman Catholics the Camdenians' *A Few Words to
Church-wardens*. In 1843, Neale and Webb criticized Pugin for his
seeming indifference to church symbolism; Pugin denied the
charge, although his subsequent writings paid greater respect to
the subject. There were several bitter exchanges between the two
parties, but these seem to have sprung not so much from any
fundamental differences in taste or artistic theory, as from their
disagreements over Christian doctrine. As a historian of the
Cambridge movement has observed on their behalf, 'Pugin's sole
fault, one feels, is that he was a Roman Catholic'.[46]

Moreover, there is a decided similarity in tone between Pugin
and the leading ecclesiologists, and it is here that Pugin had most
impact on the practice of architectural criticism. He was the first
Gothic polemicist; his *Contrasts* of 1836 and 1841 did more than
any other publication to make architectural style a subject of
emotional appeal and not simply a question of personal taste. In
this he was followed by Neale and Webb, and presently by
Ruskin. No previous writer would have excited the diplomatic
Gilbert Scott 'almost to fury' as Pugin did, and few critics before
Pugin's time would have poured such 'scorn and contumely' on
Scott as did the *Ecclesiologist*.[47] Pugin's polemics had an effect on
the vocabulary of criticism, as well as on the general tone. If the
pointed arch could be regarded as essentially Catholic, it could
equally be described as the embodiment of 'manliness';[48] and a
number of terms which had previously had a purely descriptive
function began to acquire similar moral and social connotations.
Scott remembered a friendly dispute with the Rev. Thomas
Stevens, whose church he was enlarging at about the time of *Seven
Lamps*:

> Mr Stevens got to employ the term "square abacus" as a moral
> adjective, used in the sense of manly, straightforward, real,
> honest, and all cognate epithets, and "round abacus" for what
> was milder, "ogee" being used in the sense of mean, weak,
> dishonest, &c.[49]

And when Scott himself in an Academy lecture expressed a preference for the French square abacus over the English round one, the listening students received his sentiment with a burst of applause.[50] This highly-charged atmosphere must be attributed to a large extent to the writing of Pugin and the ecclesiologists – an atmosphere in which architecture could be not only regarded as symbolic, in more senses than one, but invested in every aspect with moral overtones. *The Seven Lamps of Architecture*, which explored several means of lending to architecture a significance beyond the purely artistic, must have owed its good reception to a climate of ideas in which strong feelings could be aroused even by such an apparently harmless object as a square abacus.

## 'RUSKINIAN'

We have dealt briefly with the Lamps of Sacrifice, Truth, and Beauty in connection with ecclesiology, Pugin, and the 'artistical' interpretation of architecture. The Lamps of Memory and Power, which contain interesting analyses of the sublime and the picturesque, do not offer any fundamental innovation in art criticism; nor does Obedience, which aims mainly to recommend a universal style for the nineteenth century, and discourages idleness, the root of all evil.

There remains 'The Lamp of Life', the chapter which lies directly on the path of Ruskin's development from *The Poetry of Architecture* to *The Stones of Venice*. Here Ruskin illustrates the principle that is characteristic of him alone: that all human products, and especially architecture,

> depend, for their dignity and pleasurableness in the utmost degree, upon the vivid expression of the intellectual life which has been concerned in their production.[51]

'Life' is the appropriate term, for if a building or style is to be considered as a human personality, it should presumably exhibit signs of life as a minimum condition. One of the most important signs of life, we are told, is 'a certain neglect or contempt of refinement in execution'. Ruskin is thinking less of overall design (though this is not ignored completely) than of personal craftsmanship, shown in sculpture, mosaics, and the finishing of masonry. These signs of life, Ruskin continues, can only be seen in 'hand-work', and 'machine-work' is therefore to be despised. By machine he evidently means here anything from an engine lathe to sandpaper and polish, or even a human 'machine' working under precise instructions from a supervisor.

Ruskin gives so many reasons for the superiority of hand-work to machine-work that it is not immediately obvious which is the basic one. To begin with, he admires the irregularities and asymmetries of Italian Romanesque building, and suggests that although symmetry has its own charms, these have 'a grace about them which equality never obtained'[52] — a purely visual appreciation, it seems, firmly in the Picturesque tradition. A second possible reason for Ruskin's rejection of machine-work is that it destroys the craftsman's creativity, and gives rise to 'carvers' who take no pleasure in their carving.

'Was the carver happy while he was about it?' In his later writings (and actions), Ruskin's concern for the plight of the craftsman became unmistakable, but in 'The Lamp of Life' he seems more interested in whether a piece of workmanship *looks* as if the worker was happy while he was about it. At any rate, shortly before asking his celebrated question, Ruskin points out another respect in which hand-work is superior: it enables the spectator to see a contrast between dedicated and careless work. 'It will be plainly seen that some places have been delighted in more than others', which is more satisfying than 'the look of equal trouble everywhere — the smooth, diffused tranquillity of heartless pains'.[53]

This does not ring quite true, for Ruskin was not in the habit of commending a building for the varying quality of its workmanship, or for the contrast-value of slovenly work. Nor is he convincing in adding, by way of justification, that 'to those who love Architecture, the life and accent of the hand are everything', since previous writers on architecture had in fact taken little interest in 'hand-work'. A further consideration is not mentioned by Ruskin, but I believe it is fundamental: he had to insist on the paramount importance of hand-work, because his entire system of 'personal' analysis could not begin without it. Ruskin wanted to suggest that the stonemason actually communicated certain of his personal characteristics to his masonry. He had not yet worked out these characteristics in detail; the final list, of 'savageness', 'fancifulness' and the rest, was to appear in 'The Nature of Gothic' of 1853. He was already not satisfied with regarding architectural styles and features simply as *symbols* of human traits, as other writers had done, but was anxious to show that the frame of mind of the builders themselves was apparent in their work. This was the purpose of *The Poetry of Architecture*; even with the less promising material of 'The Lamp of Sacrifice', he seems to have had it in mind in trying to demonstrate not that a church symbolised Sacrifice in general, but that its builders could make their sacrificial spirit evident in the façades of the building. Hand-work, then, was to be the crucial means of communication. Although Ruskin had artistic reasons for his dislike of smooth, finished surfaces, he may also have been frustrated by the lack of scope they offered to his style of analysis.

So despite his growing concern for social conditions, Ruskin might not have made much of his principle that the builder transmits his mentality into his work, had this assumption not proved fruitful as a method of critical appreciation. We have observed that Ruskin was using it in his early writing, long before he had revealed any serious concern with the 'human condition'. In *Seven Lamps* also his references to the welfare of the 'carver' seem to be motivated primarily by literary expediency. There is a passage in 'The Lamp of Power' in which he attributes to rough, untreated stones 'a stern expression of brotherhood . . .' We might expect him to continue, 'between fellow-masons' or 'between master and workman', but in fact he goes on, 'with the mountain heart from which it has been rent'.[54] Even in 'The Lamp of Life', he appears to be trying out different varieties of metaphor and analogy, before developing that one which offered the greatest literary potential.

Only by looking at the contemporary literature of 1847–50 can one realise the significance of this conception of hand-work as a means of communicating personality, and see that it formed the missing link in a chain of prevalent ideas. Historians and architectural writers alike were increasingly prepared to describe architecture in human terms; many of them asserted that a style must be regarded as an expression of a civilization; but none had discovered a plausible means of connecting aspects of buildings with the qualities of a society. 'It is a mere verbal fiction', wrote the *Rambler*, 'to call anything a fine *art* which is not the *natural* expression of the inhabitants of the age and country in which it is cultivated'.[55] But the *Rambler* did not help its readers to identify such expression, and nor did James Fergusson, although, writing of architectural styles in the same year, he advised that the 'singular persistence of national character' should not be overlooked.[56] Nor did Edward Garbett, who declared that 'it is not the building we admire or condemn, but the mind that appears in it — not the design, but the spirit that presided over it, and stamped its own character thereon, in unmistakable and unalterable marks'. Garbett was explicitly looking for 'the expression of mental qualities' in architecture, but the only quality he actually described was 'selfishness'. A building looks selfish, he wrote, if it does not seem to have tried to compensate with some 'unnecessary design' for the fact that it blocks out our air, light, and view of nature[57] — an ingenious notion, but not one that could be said to link a style with a civilization.

The same aspirations are to be found outside architectural circles. William Hickling Prescott's *History of the Conquest of Peru* appeared in a London edition in 1847, and it included the following Ruskin-like sentiments:

> The painter and the sculptor may display their individual genius in creations of surpassing excellence, but it is the great monuments of architectural taste and magnificence that are stamped in a peculiar manner by the genius of a nation. The Greek, the Egyptian, the Saracen, the Gothic — what a key their respective styles afford to the character and condition of the people.[58]

Yet that key remained unturned, for the buildings of the Incas seem to have revealed to Prescott only the uniformity and ignorance of the Inca mind. His theme was taken up, however, by Edward Freeman, who placed the first of Prescott's sentences quoted above on the title-page of his *History of Architecture* in 1849, and did succeed in illustrating the principle with some broad generalisations (Roman architecture expressed 'the steady, un-daunted, unyielding will of the Roman people'[59] — a foretaste of Ruskin's 'Pride of Renaissance'). Freeman's conclusions were bound to be vague, since he was still relating supposed national character to the *overall* character of a national style; whereas Ruskin, more fruitfully but no less fallaciously, derived even the details of building practice from what he took to be the character of the society in question.

A final example of 'Ruskinian' analysis in the 1840s is a passing comment by Ayliffe Poole on the sinuous forms of Decorated Gothic in the early fourteenth century. There were those who

> might half admit a question, whether the luxury and licence of a court such as that of Edward II had not something in common with the forms which were developed by contemporary architects. The straight line, the circle, and the right angle— types, as it were, and the expressions of direct, straightforward, measured, stern duty and action,—are everywhere deserted or disguised . . .[60]

This slight (and untypical) passage draws a closer parallel between architectural details and the 'character of the time' than do Freeman, Pugin, or even the Ruskin of *Seven Lamps*. But 'The Lamp of Life' held the seeds of a much more systematic and thoroughgoing analysis on the same lines, suggesting a means by which these human qualities might actually have been transmitted. Poole was evidently afraid that his characterisation of Decorated Gothic might be thought a fanciful irrelevance, a departure from his soberly factual account; and Ruskin, claiming that in *Seven Lamps* he had tried to show 'how every form of noble architecture is *in some sort* the embodiment of the Polity, Life, History, and Religious Faith of nations',[61] seems aware that his dabblings in analogy had fallen well short of the standards of historical fact. But the method of 'The Lamp of Life' showed Ruskin that through the irregularities of handtooled masonry he could develop a form of architectural criticism which would pass muster as history. The result was *The Stones of Venice*.

# 7 Epoch Sauce and *The Stones of Venice*

The first volume of *The Stones of Venice* was a disappointment to Ruskin's father, who realised that it had not the makings of a bestseller. Ruskin's reputation by this time ensured reviews in the major periodicals which were on the whole favourable, but the public would not buy – although in the same year Ruskin's fairy-tale, *The King of the Golden River*, ran through three editions.

The difficulty lay mainly in the subject-matter. Each of the components of architecture was examined in turn, an the chapter-headings served as a warning of the unglamorous contents: 'The Arch Line, The Arch Masonry, The Arch Load, The Roof, The Roof Cornice, The Buttress . . .' Ruskin referred to the volume as 'my antiquarianism'[1], but the craze for the antiquarian study of Gothic elements was passing or passed, and a wider public wanted architectural styles set in a wider context. A decade earlier, the book might have been adopted as a manual by church-hunting undergraduates, for the various elements of building were clearly and entertainingly presented, but in the year of the Great Exhibition something more was required.

The opening chapter ('The Quarry') has a promising beginning: in the first paragraph the reader is told that the great power of England may be brought to destruction unless Englishmen remember the examples of the two other great rulers of the ocean, Tyre and Venice. Then Ruskin suggests that he is about to offer a history of Venice 'almost without reference to the construction of her senate or the prerogatives of her Doge'. Nor will he claim that Venice was great so long as her policies were motivated by religion; this would have been a difficult thesis to maintain, since for much of her history Venice was notoriously ruthless in promoting her own commercial interests. Ruskin therefore argues that Venice's health and greatness depended on the piety and nobility of her citizens in *private* life or as individuals. One or two anecdotes are offered in support, but it is made clear that most of Ruskin's evidence of the personal piety of Venetians will be artistic.

Now Ruskin is not concerned with the Venetians' following of sectarian doctrines, Protestant or Catholic, when he writes of their 'individual religion'. It is 'the *vital* religion, observe, not the formal'.[2] He ingeniously illustrates his distinction between vital religion and formal observance by arguing that the paintings of the Bellini brothers were animated with 'the most solemn spirit of religious faith', but in the work of their compatriot Titian, born sixty years later, there was no vital religion at all. True, Titian still painted dignitaries kneeling before the Madonna or St Mark, but this was mere outward show. Inwardly, 'Faith had become carnal': Titian used his sacred subjects as a means of displaying his skills of composition and colour, and his figure of Faith 'is a coarse portrait of one of Titian's least graceful female models'.[3]

The fatal flexibility of Ruskin's system is manifest. The same kind of considerations that had previously convinced Ruskin of a painter's sincere intentions are now brought in evidence of Titian's hypocrisy. But there is another point to note in this passage. In 1846 Ruskin would have ascribed the difference between the art of Giovanni Bellini and that of Titian to a difference in temparament. By 1851 his point of view had changed:

> . . . Titian and Bellini are each true representatives of the school of painters contemporary with them; and the difference in their artistic feeling is a consequence not so much of difference in their own natural characters as in their early education: Bellini was brought up in faith; Titian in formalism. Between the years of their births the vital religion of Venice had expired.[4]

Ruskin is forced to shift his ground in this way because the *Stones of Venice* trilogy is devoted to the corporate art of architecture and its relation to the 'moral temper' of Venice as a whole; so that painting too must be seen as the expression of a society. Ruskin briefly outlines in this first chapter how he will present the rise and fall of the spirit of Venice through her architecture. But now, just as our appetites are fully whetted, Ruskin proposes 'in these first following pages' to lay down the basic laws of architectural criticism — and he proceeds to do so for the rest of the volume. Readers of the first edition had to wait over two years to see the promised history in volume two.

Moreover, the piece-by-piece analysis of blocks and angles which occupies the bulk of the first volume is largely irrelevant to the main enterprise. Ruskin picks out the optimal shape for a wall cornice or a pier base on functional grounds, often very persuasively, but does not consider them as expressive of human traits. Aesthetic and constructive merits are sharply distinguished, whether in cusps, domes, roof cornices, parapets, pinnacles or buttresses. The spire of a cathedral, for instance, was built not to represent heavenly aspiration (writes Ruskin) but in conformity with the steeply-pitched domestic roofs which the northern climate demanded. He lets slip a few comments which echo the tone of *Seven Lamps*: 'the arch line is the moral character of the arch, and the adverse forces are its temptations'; [5] a series of cornices show 'the Christian element struggling with the formalism of the Papacy', and the last cornice reveals 'Protestantism — a slight touch of Dissent, hardly amounting to Schism, in those falling leaves . . .' [6] Yet these are incidental *jeux d'esprit*, and not the cumbrous lengthily-developed analogies of *Seven Lamps*. They come as light relief from the systematic cataloguing of features and functions. Ruskin uses military metaphors with the same playful intent when he envisages a battle between the various architectural elements, of which the voussoirs are the losers, for after 'their flank is turned by an invidious chamfer', they turn traitor and in despair go over to the classical camp. [7] Or there is a political metaphor, which leaves no doubts about Ruskin's reaction to the recent revolutionary stirrings. He condemns

> ornaments expressing the endeavour to equalise the executive and inventive, — endeavour which is Renaissance and revolutionary, and destructive of all noble architecture. [8]

Soon afterwards he writes scornfully of English Perpendicular Gothic, as being the worst example of

> the democratic ornament, in which all is equally influential, and has equal office and authority; that is to say, none of it any office nor authority, but a life of continual struggle for independence and notoriety, or of gambling for chance regards.

In contrast, the ornament to be admired is 'ordered, disciplined, well officered, and variously ranked'.[9]

The second volume shows an astonishing change in attitude. There are no more sneers at democracy. Ruskin no longer appears as a bigoted authoritarian, a member of the prosperous middle-classes fearful of the popular power recently exercised all over Europe. His new image is that of a man 'of the people. He stresses the inventiveness of the free workman, instanced by the medieval Venetian craftsman fashioning his clumsy but always original glassware; he approves of the northern European tendency 'to set the individual reason against authority, and the individual deed against destiny',[10] and he implies that the upper classes deserve the unprecedented hatred felt towards them by the lower classes, who are degraded to an unendurable machine-like existence. Furthermore, he writes, manual labour is not to be valued for its own sake, as several contemporaries believed, but the architect should work in the mason's yard with his men. And let

> the distinction between one man and another be only in experience and skill, and the authority and wealth which these must naturally and justly obtain.[11]

The political views expressed in this volume are not irreconcilable with those of the first, for Ruskin's ideas of social justice always involved a strong but benevolent guiding authority. But the weight of emphasis has unmistakably shifted on to the welfare of the worker: — is he to be made a tool, or a man? The message is now directed at society as a whole, not just at architects and architectural enthusiasts. Ruskin regards Gothic as admirable for the reason that this style was the product of a social system which recognised the value of each individual and allowed each man to realise his human potential.

As in the case of *Seven Lamps* it is natural to suppose that this shift of attention reflects an underlying change in Ruskin's political views at this time, and three letters composed in March 1852 (intended for publication in *The Times*) bear witness to his growing concern with social and economic questions. He was increasingly certain that the working-classes were unnecessarily condemned to meaningless and degrading labour; his sincerity is not in doubt. But once again we should not forget the additional possibility that the changes in his criticism had more literary 'internal' causes: that he developed a critical method already tried out to a lesser extent in *Modern Painters* and *Seven Lamps*, and that he came to treat the workman's spirit as the fundamental determinant of architectural style because of the rich store of vocabulary and metaphor involved. It is even possible that this literary gambit fostered in Ruskin an interest in the state of working people, as much as vice versa.

At any rate, we must investigate how the second volume of *The Stones of Venice* managed to give such a detailed account of that formerly vague entity, the Gothic spirit. In this volume Ruskin analyses two eras of Venetian building, Byzantine (including St Mark's) and Gothic. The Ducal Palace, the subject of his final chapter, combines the Gothic and Renaissance styles, but most of 'Renaissance Venice' is saved for malevolent scrutiny in the third volume. Ruskin's method of deriving age-character from art is less prominent in the Byzantine section, but as far as it goes the method is the one previously applied to individual painters. Early Byzantine Venice is supposed to have had 'a sadness of heart upon her, and a depth of devotion', and this is inferred partly from the symbols of her sculpture – peacocks for the Resurrection, a dove for the Comforter, a vine for Christ or those in union with him. But

> I lay no stress on these more occult meanings. The principal circumstance which marks the seriousness of the early Venetian mind is perhaps the last in which the reader would suppose it was traceable; – that love of bright and pure colour which, in a modified form, was afterwards the root of all the triumph of the Venetian schools of painting . . . [ Moreover ] . . . the purest and most thoughtful minds are those which love colour the most. [12]

It is by reference to painting that Ruskin tries to justify this surprising idea. With Fra Angelico (pure colours and elevated soul) it works well enough, and it is just credible that Salvator Rosa's 'gloomy' greys correspond to his life spent as 'a dissipated jester and satirist'; in general the principle serves Ruskin's desire to elevate fifteenth-century painting and deflate much of the seventeenth. But his system was threatened by such artists as Titian, Correggio and Rubens, who were famous for their 'love of colour' and yet indulged in 'sensualities' and 'coarseness' of which he could not approve. Furthermore their colours, as Ruskin admits, 'are not usually understood to be either pure or pensive'. The upshot is another of his self-defeating qualifications: *because* these painters placed their trust in the power of colour, they were enabled to stoop to the sensual depths, to descend 'as by a chain let down from heaven', without quite falling.

Next Ruskin associates purity of colour not with blitheness or *naïveté*, but with calm and serious purpose; and since he applies it to whole societies and to such vague entities as 'the Oriental mind', the correlation is not easy to establish or refute. His own supporting evidence is scriptural, relying on the eternal significance of the rainbow and of Joseph's coat of many colours. On the strength of this we are invited to believe that the colourful architecture of 'Byzantine' Venice stemmed from 'the solemnity of her early and earnest religion'.[13]

Immediately following is the justly celebrated chapter, 'The Nature of Gothic', which contains Ruskin's most compelling attempt to analyse the 'character' of a style. The essence of its success lies in his choice of attributes. The physical qualities which he takes as signs of mental qualities are already ambiguous, and can be applied to either humans or architecture with only minor modifications and a minimum of obvious metaphor. The elements of Gothic, considered 'as belonging to the building', are listed by Ruskin':

1 Savageness
2 Changefulness
3 Naturalism
4 Grotesqueness
5 Rigidity
6 Redundance

'As belonging to the builder', these become

1 Savageness or Rudeness
2 Love of Change
3 Love of Nature
4 Disturbed Imagination
5 Obstinacy
6 Generosity

How different from the lamps of 'Memory', 'Sacrifice' and

'Obedience', which could only be made relevant to architecture by complicated symbols and analogies. How different even from the criteria of purity and brightness of colour, used in the previous chapter; Ruskin could no doubt have slipped smoothly from brightness of colour to brightness of character, but unfortunately he wanted to reach an opposite conclusion, and had to resort to Biblical blustering.

Because the moves from physical to mental characteristics are so slight, Ruskin's strategy is disguised. He does not at first seem anxious to sell the Gothic style to his readers. We feel that he has given a neutral description of the outward features of the style, and then offered the subjective equivalent, without necessarily *admiring* the character delineated thereby. That character is now 'generous', it is true, but also 'obstinate' and 'rude' and his (or its) imagination is 'disturbed'. Ruskin cunningly waits for the detailed exposition of each trait before persuading us that this savage, obstinate character is in reality most attractive: 'savageness' turns out to be 'wolfish life', 'changefulness' becomes 'the restlessness of the dreaming mind', and 'obstinacy' is transformed into 'resolute independence'. Gothic emerges as a storybook hero, a noble, romantic character with a few attractive vices. A less deceptive summary of Ruskin's characterisation of the Gothic spirit would be as follows —

1 Inventiveness
2 Boundless Imagination
3 Frankness and Sympathy with Nature
4 Fantastic Imagination
5 Independence and Energy
6 Enthusiasm and Humility.

Ruskin has no difficulty in deriving many more commendable human qualities from each of his six features 'as belonging to the building'. In fact this chapter might have shown an articulate opponent of Gothic, had there been any such, how to attack the style by the same means. From the same set of external attributes, the following traits could have been inferred without any greater distortion:

1 Crudeness
2 Disorder and Anarchy

 3 Naïvety and Lack of Invention
 4 Obscenity
 5 Stubborn Awkwardness
 6 Extravagance.

If Ruskin's tastes had been those of the early eighteenth century, he could no doubt have made a villain out of Gothic along these lines. Alternatively, his original list might be applied, with a little ingenuity, to styles other than Gothic. We may notice that Ruskin's Gothic virtues here, unlike those in *Seven Lamps*, are not particularly religious (although he cannot resist a reference to 'the Protestant spirit of self-dependence and inquiry' expressed in the 'rigidity' of northern Gothic decoration[14]). The simpler secular qualities could be associated with visual counterparts without requiring such patent contrivance as did the religious qualities, and even transforming 'redundance' into 'humility', the most mysterious manoeuvre of the chapter, seems straightforward by comparison with the earlier work. When in 1921 Professor Percy Gardner put forward eight 'lamps of Greek art', he claimed to be following the lead of Ruskin's *Seven Lamps*, but his traits are in reality of the type set out in 'The Nature of Gothic'. Gardner's list consists of Humanism, Simplicity, Balance and Measure, Idealism, Naturalism, Patience, Joy, Fellowship.[15] (Ruskin would have denied that the last four were represented in Greek art, and claimed them for Gothic.) Some of Gardner's derivations are just as arbitrary as Ruskin's, but his essay is still in print, and the method has not yet lost its fascination.

In this second volume, it is not clear how far Ruskin intends us to believe that the builders of Gothic architecture in fact possessed the qualities which he presents as 'the Gothic spirit'. Only in the last chapter ('The Ducal Palace') is there a systematic attempt to demonstrate a gradual change in the Venetian character, based mainly on the difference between Gothic and Renaissance treatments of virtues and vices in sculpture and literature. Throughout the volume, Ruskin brings forward purely artistic evidence of national character, and uses it either to settle questions over which more orthodox historians had disagreed or to take the place of more orthodox historical evidence. The following is a typical example, which also shows that Ruskin had not abandoned his faith in the significance of facial features:

And this profession of their faith may be interpreted in two ways. Most modern historians would call it, in common with the continual reference to the principles of justice in the political and judicial language of the period, nothing more than a cloak for consummate violence and guilt; and it may easily be proved to have been so in myriads of instances. But in the main, I believe the expression of feeling to be genuine. I do not believe, of the majority of the leading Venetians of this period whose portraits have come down to us, that they were deliberately and everlastingly hypocrites. I see no hypocrisy in their countenances. Much capacity of it, much subtlety, much natural and acquired reserve, but no meanness . . .[16]

Ruskin offers no independent reasons to suppose that the Venetians had the moral inclinations he attributes to them. At one point he suggests that the simple architectural decoration of the thirteenth century was linked to 'a singular simplicity in domestic life', but by way of corroboration he quotes a passage from Cary's translation of Dante's *Paradiso* which refers to a lady 'with no artful colouring on her cheeks' and sons 'well content With unrobed jerkin'[17] – slender evidence indeed, especially as Dante was describing not Venice but Florence.

The third volume of *The Stones of Venice* is a different proposition again. It clearly puts forward a historical thesis, that the society of Venice suffered a general decline in the later fifteenth and sixteenth centuries. There is some reference to the social customs of the time, and as each stage of the Renaissance is described in turn, Ruskin conveys the impression that he has a knowledge of its social and spiritual phenomena beyond that which he detects in its architecture. This is the only one of the three volumes which invites comparison with contemporary histories of Venice, of which the best-known in England was contained in Sismondi's *Histoire des Républiques Italiennes au Moyen Age*. Ruskin was reading this work on his all-important tour of Italy in 1845; at Lucca his breakfast consisted of 'coffee, eggs, and a volume of Sismondi', while at Pisa Sismondi helped him 'feel what I had to look for in the Campo Santo'.[18] Ruskin used the Frenchman's history in writing *The Stones of Venice* and *Val d'Arno*, and despite some grumbles about Sismondi's republican prejudices, seems to have maintained a high opinion of his work. But there is a major difference between the two writers. Although both made great play with the idea of national character, and although in 1845 Ruskin was interested in Sismondi's theory that it was largely determined by political structure, he subsequently took an opposite view. It is not clear what Ruskin regarded as the fundamental cause of moral and artistic decline in *The Stones of Venice* – he implies that civilizations, like individuals, advance through their own virtue and decay, through their own pride – but the cause certainly did *not* lie in political events, he believed; to Ruskin politics were merely an offshoot from a grand process of corporate character development.

This third volume opens with an uncompromising interpretation of early Renaissance art as the product of spiritual decadence. We are told of its 'luscious' ornament, its 'idle subtleties of fancy', and its lack of the 'temperance' necessary to all great art. 'The fatal weariness of decay' is already indicated in the later Gothic crockets and finials of Venice, and her capitals decline 'into luxury and effeminacy as the strength of the school expires'. In the next chapter Ruskin associates these failings with the 'infidelity' of the Renaissance, which he attributes to the worldliness and decadence of the Church, to the antagonism between Romanism and Protestantism (detrimental to both) and to the renewed study of classical literature.[19]

Professor Rudolf Wittkower has made a well-known attack on Ruskin's belief that Renaissance architecture was pagan and profane, calling a passage from Ruskin's third volume 'the extreme statement of misrepresentation'.[20] He rightly calls attention to the fact that Ruskin was most unfair in picking out Renaissance architecture as particularly irreligious. However Wittkower goes further. He points to the arguments by which Alberti and his successors justified their designs, their regard for the circle and its centre as symbols of God, their debt to Plato's cosmology and to Pythagoras' universal ratios; and he presents these facts as if they refuted Ruskin's interpretation.[21] But Ruskin would have found them beside the point. *The Stones of Venice* presents architecture as an *unconscious* expression of national character. It is concerned with moral traits in a broad sense, not with metaphysical theories, and with societies rather than individuals. Geoffrey Scott's critique in *The Architecture of Humanism* more clearly exposes Ruskin's unwarranted analogies, although this book itself makes some over-ambitious inferences of the mentality which gave birth to the Renaissance and Baroque forms.

However, the charge of worldliness is the least original aspect of Ruskin's critique, and also the aspect on which he places least emphasis. His basic quarrel with the Renaissance is more subtle. He distinguishes between the change in formal elements, from Gothic to classical, and what he sees as a change in approach and building method, leading to an increasing demand for perfection. If either innovation had taken place without the other, Ruskin speculates, the effects might have been less damaging. But he is concerned less with the inadequacies of the forms of the Renaissance than with its 'corrupt moral nature'.[22]

This corrupt spirit of the 'Roman Renaissance' is analysed into four elements: Infidelity, which we have already mentioned, and three varieties of Pride. Of these the least dangerous is 'Pride of System', that is, the reduction of arts and sciences to rules and formulas at the expense of individual inventiveness. The brunt of Ruskin's onslaught is borne by 'Pride of Science' and 'Pride of State', themselves sources of Infidelity. 'Science', in the context of Renaissance painting, means the laws of perspective, anatomy, and accurate drawing. But according to Ruskin, a mastery of these leads to a deadening of the imagination and human feelings which are essential to art in its true sense. He allows that 'the schools of knowledge' can portray the commonplace external aspects of nature, but insists that they cannot deal with what is of the spirit, which is the only worthwhile occupation of art.[23]

'Pride of State' is the Renaissance antithesis to 'The Nature of Gothic'. In contrast to the guided individuality of Gothic architecture, that of the succeeding style yields 'an expression of aristocracy in its worst characters; coldness, perfectness of training, incapability of emotion, want of sympathy with the weakness of lower men, blank, hopeless, haughty self-sufficiency'. Whatever excellence it may have is erudite, so that it offers nothing that the common man can enjoy, and in fact is 'full of insult to the poor in its every line'. Ruskin uses tomb sculpture to illustrate the way in which this form of pride accumulated.

But when we have finished the book, after struggling through a chapter on grotesques whose arguments are as contorted as its subject, we realise that the historical framework is largely an illusion. The references to the political and religious life of Venice are related only to details of Ruskin's interpretations. Although he evidently believed that societies whose spiritual state was admirable were rewarded by material prosperity, he did not utilise facts that would (on this principle) strengthen his case, such as the great increase of wealth and territory in the first two decades of the fifteenth century, which for Ruskin was the climax of Venice's 'central epoch'. Nor, of course, did he give any account of considerations which would weaken his argument – in particular, the continued expansion of Venetian power on the mainland in the later fifteenth century, when Venice was (in Ruskin's scheme) declining. We are not, after all, offered an outline of the course of Venetian history with which the development of its art might be correlated; as in the second volume, Venice is seen almost exclusively through her art, and artistic evidence retains its supreme authority.

Acknowledging the insidious eloquence of *The Stones of Venice*, one cannot help wondering why no English writer of the earlier nineteenth century tried to do for Greek architecture what Ruskin did for Gothic – an easy enough task in principle, as Professor Gardner has more recently shown. We have mentioned Edward Freeman's brief comparisons drawn in 1849 between the supposed characters of Greek races and their architectural styles, but in all the writings of contemporary specialists in Greek architecture, such as 'Athenian' Aberdeen, William Wilkins, C. R. Cockerell and Francis Penrose, no attempt was made to interpret the art of classical Greece in human terms, despite the example set briefly by Winckelmann in the 1750s.[24]

In general we might put this down to inevitable fluctuations of taste, and suppose that the newer fashion for the Middle Ages attracted the most imaginative writers. A Victorian architect recalled that Pugin's *Contrasts* 'might easily have been exposed by anyone of equally strong convictions on the other side, had there been any such person or such convictions, but the ardent spirits at that time were all in the camp of the medievalists'.[25] No doubt this in turn was partly because several of the 'ardent spirits' were ardently Christian, and aware of the close links between their religion and Gothic building; by comparison (as a manual of the time repeated), 'Grecian and Italian forms have little language for the Christian mind'.[26]

A further reason must be that the very idea of 'expressive' art was not congenial to many worshippers of Greek and Roman civilization. It was not so much that Greek and Gothic architecture represented different mental qualities as that Gothic represented mental qualities of some kind while Greek did not at all. It was felt that the merits of the latter lay rather in the realms of abstract beauty and fine geometry. The same was held to be true of Greek sculpture: in *Modern Painters* Ruskin wrote that ancient statues never expressed any elevated character by their faces, for 'the Greek could not conceive a spirit'.[27]

In his later lectures, he claimed that Greek sculpture was 'faceless', 'independent, not only of the expression, but even of the beauty of the face'.[28] (As regards the first-hand evidence available in England, Greek sculpture was indeed 'faceless', since of all Elgin's human figures from the Parthenon pediments, only the so-called Theseus in the east pediment still had a head.) Here Ruskin articulated what had often been accepted implicitly, though few had dared to show such open disrespect for Greek art.

Ruskin has often been criticised for neglecting the three-dimensional aspects of architecture; and (with some exceptions) he did indeed neglect volumes in favour of surfaces, because surfaces were the crucial element in his approach. The walls of a building formed the point of direct contact between workman and artefact, the point at which (as Ruskin saw it) the workman's qualities were transmitted to the building. For Ruskin, the workmen were the representatives of the age-spirit. The proportions and masses of the building did not lend themselves to Ruskin's treatment, and in any case they were likely to be determined by a small group or by an individual architect of unknown character. An appendix of *Seven Lamps* is devoted to the architects of the Ducal Palace, but there is no suggestion that their particular personalities were relevant to its design. Even the functional aspects of a building (again the responsibility of a select few) are not regarded by Ruskin as evidence of character, although they may betray intelligence or a lack of it: 'the intelligent part of man being eminently, if not chiefly, displayed in the structure of his work, his affectionate part is to be shown in its decoration.'[29] In short, the more consciously and intellectually conceived aspects of architecture were less likely to serve as agents of the age-spirit. Thus it is not surprising that of the six elements which make up 'The Nature of Gothic', Ruskin's

most neatly fashioned piece of character inference, three apply
solely and the other three chiefly to surface ornament.

So while Ruskin's methods of criticism had developed con-
siderably in the space of a decade, the development was on the
whole consistent. From reading faces as evidence of character,
Ruskin and his contemporaries exploited the technique to use
other aspects of paintings as evidence of their creators' personalities; and Ruskin further extended the technique from
painting to architecture, and from individuals to societies. By the
final volumes of *The Stones of Venice*, he was reading the faces of
buildings as confidently as he read the faces of portraits. Several
critics had set out on the same road, but none followed it so far.
Only Ruskin could render plausible the extravagant inferences and
tottering generalisations which the method entailed, or describe its
leading principle with such revealing accuracy:

> I do with a building as I do with a man, watch the eye and lips:
> when they are bright and eloquent, the form of the body is of
> little consequence.[30]

\*          \*          \*

Of all his books, the second volume of *The Stones of Venice*
remains Ruskin's masterpiece. The purple passages in 'The Nature
of Gothic', the chapter later reprinted by William Morris's
Kelmscott Press, have not faded:

> It is that strange *disquietude* of the Gothic spirit that is its
> greatness; that restlessness of the dreaming mind, that wanders
> hither and thither among the niches, and flickers feverishly
> around the pinnacles, and frets and fades in labyrinthine knots
> and shadows along wall and roof, and yet is not satisfied . . .'[31]

And so on. Ruskin's indictment of mindless labour, of degrading
men into machines, is likewise as applicable to the twentieth
century as it was to the nineteenth. All this is held together by a
skilfully-wrought framework of 'cultural history', which lends
weight to what might otherwise seem flippant and fanciful. At last
Ruskin had found the formula best suited both to his talents and to
the market. This volume was the first of Ruskin's books to be
reviewed by *The Times*, and their notice was long and favourable.
The *Daily News* stated, significantly, that 'Mr Ruskin is the first

really popular writer we have ever had upon architecture; and, paradoxical as it may seem, it is because he is almost the first truly profound writer we have had on that subject'.[32]

Histories of art are rarely popular, but *The Stones of Venice* cannot properly be described as a history of art. If the art historian's task is to consider historical contexts in order to interpret works of art, then Ruskin did the reverse: he considered works of art in order to interpret historical contexts. *The Stones of Venice* is a kind of history of ideas, akin to the German discipline of *Geistesgeschichte* in its assumption that there is some essential factor which unites all the cultural products of an age, a factor which is often seen as a frame of mind, or a cluster of attitudes — in short, a personality.

As a historical study, *The Stones of Venice* is open to many of the objections to which all *Geistesgeschichte* is subject.[33] On the other hand, a number of twentieth-century historians have found its historical methods convincing,[34] and the principle that art-forms are to a large extent 'expressions of a socially-conditioned world-view'[35] has an ancestor in Ruskin as well as in Marx.

Ruskin despised what little he knew of German literature and philosophy, and he would have been indignant at the notion that his work had anything to do with Germany. Indeed the idea that the arts of a society flourished or declined together had long been familiar in Britain as well as on the Continent. Eighteenth-century writers had repeatedly debated whether climate, commerce or political system had the greatest influence on cultural fluctuations. (The painter James Barry was piqued by Winckelmann's suggestion that England's artistic genius was inhibited by her cloudy skies.) 'The spirit of the age affects all the arts', wrote David Hume[36] — but he and his British contemporaries made little attempt to *define* that spirit. Only in Germany was the age-spirit characterised: Winckelmann promoted classical Greece as a civilisation of 'noble simplicity and quiet grandeur', Herder was encouraged to offer a parallel interpretation of the Middle Ages, and Schelling and the Schlegels also followed Winckelmann's lead. As early as 1778 Winckelmann's method was criticised, astutely, in terms that could apply equally well to Ruskin:

More than once Winckelmann first put his imagination to work to invent the style of an age or an artist and make it seem likely;

then he derived from this judgements for the whole history of the era, from which he again derived a number of other things. [37]

Winckelmann's British readers were not much interested in his historical approach. They admired his passion for antiquarian research, just as they admired the 'antiquarianism' of Horace Walpole and Seroux d'Agincourt. It was not until the Victorian era that a need was felt in Britain for wider interpretations of art in terms of the social and religious attitudes of its time. Well aware of the earlier German developments, Anna Jameson in 1848 looked back with disdain upon the arid arguments of Richardson and Reynolds:

> In those days we had Inquiries into the Principles of Taste, Treatises on the Sublime and Beautiful, Anecdotes of Painting, and we abounded in Antiquarian Essays on disputed Pictures and mutilated Statues: but then, and up to a late period, any inquiry into the true spirit and significance of works of Art, as connected with the history of Religion and Civilization, would have appeared ridiculous – or perhaps dangerous . . .

Connoisseurs, she continued, had been concerned with the authenticity of a work, but not with its spirit, nor with the artist's intentions. But now some were beginning to suspect that pictures offered 'more than mere connoisseurship can interpret; and that they have another, a deeper significance than has been dreamed of by picture dealers and picture collectors, or even picture critics'. [38]

Mrs Jameson may well have had in mind Friedrich Schlegel and Alexis-François Rio as exemplars of this new interest in broader cultural factors. We have already mentioned Schlegel's influential emphasis on the intentions and spiritual state of the individual artist, but equally novel to English readers was his treatment of the art of a period as the product of a general age-spirit – especially as applied to Gothic architecture and the paintings of the earlier Italian masters. One instance of the effect which this produced in England occurs in a letter to Constable from his friend and patron Archdeacon Fisher, written it seems to distract Constable from brooding over the recent death of his wife.

> I met in Schlegel a happy criticism on what is called Gothic architecture. We do not estimate it aright unless we judge of it

by the spirit of the age which produced it, and compare it with
contemporary productions . . .[39]

Fisher may not have taken Schlegel at his most profound, for he
concludes that when we look at a cathedral, we should imagine
mitred abbots and mailed knights processing down its solemn
aisles, but he does add that 'I . . .have enlarged a little on his
notion, since he only hints at the thing'. Others took the 'spirit'
more seriously, and foremost among those who treated art 'as
connected with the history of Religion and Civilization' was the
much-admired Rio. Like his mentor Friedrich Schlegel, Rio
interpreted the mentality of paintings at a social as well as at a
personal level. He attributed the achievements of mid-fourteenth
century painting to the 'marvellous unity' of the period, in which
artists of every kind worked for God's glory, impelled by a
common source of inspiration, and in an atmosphere of intimate
sympathy between artists and people. The Frenchman's book was
a lament for the losing battles fought by true (Roman Catholic)
religion against the pagan influx of luxury, frivolity, classical
pedantry and vanity. In the final chapter on Venice, Rio made a
most determined effort to show that Venetian art was the
necessary product and faithful mirror of the '*génie national*'.[40]

Ruskin's *Stones of Venice* was the direct inheritor of this strategy,
but most of his English readers would not have encountered the
strategy before – unless, like Carlyle, they were familiar with
German historiography, or else, like Lord Lindsay and Anna
Jameson, they had digested the writings of Rio. Francis Palgrave
was another who was impressed by Rio's 'epoch sauce' (to borrow
a phrase of Bernard Berenson's[41]): in September 1840 Palgrave
contributed to the *Quarterly* a remarkable review of Vasari's *Opere*,
arguing in effect that the great ages of art were those in which
painting and architecture embodied the feelings and spiritual state
of the whole people. As Ruskin was later to do, Palgrave made use
of this analysis to denounce the mechanised art of his own day and
its stifling of free expression. He likened machine-produced
designs to music from a barrel-organ: never a false note, but it soon
palls.

It is fair to conclude that Rio paved the way for the success of
*The Stones of Venice* among a small but influential group of people.
It is notable that Rio had closer personal contacts with the literary

figures of early Victorian England than with the painters and critics of art. Through his friend Monckton Milnes he met Rogers, Hallam and Macaulay, and later Tennyson, Wordsworth, Landor, Gladstone and Carlyle, On the other hand there were several hard-headed scholars who rejected the Rio-Ruskin approach. One was Charles Eastlake, who pointedly ignored Rio's book[42] and whose wife became Ruskin's sharpest critic; and another was C. R. Leslie, the biographer of Constable and a firm opponent of transcendental explanations, who rejected the notion of Fra Angelico's pencils operating by the immediate direction of Heaven; the friar was capable of painting a picture in which 'the principal face, and that, too, of a divine personage, squints'.[43]

# 8 Turner and the Pre-Raphaelites

The painting of J.M.W. Turner was the deepest and most enduring of Ruskin's enthusiasms. In 1838 John James Ruskin, who was a collector of contemporary English pictures, began to give Turner watercolours to his son. His New Year's gift in 1844 was an oil, the 'Slave Ship' which Ruskin had just praised so memorably in his first book. By this time Ruskin had begun to buy Turners on his own account, but his requests to his father for more money with which to buy them were not always successful, mainly because John James, the prudent businessman, was reluctant to invest disproportionately in any one artist.

But the young Ruskin was prepared to pay for Turner water-colours sums which shocked his father, and he feasted on those he possessed. 'The exquisite pleasure that every new one gives me is like a year added to my life', he wrote to his father in January 1852.[1] Turner had died the month before; Ruskin wrote from Venice, asking his father to try to buy some of Turner's sketches ('I can . . . reason out a great deal of the man from them which I cannot get from the drawings').[2] This plan had to be abandoned when Ruskin heard that he had been made an executor of Turner's will (although he subsequently renounced his executorship). Instead Ruskin entered into Turner's dream of a 'Turner's Gallery', to be added to the National Gallery, and he hoped he might be put in charge of the new extension if it were created. But he had to be content with persuading the Trustees to let him sort out the drawings – nearly 20,000 of them – which Turner had left. He bought and sold Turners frequently: the list of works by Turner which Ruskin owned at one time or another numbers nearly 300.[3] He continued to promote Turner's work until late in life, by giving many of his Turners to Oxford and Cambridge, by arranging loans and exhibitions, and of course by his writing.

We have seen that although Ruskin's theme was Turner's Truth, the Truth on which Ruskin insisted was a matter of original conception and profound sympathy, and thus could be extended without much difficulty into an analysis of character. By this means Turner became a victim of Ruskin's personal criticism, which could be savage in attack but embarrassingly fulsome in defence.

Even the first volume of *Modern Painters* perplexed reviewers by its worship of the artist. 'The Turneric might have been advocated without such an especial idolatry of the artist himself', wrote one.[4] As a result of comments like this, Ruskin removed from subsequent editions a passage referring to 'Turner – glorious in conception – unfathomable in knowledge – solitary in power . . . sent as a prophet of God to reveal to men the mysteries of His universe, standing, like the great angel of the Apocalypse, clothed with a cloud . . .'[5] But from 1846 onwards he adopted a different form of Turner-worship. At first, Ruskin was understandably less willing to infer Turner's character from his art than the characters of the early Italians from theirs. The 1846 edition of volume one took a much more sober view of Turner than the two previous editions had done:

> I conceive of him to be the most powerful painter whom the world has seen, and that he was prevented from being also the most perfect, partly by untoward circumstances in his position and education, partly by the very fulness and impetuosity of his own mind, partly by the want of religious feeling and its accompanying perception of beauty; for his noble treatment of religious subjects . . . is wanting in the signs of the more withdrawn and scared sympathies.[6]

When Ruskin returned to the subject of Turner and his art five years later, having married and written *The Seven Lamps of Architecture* in the meantime, he was more prepared to draw conclusions about Turner the man. The occasion was Ruskin's pamphlet *Pre-Raphaelitism* of 1851, of which the bulk was devoted to Turner. Not much was said here about the Pre-Raphaelite Brothers, and what there was did not always flatter them. (Millais was credited with a quiet temperament, a feeble memory, no invention, and excessively keen sight.[7]) Ruskin divided Turner's work into three periods, neatly summarising the characteristics of each, and paying special attention to the 'characters of mind' displayed in each case.

During the first period, up to 1820, Turner painted nearly every kind of subject – town, country and marine, domestic, biblical and historical. We might suppose that this variety would make it difficult for Ruskin to divine Turner's state of mind at this time, but he turned it to his own advantage, claiming that Turner's 'utter forgetfulness of self' is shown thereby, and that the painter 'appears as a man of sympathy absolutely infinite'. This 'sympathy' he also discovered through Turner's 'subtle power of expression' – not human expression, for Turner was not renowned for his figures and faces, but the essential character of material things, 'the thorough stiffness of what is stiff, and grace of what is graceful, and vastness of what is vast'. The crucial assumption here is that 'the man who can best feel the difference between rudeness and tenderness in humanity, perceives also more difference between the branches of an oak and a willow than anyone else would'. [8] Ruskin was not the only early Victorian writer to believe this, but it seems an unlikely proposition today.

We need not assume that Ruskin was primarily interested in discovering the hidden truths of Turner's inmost being, if we bear in mind again that Ruskin's critical approach and much of his critical vocabulary depended on the principle that artistic abilities stem from moral qualities; to put it briefly, moral qualities of one kind or another had to be assumed before the criticism could begin. From the critic's point of view it did not matter greatly whether Turner or the stonemasons of medieval Venice actually possessed the qualities he ascribed to them, so long as they could plausibly be imagined to have them – that is, the attributions had to stop short of obvious fantasy.

Ruskin's conception of Turner's character is not easily reconciled with others' opinions of the painter. The man whom Emerson called 'a cross grained miser' and whom Hoppner had criticised for his 'manners so presumptive and arrogant' became in the words of Ruskin (who had first met Turner when the latter was 65) a man of 'chastened and exquisitely peaceful cheerfulness, deeply meditative'. [9]

In November 1856 the Turner Gallery was opened at Marlborough House, and the notes which Ruskin published on the pictures exhibited there show how far his critical approach had

altered since he first emerged as Turner's champion. In those days
he was concerned to show that Turner's pictures displayed both
essential Truth and 'truth to nature', just as his initial defence of the
Pre-Raphaelites emphasised their 'accuracy' of colour and perspective. Then, as a second stage, his booklet *Pre-Raphaelitism*
(1851) linked Turner and the Pre-Raphaelites in a more ambiguous fashion, and contrived to suggest that 'painting from
nature only' meant something like 'pursuing one's individual
vision'. By 1856 much of the ambiguity was resolved: by 'Pre-
Raphaelite painting' he now had in mind little more than bright
colour and scrupulous detail, and he no longer tried to establish
Turner's fidelity to Nature, nor to link him with Pre-
Raphaelitism, which was generally agreed to have been one of
Ruskin's least convincing manoeuvres. Instead, he chose to find in
Turner's pictures expressions of deep feeling and significant
meaning. So Turner's early 'Shipwreck' 'is only one of many, in
which he strove to speak in sympathy with the mystery of human
pain', and his 'Phryne going to the Bath' (1838) 'is definitely
painted as an expression of the triumph of Guilt'. Even Ruskin
must have realised that some of these insights were a little far-
fetched, for he added ingenuously, 'there is something very strange
and sorrowful in the way Turner used to hint only at these under
meanings of his . . . '[10]

As before, Ruskin claimed that Turner was distinguished from
all other modern landscape painters by his 'strange human
sympathy', but he now brought forward fresh evidence. Whereas
Turner's rivals inserted figures into their pictures to add superficial
interest, Ruskin suggested, Turner made his figures play some
important role. The weakness in this thesis is that Turner was
notoriously unorthodox in his drawing of the human figure; in
'Phryne' the figures looked like rag dolls to the *Athenaeum*'s critic,
and like 'chalk puppets' to Ruskin himself. After a vain attempt to
excuse this supposed fault, Ruskin had finally to confess that of all
the mysteries of Turner's art, his figure painting was the most
mysterious of all.[11]

Ruskin also discussed more technical aspects of Turner's artistic
developments, such as his changing colour preferences and
treatment of light and masses. But the overall impression given by
these notes is one of a development and decay in Turner's *character*.
More ambitiously than before, Ruskin not only read elaborate

'expressions' into the paintings, but also treated them as issuing from Turner's own feelings and personality. Turner's earlier work demonstrated 'the evidently stern and pathetic temper of his maturing mind'; in middle life, 'he mocks no more, he weeps no more' (and so would have been better fitted to paint Byron's 'Childe Harold' when he was younger); and in Turner's final years Ruskin found, but declined to specify, 'the *distinctive* characters indicative of mental disease'.[12] To Ruskin, every artistic change implied a psychological change; and the longer Turner lay in his grave, the more liberties Ruskin could take in divining his soul.[13]

This seems to be a general rule in Ruskin's art criticism: the more remote in time the painter under inspection, the more ambitious the character analysis. In writing of painters who were still alive and known, including the Pre-Raphaelites, Ruskin had to restrain his imagination. There is a passage in the second volume of *Modern Painters* which condemns 'sensual' painters, mentioning Correggio by name, and adding 'excepting always Etty'; a later footnote reads, 'not in the least excepting him – this sentence, I fear, is mere politeness to a painter then living'.[14] Similarly, in Ruskin's *Academy Notes* of 1855–9 there could be no question of referring the features of each picture to the character of its painter. Nor did he invoke any decadent tendencies of the times, but on the contrary reported a steady improvement in the general standard of painting, with many paintings 'struggling forward out of their conventionalism to the Pre-Raphaelite standard'.[15]

Since neither of these two favourite critical strategies was open to Ruskin here, his artistic preferences emerged uncluttered by theory or rhetoric. He admired meticulous and accurate detail, though not in all circumstances, or as an end in itself: a 'Spring Evening' was described as 'merely good pre-Raphaelite work, certainly showing no evidence whatever of inventive power'.[16] He paid some attention to drawing, arrangement of masses, and perspective, and considerable attention to fine discriminations of colour. But the dominant terms of reference are 'expression' and 'feeling' – as they might perhaps be in a passage of twentieth-century art criticism, but would certainly not have been a generation before Ruskin.

Both facial expression and general emotional tone attracted his interest. The former, he suggested, should not denote strong emotions so much as subtle ones. Thus he advised Mr Phillip to refine his style so that he might 'represent not merely the piquancy, but the wayward, half melancholy mystery of Spanish beauty'.[17] He praised C. R. Leslie as the great master of 'the phases of such delicate expression on the human face as may be excited by the slight passions or humours of the drawing-room or boudoir';[18] and on Miss Boyce's 'Elgira', Ruskin's comment is worthy of Winckelmann:

> As we watch the face for a little time, the slight arch of the lip begins to quiver, and the eyes fill with ineffable sadness and on-look of despair.[19]

No less than Winckelmann, nineteenth-century interpreters of finely judged expressions ran the risk of counter-interpretation, and indeed the more subtle the expression, the more scope there was for disagreement over its meaning. When William Roscoe claimed that Leonardo's 'Last Supper' showed Christ with an expression of 'unshaken firmness', the *Edinburgh Review* preferred to think that the face radiated 'benevolence, mildness, forgiveness, melancholy', and also found Roscoe mistaken in his reading of the faces of all the apostles.[20] Ruskin's criticisms were often liable to this kind of flat contradiction. He mentioned one of Leslie's scenes from Don Quixote, on view in the 1855 Academy exhibition, in praising Leslie as the master of delicate expression; but of this same picture, the *Athenaeum* wrote disapprovingly that 'in no face is there much expression, but in that of the right-hand attendant, and that might as well as away'.[21]

Ruskin saw human faces in some unlikely places: in the brick building which 'wherever it intrudes its good-humoured red face, stares plaster and marble out of countenance . . .'; in a simple Italian window, which had 'much the same relation to a glazed window that the hollow of a skull has to a bright eye'; and in a grotesque Gothic roof, which had 'a certain charm like that of cheerfulness in a human face'. Ruskin also drew on other even less probable parts of the human anatomy for his metaphors: English trees are said to 'grow in paroxysms of *mauvaise honte*, sticking out their elbows everywhere in the wrong places'; and as an astonished reviewer pointed out, 'he calls the joints of boughs their "arm-pits"'.[22]

It seems sometimes as if Ruskin could hardly help seeing people and personalities wherever he looked. And the same may be true of his analyses of the characters of artists — which, in the context of his art criticism as a whole, appears not so much a consciously contrived policy as the inevitable response of an arch-anthropomorphist in an age of anthropomorphism. Ruskin was prone to seeing great human significance in the smallest detail (he 'discovers the Apocalypse in a daisy', as the *Athenaeum* put it),[23] and this habit of mind links his interest in facial expression with his 'artist-oriented' criticism. When Ruskin was prevented from finding the entire personality of an artist (or his age) revealed in the colours of his palette or in the style of his window-carving, he was still able to discern in a figure on canvas the most intricate mental characteristics, on the basis of a few ambiguous brush-strokes.

This raises an interesting question concerning Ruskin's criticism of the Pre-Raphaelites. Pre-Raphaelite painting is today often distinguished from contemporary efforts by its emotional expressiveness — by its ability to evoke a sense of pathos without quite lapsing into sentimental melodrama; and it is the 'soulful' qualities of even the earlier Pre-Raphaelites that are supposed to have influenced the European Symbolist movement of the later nineteenth century.[24] An important element was the aura of restrained, romantic religious emotion introduced by Rossetti at an early stage and imitated by his disciples. Rossetti summarised Pre-Raphaelitism as 'réalisme emotionnel mais extrèmement minutieux'.[25] Now Ruskin paid his respects to the realism; but why did he make so little mention of the emotional aspect?

Briefly, the circumstances were these. In the autumn of 1848, three young artists, Dante Gabriel Rossetti, William Holman Hunt and John Everett Millais, admiring Lasinio's engravings of the Campo Santo frescoes which had occupied Ruskin three years before, decided to call themselves the Pre-Raphaelite Brotherhood — a group which soon included four others in addition. At first the Brothers' exhibited works were well received, but early in 1850 the meaning of 'P.R.B.', the initials with which their pictures were signed, was let slip to the public: a series of scornful articles followed, written by reviewers who smelt a plot against all that was respectable and Protestant. The most unpleasantly violent came from the pen of Charles Dickens, who described the central figure in Millais's 'Christ in the House of his Parents' as a 'hideous, wry-necked, blubbering, red-haired boy in a night-gown, who appears to have received a poke playing in an

adjacent gutter'.[26] Potential buyers shied away. However, at the
opening of the 1851 Summer Exhibition of the Royal Academy,
Ruskin's attention was drawn to the Pre-Raphaelites' contribution; he took up their cause energetically, beginning with two
letters to *The Times*.

The first of these two letters of May 1851 praised the 'perfect
truth, power and finish' of parts of the pictures by Millais, Holman
Hunt and Charles Collins in that year's Academy exhibition. The
second letter admired Hunt's 'Valentine and Sylvia' for 'its
marvellous truth in detail and splendour in colour', but it also
attended to the facial expression of the figures: the conception and
execution of 'Valentine and Sylvia' are said to 'fail in making
immediate appeal to the feelings, owing to the unfortunate type
chosen for the face of Sylvia'. The left-hand figure of Millais's
'Return of the Dove to the Ark' was also 'unredeemed by any
expression save that of dull self-complacency'; let the spectator
contemplate instead 'the tender and beautiful expression of the
stooping figure . . .'[27] There are other adverse comments of
various kinds in each letter, and at this stage Ruskin seems not to
have cast the Pre-Raphaelites in any one particular role.

Then in August his pamphlet *Pre-Raphaelitism* appeared, and
clarified the image of the Pre-Raphaelites: the preface praised them
for fulfilling to the letter the advice of *Modern Painters*, to 'go to
nature in all singleness of heart, and walk with her laboriously and
trustingly'.[28] But the pamphlet made it clear that this was not the
supreme purpose of art. Ruskin drew a contrast between faithful
representation of natural objects (referring by implication to the
Pre-Raphaelites) and original, imaginative painting; and it was the
second of these which occupied 'the highest, the noblest place'. He
argued that careful copying was valuable as a training, as an
historical record, and especially as a revolt against the prevailing
system, corrupt with conventions of 'ideal beauty', banal subject-
matter, and artificial contrasts in lighting and colour;[29] but it was
not great art. While Ruskin may have been the Pre-Raphaelites'
saviour, he did not hide his reservations. 'They are working too
hard', he remarked later in the pamphlet, and 'missing the fine
effects which a broader, less meticulous treatment could achieve'.[30] In his fourth Edinburgh lecture, delivered two years later,
Ruskin again cast doubts on the 'laboriousness' he had recom-
mended in that over-remembered passage; he also repeated that

Pre-Raphaelite painting could not rank in the highest class as long as they selected their subjects only from nature. But painters must be '*educated* on the severest Pre-Raphaelite principles'.[31]

Moreover, Ruskin did not praise the Pre-Raphaelites for their fidelity to natural forms so much as applaud them, together with Turner, for being true to their own personal visions. Indeed, he claimed, all great painters became great 'by painting the truths around them as they appeared to each man's own mind, not as he had been taught to see them'. There was no single correct rendering of nature on canvas, no single truth, but various kinds of truth corresponding to the various powers and perceptions of artists.[32] By this rather devious means he managed to suggest that Millais and Turner were equally 'truthful'.

Ruskin's letters and pamphlet of 1851 undoubtedly enhanced the reputation of the Pre-Raphaelites, but it is less certain whether they persuaded critics and public to regard the group in his own terms. The P.R.B. was generally thought to favour precise detail, clear contours and (in some eyes) deliberate ugliness, and to oppose bravura and 'slosh'; their bright colours aroused considerable comment ('at present the Pre-Raphaelites and their followers see no medium between treacle and duckweed. Liquorice and emeralds are their war-cries . . . '[33]); and they were seldom believed to be imitating paintings executed before Raphael. In all these respects public opinion coincided with Ruskin's. But throughout the 1850s, the periodical notices continued to observe what Ruskin had conspicuously neglected, the emotional qualities of Pre-Raphaelite art.[34] The first painting to be exhibited with the initials 'P.R.B.', Rossetti's 'The Girlhood of Mary Virgin', reminded Frank Stone in his review for the influential *Athenaeum* 'of the feeling with which the early Florentine monastic painters wrought'.[35] In the following year Stone was less appreciative, but he still wrote that the Brotherhood was 'making sentiment and expression the great ends, and subordinating to these all technical considerations'.[36] The *British Quarterly Review* of 1852 remarked on 'the peculiar sentimental tendencies of at least a portion of the Pre-Raphaelites';[37] and Théophile Gautier attributed to the earlier Millais not only 'la couleur de vitrail de Van-Eyck et le minutieux réalisme d'Holbein', but also (and firstly) 'la simplicité pieuse d'Hemmling'.[38]

Of course, the sense of piety or poignancy in some Pre-

Raphaelite paintings is not something distinct from their more obvious physical characteristics. The twilight colours of Millais's 'Autumn Leaves', for example, contribute greatly to the painting's evocative atmosphere (and Ruskin did call it 'by much the most poetical work the painter has yet conceived'[39]); the same is true of the golden light of Hunt's 'Haunted Manor', or the slightly sickly tones of Dyce's 'Pegwell Bay'. Another important contributor is the facial expression of the figures, as Ruskin recognised in his first letter to *The Times*, and in several subsequent notices of Pre-Raphaelite pictures: Arthur Hughes's 'April Love' (plate 7a) was 'most subtle in the quivering expression of the lips',[40] and Hunt's 'The Awakening Conscience' was admired for 'the countenance of the lost girl, rent from its beauty into sudden horror; the lips half open, indistinct in their purple quivering, the teeth set hard, the eyes filled with the fearful light of futurity . . .'[41] (Here again there was scope for disagreement – the *New Monthly Magazine* reported that 'the expression on her countenance is that of one who is shivering dreadfully'.[42]) However, Ruskin did not mention poignant facial expression as being a Pre-Raphaelite speciality, although he might with some justice have done so. Each of the first three paintings to carry the initials 'P.R.B.' was praised by other critics for the expressively subdued faces of their characters. The following year, even Frank Stone's adverse notice of Rossetti's 'Ecce Ancilla Domini' found that 'a certain expression in the eyes of the ill-drawn face of the Virgin [plate 7b] affords a gleam of something high in intention.'[43] Facial expression was one of the controversial aspects of Millais's so-called 'Carpenter's Shop': many disliked it, but the *Illustrated London News* believed that only in Dyce's work was there 'sincerity of look in the heads of the principal figures at all comparable to this'. It also seemed to think that this aspect of the picture constituted its 'Pre-Raphaelism'.[44]

In the Academy exhibition of 1852, the faces of Millais's 'Ophelia' and 'Huguenot' drew lavish praise. The picture of the Huguenot refusing to wear the armband that would save him was hailed almost unanimously as the gem of the exhibition, wrote the *British Quarterly*, and 'the special feature of the picture is the face of the lady [plate 7d]. It is a poem in itself . . .'[45] *Fraser's* devoted more column inches to the 'condensed pathos' conveyed by the faces of this painting than to its colouring or fidelity to natural detail; it also appreciated the pathos in the face of Ophelia (plate

7c), and its 'curious kind of gay, yet melancholy beauty'.[46] Gautier wrote of 'sa bouche entr'ouverte par un sourire extatique',[47] and Tom Taylor, hitherto hostile to the Pre-Raphaelites, confessed himself converted by these two pictures, and seemingly by their faces above all. He was haunted by that of the drowning Ophelia, he said, until he was blinded with tears; of 'The Huguenot', 'what I first see, in spite of myself, is the subtle human expression of those two faces'. When looking at Millais's two pictures 'I commune with the painter's thoughts'.[48]

To commune with the painter's thoughts on the basis of his figures' expressions was above all a speciality of Ruskin's — and yet he did not approach the Pre-Raphaelites in this way. Was he perhaps insensitive to emotional tone at this time? His *Academy Notes* show that, on the contrary, he was well aware of the difference between poetic and banal sentiment. For example we might well agree with Ruskin that around 1856—7 Millais's art took a dramatic turn for the worse, and that this lay basically in 'a warping of feeling' rather than in any errors of draughtmanship. And Ruskin was less enthusiastic than many over Sir Edwin Landseer's animal paintings: while they applauded the noble sentiments of 'Saved', in which a dog has rescued a child from drowning, he merely observed that the child's clothes should have been made to look wet. Of Augustus Egg's moral tale, 'Come, Rest in this Bosom', his comment was that 'the subject of prison sentiment is both painful, useless, and hacknied [sic ]'; and while he briefly commended the 'delicacy' of Arthur Hughes, he was not impressed by the agonies of W. L. Windus's 'Too Late', nor by the crudeness of Maclise, whose 'Orlando' should have shown 'calmness and steady melancholy' instead of a 'sentimental grimace'.[49]

Ruskin was also conscious that clear, meticulous details could intensify the mood of a painting — an effect which has become more evident as a result the Surrealist movemnt of the twentieth century. He pointed this out in referring to Hunt's 'The Awakening Conscience'.

Nothing is more notable than the way in which even the most trivial objects force themselves upon the attention of a mind which has been fevered by violent and distressful excitement. They thrust themselves forward with a ghastly and unendurable distinctness . . .'[50]

He repeated this observation soon afterwards in relation to architecture, and in 1865 Ford Madox Brown introduced 'The Last of England' in similar terms, writing that he had reproduced minute details to increase the pathos of the subject.[51] It follows from this principle that not all subjects are equally well served by Pre-Raphaelite detail, as Ruskin was well aware, for the champion of Turner and Tintoretto was hardly likely to object to Millais's freeer, more painterly manner in itself. He was prepared to say of Millais's 'The Rescue', a post-P.R.B. and rather sentimental picture, that there was 'a true sympathy between the impetuousness of execution and the haste of the action'.[52]

So Ruskin was not one to miss the 'feeling' of a picture, but in the case of the Pre-Raphaelites he commented on it only occasionally and incidentally. One such occasion was the appearance of John Brett's 'Val d'Aosta' in the Academy exhibition of 1859, a painting which he admired as a 'historical landscape'. Yet 'it has a strange fault, considering the school to which it belongs, – it seems to me wholly emotionless'. The way in which Ruskin continues his argument offers a clue to his general reticence on the subject of Pre-Raphaelite emotion. 'Not but that I believe the painter to be capable of the highest emotion: anyone who can paint thus must have passion within him; but the passion here is assuredly not out of him.'[53] The point is that Ruskin still believed that art expressive of noble emotional qualities must have sprung from an appropriately equipped soul; and he knew the souls of the principal Pre-Raphaelites too well. He could just persuade himself, against most of the evidence, that Turner's pictures were a manifestation of his all-embracing heart, but he could not in the end deceive himself over the prickly Ford Madox Brown, or Millais who had married his ex-wife, or Rossetti the sensualist.

Millais had been Ruskin's greatest hope, and it was Millais whom he first took under his wing. But by the time Millais had painted 'Sir Isumbras at the Ford', Ruskin might have felt (if his taste in metaphors had been less refined) that he had hatched a cuckoo. On the other hand the dedicated Holman Hunt, who had been deeply impressed by *Modern Painters*, might have qualified for the noble role in which Ruskin perhaps wished to cast him, and indeed he declared that Hunt's 'The Light of the World' was 'the most perfect instance of expressional purpose with technical power, which the world has yet produced'. But the *combination* of these two was important to Ruskin, and Hunt could not always supply it. His 'Scapegoat' was heavy with symbolism, but despite its devout intentions, Ruskin had to condemn the picture as an artistic failure. For 'while the expression is always to be the first thing considered, all other merits must be added to the utmost of the painter's power'.[54]

To a much greater degree than Holman Hunt, the German Nazarene painters and their followers had a reputation for portraying pious facial expression. But again Ruskin, who was prejudiced against contemporary German culture in general, could not accept that these artists were sincere, and so he condemned them on two charges. One was a criticism similar to that of Hunt – that they concentrated on the expression of the human countenance, and did not pay enough attention to 'technical excellence'; but secondly, since on Ruskin's principles the faces in their pictures should still indicate devotion and nobility of mind on the part of the painters, he accused them of affectation: 'the [modern German] artist desires that men should think he has an elevated soul . . . He lives in an element of what he calls tender emotions and lofty aspirations; which are, in fact, nothing more than very ordinary weaknesses or instincts, contemplated through a mist of pride.'[55]

Marcel Proust believed that beause Ruskin wanted to present art as a statement of truth, rather than as something of beauty, he was forced to lie to himself about his own reasons for his likes and dislikes.[56] No doubt this applies to Ruskin's reluctance to comment on the expressive qualities of the Pre-Raphaelites, although in theory he placed them in 'the Great Expressional school'. One of his enemies had made a similar observation on Ruskin's criticism at the time: Elizabeth Eastlake, reviewing *Modern Painters*, declined to criticise the Pre-Raphaelites, 'their merits being, in our judgement, great, and their faults sufficiently censured by Mr Ruskin's praise'.[57] If she meant that Ruskin underrated their lyrical qualities, her point seems a sound one. In the following year, Ruskin even told the Society of Arts that 'the prosaic Pre-Raphaelites' 'were more noteworthy than the poetical Pre-Raphaelites', on the unconvincing grounds that in a scientific age there was more scope for improvement in truth than in imagination.[58]

The third of the leading Pre-Raphaelite trio, Dante Gabriel Rossetti, might seem at first to have been the least likely to fulfil

Ruskin's aspirations. Their ten-year association, which began in 1854 when Rossetti was in his mid-twenties, was in many ways the most improbable and intriguing relationship of Ruskin's life. As characters, the Bohemian Rossetti and the punctilious, over-correct Ruskin could scarcely have been more different, and yet each derived from the other a particular kind of benefit.

Ruskin's family, as we have seen, was solidly middle-class. His father had worked for nine years without a holiday (Ruskin recorded) to pay off the debts incurred when his own father's grocery had failed. He was prudent, respectable, socially ambitious and (aided by a post-Napoleonic boom in sherry sales) wealthy. In contrast, Rossetti's father Gabriele had been a leading member of the Carbonari, an underground group who had agitated for a liberal constitution in the Kingdom of Naples. They were successful, for a brief period, and crowds in the streets had sung an 'Ode to the Dawn of Constitution-Day' which Gabriele had composed. When King Ferdinand abolished the new constitution Gabriele was condemned to death, but being on good terms with the wife of a visiting British admiral, escaped on a British ship.

Rossetti's maternal uncle, John William Polidori, displayed literary talents of another kind in his Gothic tale *The Vampyre*. While the Ruskin parents were reading Byron's works in their suburban drawing-room, Polidori was travelling on the Continent as Byron's personal physician, until, faced with a gambling debt, he killed himself with an enormous dose of poison. One is reminded of Rossetti's own attempted suicide by laudanum half a century later, and of Rossetti's boast to Hall Caine: 'I judge I've taken more chloral than any man whatever.'[59]

So Rossetti was brought up in a house full of expatriate Italian radicals, writers and musicians, in a very different atmosphere from that which hung over the Ruskin home. In both households literature was encouraged, Walter Scott and Shakespeare being favourite authors; but whereas the Ruskins laid heavy emphasis on Bible-learning and evangelical doctrine, with 'Byron at the dessert' as a concession, the young Rossetti devoured novels, plays and poetry in three languages. ('It may be feared there was no solid reading', wrote his brother William.) In 1846, when Ruskin was an orthodox and promising young man with two volumes of *Modern Painters* in print, Rossetti entered the Royal Academy Schools, 'rolling carelessly as he slouched along, pouting with parted lips, staring with dreaming eyes', as Holman Hunt recalled.[60] To another fellow-student Rossetti's pale, hollow cheeks already indicated 'the waste of life and midnight oil to which the youth was addicted'.[61] After two years, dissatisfied with his progress, he went to study under Ford Madox Brown; later that year he met Holman Hunt and Millais, and the Pre-Raphaelite Brotherhood was formed.

Ruskin did not at first notice Rossetti's paintings, and his famous defences of Pre-Raphaelitism in 1851 made no mention of him. Then in 1853 Ruskin praised Rossetti's work in a letter to MacCracken, one of the painter's early patrons, and early in the following year MacCracken sent Ruskin a Rossetti watercolour, 'Dante Drawing an Angel on the First Anniversary of the Death of Beatrice', for his opinion. Ruskin wrote immediately to Rossetti praising his 'thoroughly glorious work', and a few days later called to see him at 14 Chatham Place.

It must have been a novel experience for Ruskin to meet that sophisticated cosmopolitan figure at his unkempt house overlooking the Blackfriars mud, although Rossetti had not yet entered the dimly-lit opulence of Cheyne Walk, nor indulged in the mistresses and marsupials that enlivened his later life. Ruskin was nevertheless anxious to buy Rossetti's work, and Rossetti was flattered but surprised by the influential critic's attention. He wrote to Ford Madox Brown:

> His manner was more agreeable than I had expected, but in person he is an absolute Guy — worse than Patmore. He seems in a mood to make my fortune.[62]

William Rossetti, in his memoir of his brother, unfortunately chose to omit the central clause above ('in person . . .'), thus giving a misleading impression to a generation of biographers who quoted that passage from the memoir. Still, there has never been any doubt that Rossetti sometimes found his patron irritating and absurd. Ruskin was a frequent visitor to Chatham Place, and his letters are full of half-teasing criticism of Rossetti's painting, his writing and even his living habits.

> If you wanted to oblige *me*, you would keep your room in order and go to bed at night . . . Take all the pure green out of the flesh of the Nativity I sent and try to make it a little less like

worsted-work by Wednesday . . . You are a conceited mon-
key, thinking your pictures right when I tell you positively they
are wrong. What do you know about the matter, I should like to
know. [63]

William Rossetti considered, later, that all this was simply
evidence of Ruskin's pleasant *badinage*, his 'exquisite amiability',
but I doubt if Dante himself took it that way, and his letters to
Thomas Woolner and Ford Madox Brown contain some sardonic
references to 'The Great Prohibited', as he called Ruskin. Woolner
and Brown themselves disliked Ruskin, particularly Brown,
whose work Ruskin had consistently ignored. Their first meeting
was a disaster, moreover. Brown's record of the event in his diary is
a masterpiece of self-congratulation.

. . ."enter to us" Ruskin. I smoke, he talks divers nonsense about
art hurriedly in shrill flippant tones. I answer him civilly, then
resume my coat and prepare to leave. Suddenly upon this he
says, "Mr. Brown, will you tell me why you chose such a very
ugly subject for your last picture ['An English Autumn
Afternoon']?" . . . I, being satisfied that he intended imperti-
ence, replied contempuously, "Because it lay out of a back
window", and, turning on my heel, took my hat and wished
Gabriel good-bye. [64]

One cannot blame Brown, who was not renowned for his sense
of humour. But the interesting aspect of the affair is how little
Rossetti shared his friend's hostility to Ruskin. Of course, Ruskin
was a great provider of the 'tin' so necessary to Rossetti, who
seemed always to be on the point of a visit to the pawnbroker, and
he could give valuable publicity to the artist's work. Yet Rossetti
was an extremely independent figure, who repeatedly failed to
fulfil his commissions; he was quite capable of dismissing Ruskin,
or at least of dealing with him on a more formal basis. Rossetti's
was the more mature, the stronger character, and he surely saw
that Ruskin's teasing and niggling represented a desperate desire
for friendship. Ruskin had friends enough in his later life, when he
appeared as a lovable, eccentric sage. But in the very month (April
1854) in which he met Rossetti, his wife left him. He had his
supporters, but as he wrote to Rossetti in 1855, 'I have no
friendships, and no loves'. [65]

Rossetti on the other hand, while not especially demonstrative, always attracted friends; there was always a 'Rossetti circle', although its members changed. The P.R.B. too was a close personal association – 'we were really like brothers, constantly together', wrote William Rossetti, the non-professional secretary of the group. And Rossetti had the great gift of not taking himself too seriously; he lacked the protective wall of dignity and self-esteem which cut off so many of his contemporaries (such as Brown and Ruskin) from one another. He did more than play up to Ruskin; in tolerating Ruskin's patronising banter, he responded to his emotional needs and offered an element of genuine human contact which Ruskin was rarely able to experience. Despite Ruskin's material generosity to Rossetti, I believe he received from the painter more than he gave.[66]

Even those who had no great respect for Ruskin's artistic opinions paid tribute to his eloquence. One such was Arthur Munby, the admirer of working women and author of fascinating diaries; another was Rossetti. 'Such flaming diction, such emphasis, such appeal', commented Rossetti[67] on an impromptu speech of Ruskin's at the newly-founded Working Men's College, at which Ruskin, Rossetti and Munby were all lecturers. Ruskin taught his students to represent rocks and leaves in minute, hard-edged detail, while Rossetti (whom Ruskin had persuaded to offer his services) taught figure drawing by means of bold exercises in colour and shade, paying little attention to outline. Rossetti's classes are said to have been unorthodox, but often inspiring, as one can well imagine – with his magnetic personality, demonstrations of rich colour-schemes, and down-to-earth approach: 'Get rid of that academic fribble! Paint only what you see!'[68]

The subject of Rossetti's greatest pictures at this time, the Beatrice to his Dante, was the long-suffering Lizzie Siddal, who had modelled for Millais's 'Ophelia' and several other early Pre-Raphaelite works before Rossetti monopolised her. She also painted a little herself, encouraged by Rossetti, and Ruskin offered her a regular income in return for her drawings. It is doubtful whether Ruskin really thought she had genius, as he said, any more than Rossetti respected Ruskin's art criticism; but Ruskin must have seen in Rossetti's relationship with Lizzie Siddal something of what he and Effie had lacked. One may even detect in Ruskin's drawings of Rose La Touche – the most enduring love of his life, whom he first met in 1858 – a hint of the manner of Rossetti's portraits of his own ill-fated love.

Rossetti married Lizzie in May 1860, and thereafter Ruskin and Rossetti grew increasingly further apart. Lizzie, always in bad health, had a baby stillborn the following year, and died tragically in 1862 after an overdose of laudanum. Rossetti moved to Cheyne Walk, Chelsea, and began to install his salamanders, peacocks and kangaroos: Ruskin proposed renting a room there, but it would hardly have been a successful arrangement. He continued to pay tribute to some of Rossetti's paintings, notably 'Beata Beatrix', his softly radiant monument to Lizzie's memory. However, Rossetti had started to paint in a heavier and more sensuous manner, with Fanny Cornforth and Alexa Wilding his principal models, a style which was to reach its climax under the languorous spell of Jane Morris. Ruskin recognised the power of these paintings, but could not approve. In 1868 he called on Rossetti and suggested in vain that they co-operate in one of the social ventures to which Ruskin was now committed. The two men seldom met again.

So by 1860 Ruskin could hold no more illusions about the personalities of the Pre-Raphaelite trio. It is significant that when Ruskin now came, at last, briefly to infer the Pre-Raphaelites' character from their art, his analysis was hostile. In August 1851, when he had scarcely known them as individuals, he had mentioned their 'strength of character' and their 'earnestness', but in the final volume of *Modern Painters* of 1860 he knew them very much better, and regarded their partiality for small, sharp forms in a different light:

> . . . Which modes of choice proceed naturally from a petulant sympathy with local and immediately visible interests or sorrows, not regarding their large consequences, nor capable of understanding more massive view or more deeply deliberate mercifulness; – but peevish and horror-struck, and often incapable of self-control, though not of self-sacrifice.[69]

By this time, however, changes had become evident in Ruskin's overall approach. In the third volume of *Modern Painters*, which appeared in 1856, he was still describing paintings and literature in terms of the presumed moral traits of their authors, but the individuals he examined were now treated as representatives of a whole age. Homer stood for 'the Greek mind', and Scott and

Turner for 'the modern mind'. Ruskin was in effect following the policy which he had used successfully in his previous major work, *The Stones of Venice*, in which the development of Venetian architectural styles was made to correspond to a development in the corporate mind and soul of Venice. In subsequent writings Ruskin was generally more concerned to discover in paintings indications of large-scale social trends than to draw conclusions about the personality of individuals. Turner remained an exception: Ruskin continued to see all sorts of moral traits revealed in his hero's work, and sometimes simply lauded Turner's character with anecdotes and reminiscences. The materials for his unfinished book *Dilecta* included a phrenologist's report made from a cast of Turner's head after his death, and among a suitable list of virtues are some unexpected items, such as: 'having large veneration, he must be an earnest worker in a religious cause'.[70]

From this time onwards the idea that art manifests its creator's character together with the status of facial expression in art began to lose favour both in Ruskin's own mind and in other artistic circles. Critics like Charles Leslie and Elizabeth Eastlake, who were not given to rhapsodies over soulful eyes or twitches of the mouth, were equally reluctant to interpret a work of art as if it laid bare the character of its creator. Artists dead and alive were expected to be more detached from their work than Ruskin would have believed possible. Lady Eastlake's opinion of Raphael as an artist waxed higher and higher, she wrote to Layard in 1882, but she had doubts about the painter's personality: 'the *man* was doubtless very nice, but he does not come up to a high standard, and I hate the courtier-like characters of the time.'[71]

In the 1890s the reaction against Ruskin's approach reached a peak. But it is interesting to note that Oscar Wilde, a symbol of the period in many ways, nevertheless did not follow the pattern of reaction in *The Picture of Dorian Gray*. In this novel an immaculate portrait is painted of the young, beautiful and innocent Dorian Gray; then as Dorian sinks gradually into unspeakable depravity, his own face remains as flawless as ever, but the features of the portrait grow more and more hideously contorted. If only Wilde had decided that the picture of Dorian Gray should be a self-portrait, the book might have been considered a perfect example of Ruskin's principle that art mirrors the creator. Even as it stands, the novel's theme runs counter to the dominant aesthetic of the

1890s, as Robert Hichens observed in his sympathetic satire of *fin-de-siècle* attitudes, *The Green Carnation*. A wearer of that emblem of decadence is made to declare the very antithesis of Ruskin's beliefs:

> It is quite a mistake to believe, as many people do, that the mind shows itself in the face . . . Our faces are really masks given to us to conceal our minds with . . . No more preposterous theory has ever been put forward than that of the artist revealing himself in his art . . . Oscar Wilde was utterly mistaken when he wrote The Picture of Dorian Gray. After Dorian's act of cruelty, the picture ought to have grown more sweet, more saintly, more angelic in expression.[72]

# 9  The Scourge of Society

> While all the world stands tremulous, shilly-shallying from
> the gutter, impetuous Ruskin plunges his rapier up to the very
> hilt in the abominable belly of vast blockheadism, and leaves it
> staring very considerably.
>
> J. A. Froude, *Carlyle's Life
> in London*, 1884

In the later 1850s Ruskin's life and attitudes changed profoundly.
He completed *Modern Painters* and undertook no more major
artistic works, turning instead to social and economic criticism; he
was 'unconverted' from the last vestiges of his evangelical faith; he
fell in love with the 11-year old Rose La Touche, and found his
happiest moments of relaxation in the company of little girls.
Ruskin's last forty years are rich in biographical detail, and offer a
fascinating display of the disintegration of a brillant mind,[1] but to
the student of ideas they are largely disappointing. While his earlier
books were read by a rapidly increasing number of people, he lost
touch with the movement of ideas in art and art criticism, and
remained an elevated but static figure. His most popular book of
all, *Sesame and Lilies* (1865), did not so much challenge the values
of the time as enshrine them, and as Ruskin himself had once
recognised, he was at his best only when struggling against the
stream.

This change of direction is symbolised by his 'unconversion',
which he had been approaching for some years. The culmination
occurred in 1858, at Turin. In the local chapel he heard the
preacher, 'a squeaky little idiot', tell his small congregation that
'they were the only children of God in Turin': how feeble was this
small-minded Protestantism, Ruskin thought, compared with
Veronese's magnificent 'Solomon and the Queen of Sheba' in the
city art gallery, which he saw glowing in the warm afternoon

light, while a military band played in the courtyard outside.[2]

Now Veronese was, *par excellence*, a gorgeous, sensual painter, far removed from Fra Angelico and the early Italians whom Ruskin had so admired ten years before. So when Ruskin finally rejected the religion of his parents ('I came out of that chapel . . . a conclusively *un*-converted man'), he simultaneously made a drastic revision of his artistic priorities. The fifth and last volume of *Modern Painters*, published two years later, made this clear to all. So-called Christian art, the art revered by Rio, was at fault 'in its denial of the animal nature of man';[3] it was therefore swept away, wrote Ruskin, by the strong truth of Titian, Giorgione and Veronese, who painted the female body as fearlessly and majestically as they painted religious subjects. 'A good, stout, self-commanding, magnificent Animality is the make for poets and artists, it seems to me.'[4]

Another curious event may have contributed to Ruskin's worldly mood. While sorting through the thousands of drawings Turner had left, he had come across a parcel of erotic sketches. In December 1858 he and the Keeper of the National Gallery had them burnt on the grounds that 'the authorities have not thought proper to register the reserved parcel of Turner's sketchbooks, and have given no directions about them', and that 'the grossly obscene drawings contained in them could not be lawfully in anyone's possession', as he wrote later.[5] But in 1860 Turner's name appeared in Ruskin's list of great and 'boldly Animal' artists; possibly that bundle of sketches had helped to open the critic's mind to the more evident sensual delights of art.

This upheaval in Ruskin's artistic priorities was one strong reason, I think, for his turning to other subjects. Many of the assumptions underlying the earlier volumes of *Modern Painters* were shaken; the crusading fervour with which he had praised Fra Angelico's pure emotion could not so easily be used to promote 'strong and frank animality' in art. In any case, Ruskin's new list of heroes consisted of artists whom less adventurous souls had appreciated all along – Homer, Shakespeare, Titian, Michelangelo. Ruskin's principles of art were not the gospel they had once been.

His lectures of 1859 (reprinted as *The Two Paths*) show his disillusion clearly. Why was it that the virtuous Scots despised art, while the mutinous Indians loved it? Art always seemed to be

associated with sensuality, idolatry and cruelty, he claimed – his
habit of overstatement had not deserted him. His broadened
sympathies are evident, too, in the unaccustomed words of praise
for ancient Greek art and for architects in the Renaissance tradition
(although not for Joseph Paxton or his Crystal Palace), and both
Velazquez and Sir Joshua Reynolds are strongly commended.
'Observe, I do not say in the least that in order to be a good painter
you must be a good man', declared Ruskin, who in the past had
said just that; 'but I do say that in order to be a good natural painter
there must be strong elements of good in the mind, however
warped by other parts of the character.'[6]

Completing *Modern Painters* was now an effort to him, and he
wrote despairingly to Elizabeth Barrett Browning of

> . . . discovered uselessness, having come to see the great fact
> that great Art is of no real use to anybody but the next great
> Artist; that it is wholly invisible to people in general – for the
> present – and that to get anybody to see it, one must begin at the
> other end, with moral education of the people . . .[7]

And so in one sense, Ruskin became a social critic in reaction to
his lost faith in art. He had lost confidence in his old message, and
needed to break fresh ground. His teaching at the Working Men's
College must have helped to open his eyes to reality. As an
instructor at the College, he reported to a Select Committee on
Public Institutions that to keep art galleries available to the public
in the evenings would be of minimal benefit to working people as
long as their awareness was deadened by the conditions of their
daily work.

But viewed in a larger context, Ruskin's social criticism
followed naturally from what (I have argued) was from the start
one of his leading preoccupations with any building or painting –
what sort of person, or society, could have produced it? We have
seen him taking this question gradually more seriously, and (as his
interest in architecture grew) allowing the social interpretation to
dominate the personal. *Seven Lamps* had mentioned stonework
fashioned through 'heartless pains', without visible creativity or
enjoyment; in *The Stones of Venice* he turned this theme into an
attack on 'the modern English mind', with its inhuman craving for
perfection. Modern English accurate work signified slavery and
degradation into a machine, which was the root cause of the

workers' 'universal outcry against wealth, and against nobility'.

> It is not that men are ill fed, but that they have no pleasure in the
> work by which they make their bread, and therefore look to
> wealth as the only means of pleasure. It is not that men are
> pained by the scorn of the upper classes, but they cannot endure
> their own; for they feel that the kind of labour to which they are
> condemned is verily a degrading one, and makes them less than
> men. Never had the upper classes so much sympathy with the
> lower, or charity for them, as they have at this day, and yet
> never were they so much hated by them . . .[8]

Ruskin wrote this in Venice, but he was taking a close interest in
English affairs, as reported in the cuttings sent by his father. 'These
news from England are really too ridiculous', he wrote to John
James on 6 March 1852, referring presumably to the Tory threat,
led by Disraeli in the Commons, to abolish free trade and to
reinstate some form of protection. 'I can stand it no longer. I am
going for three days to give the usual time I set aside for your letter
to writing one to *The Times* – on Corn Laws, Election, and
Education.'[9]

The letters were written, and sent to John James, who was
offended – not simply by his son's dismissive reference to the
Chancellor of the Exchequer as 'a witty novelist', but by their clear
antagonism to his own staunch Tory principles. Instead of import
duties Ruskin proposed that heavy taxes be placed on luxury
goods, declaring that the luxury of the rich caused the downfall of
kingdoms. Cigars[10] and excessive jewellery were examples of
taxable luxuries; whether he would have added sherry is debatable.
There should also be a permanent system of graduated income tax,
and a tax on property over £10,000.

The second letter, on 'Election', rather ambiguously advocated
universal male suffrage, but a suffrage weighted so that (as Ruskin
put it in a reassuring letter to his father) 'one man of parts and rank
would outweigh in voting a whole shoal of the mob'.[11] The third
letter, on education, was embodied in an appendix to the last
volume of *The Stones of Venice*, which disparaged 'erudition' and
called for an education designed to fit each person for his work in
life. But the housing, clothing, feeding and educating of all
children should be the responsibility of the state.

When John James decided not to pass these letters on to *The*

*Times*, Ruskin did not make any strong protest; he was not yet completely sure of his best point of attack. His onslaught was delayed until 1857, when he gave two lectures in Manchester on 'The Political Economy of Art' (later republished as *A Joy for Ever*) – the most lucid and forceful lectures he ever gave. He did not, of course, keep to the subject of art. He opened with an uncompromising attack on the philosophy of *laissez-faire*. The 'let alone' principle was the principle of death, certain to bring ruin and degradation; instead, Ruskin believed in the strong authority of a paternal government, a government which *should* interfere in the lives of its citizens. Government should 'direct us in our occupations, protect us against our follies, and visit us in our distresses'. Ruskin had no time for the Liberty which John Stuart Mill was to defend eloquently two years later. He moved on to attack the mass-production of worthless objects, and in passing poured scorn on the extravagance of a London season, with its ball-dresses soon discarded – blankets should have priority of manufacture over jewels and lace. In the second lecture, recommending the principle of co-operation as superior to that of competition, he suggested that trade guilds might be re-established, to enhance the craftsman's status and to replace the system of private patents with open communication of ideas.

The climax of this train of thought, and in some ways the climax of his life's work, was reached in the four short pieces which he wrote for the new *Cornhill Magazine* in 1860. John James was reluctant to let them slip into print, and sure enough, once printed they were badly received. Ruskin had previously been sensitive to hostile criticism, but on this occasion he was prepared for abuse and almost welcomed it. Two years later, when the essays were published in book from as *Unto This Last* (first in a series of dreadful allusive titles), Ruskin was sure that they were the truest and most useful things he had ever written. Only Carlyle shared his opinion, but Carlyle's was one of the few opinions about which Ruskin now cared – Carlyle the isolated, bombastic prophet, exposer of 'shams' and author of the most scathing of all attacks on the Victorian *status quo*. Ruskin made no secret of his great debt to his 'master' Carlyle, 'whom I read so constantly, that, without wilfully setting myself to imitate him, I find myself perpetually falling into his modes of expression'.[12] (Fortunately Ruskin's prose was never quite as tortured as Carlyle's.) *Unto This Last* was

Ruskin's tribute to Carlyle, his attempt to do in his own way what Carlyle had done in *Past and Present*.

Ruskin's theme was the error of traditional 'political economy' in regarding human beings simply as 'covetous machines', instead of recognising that working people could be motivated by 'social affection', in the form either of respect for their employer or of *esprit de corps* among themselves. To create the conditions in which these emotions might be brought into play, Ruskin proposed that workers be paid a guaranteed, steady wage irrespective of fluctuations in demand for their products. The effect, Ruskin predicted, would be to prevent workers from alternating between three days of violent labour and three days of drunkenness.

The unwelcome inference to be drawn was that employers were at least as much to blame for the state of their employees as were the employees themselves. Ruskin wrote of employers 'raging to be rich', and 'the masters cannot bear to let any opportunity of grain escape them'.[13] The second essay went further, suggesting that the very possession of 'riches' entailed the relative poverty of others:

> The force of the guinea you have in your pocket depends wholly on the default of a guinea in your neighbour's pocket. If he did not want it, it would be of no use to you; the degree of power it possesses depends accurately upon the need or desire he has for it, — and the art of making yourself rich, in the ordinary mercantile economist's sense, is therefore equally and necessarily the art of keeping your neighbour poor.[14]

And yet Ruskin did not come to the point of proposing a redistribution of wealth: he was opposed to inequalities of wealth which had been 'unjustly established'—

> But inequalities of wealth justly established, benefit the nation in the course of their establishment; and, nobly used, benefit it still more by their existence.[15]

Again and again Ruskin writes paragraphs that attack the very roots of capitalism (to use Ruskin's term) — passages which, no doubt, account for the well-attested influence of the book on Tolstoy, Gandhi and the British Labour movement. But then he draws back from the conclusion that seems inescapable. In a footnote near the end of the last essay Ruskin denies that he favours a redistribution of wealth; not one whit. The rich should keep their riches, but use them to better purpose. The final message of the essays is not that the system should be changed, but that happiness and nobility are more valuable than 'riches' as generally understood; and that men should pursue simpler pleasures and despise luxury.

Nevertheless, the *Cornhill* essays outraged many of their readers, so much so that Thackeray, the editor of the magazine, had to bring the series to a premature close. Some made the legitimate criticism that Ruskin had misrepresented the theorists he attacked, Ricardo and especially Mill; but the more abusive critics ('hysterics . . . imbecility . . . blubbering . . . snivels') had been touched on a very sensitive spot. It was a gross calumny on the nation, claimed the *Saturday Review*, to suggest that the rich were responsible for the state of the poor. This violent response illustrates the insecurity which, in the middle of the mid-Victorian economic boom, lay not far from the surface. Even at the peak of prosperity and confidence the evidence of working-class misery was plain to see, and sudden collapses meant bankruptcy for a few and unemployment for many – 11.9 per cent of the working population in 1858.[16] The ranks of the middle-classes (from tradesmen to 'professional' men) were swelling and prospering, while for working men and women standards of living improved little if at all. The only 'boom' for the working-class was the great increase in numbers of domestic servants.

Child labour was still ruthlessly exploited, and although in the year of Ruskin's *Cornhill* articles the minimum age for underground coal-mining was raised, it was raised only from 10 to 12. Female labour was seen as especially good value, and by 1860 the textile factories employed more women than men; the working week had by this time been shortened to a mere 60 hours. There was poor relief, and a good deal of charitable activity on the part of the better off, but the oft-preached ideal of self-reliance could only be achieved by means of the steady and adequate income which *Unto This Last* proposed.

But *Unto This Last* was not in the final analysis written from humanitarian motives. Ruskin was not fully aware of the appalling conditions which persisted in the manufacturing towns where he lectured. There are occasions when it is hard not to suspect that his hatred of mass industrialisation was, at bottom, aesthetic. (Nearly the whole of the north was a coal-pit, he complained in 1859, and the south could well become a brickfield.) A man more concerned with practicalities would not have contrasted the polluted streams of Rochdale with anything so remote as medieval Pisa with its 'troops of knights'.[17] William Morris's vision of utopia by the Thames is much more compelling. Ruskin's ideal was working man fulfilled in his work, docile and respectful to his employer. He did not believe in the power, or potential power, of working people as a class; like Dickens in *Hard Times*, and George Eliot in *Felix Holt the Radical*, Ruskin exhibited a fear and distrust of the working-class *en masse*, whether organised or disorganised. Indeed his ideal of the relationship between classes runs parallel to his ideal of the relationship between the sexes. Both the workman and the woman must always be conscious that thinking is not their sphere. 'The first character of the good and wise man at his work [is] to know that he knows very little; — to perceive that there are many above him wiser than he.'[18] The workman should be like a trusting child, faithful, cheerful and humble.

Ruskin's politics cannot be summed up in a single phrase, but Bernard Shaw's description of him as a 'Tory Communist' comes close. Ruskin called himself 'a violent Tory of the old school'[19] and within the same year 'a Communist of the old school — reddest even of the red'[20] (by contrast to the 'new' school of destructive Paris *communards*); but the two descriptions are not as contradictory as they might at first seem. Ruskin had no time for liberalism or democracy, and insofar as 'socialism' meant a desire for equality of income or property, he had no time for that either. He visualised society as a organism consisting of interdependent parts, in which various ranks fulfilled their complementary but separate functions. He shared with many other critics of Victorian society a deep sense of the need for strong authority; on the other hand he believed in communal, non-competitive work — but within the existing strata of society, not across them. Indeed the effect of Ruskin's proposals would be to reinforce class distinctions; he suggested that maximum limits should be assigned to incomes *according to classes*, and even that each rank should adopt and adhere to its own distinctive form of dress. It is not surprising that in 1919 an audience laughed when Shaw spoke of Ruskin as a prophet of Bolshevism. And yet the parallel between Ruskin and

Lenin was not so far-fetched: 'The Russian masses elected a National Assembly: Lenin and the Bolshevists ruthlessly shoved it out of the way';[21] Ruskin, too, wanted powerful government on behalf of the people, but certainly not by the people.

*   *   *

Ruskin's intrusion into the arena of political economy coincided with his entry into another kind of *milieu* entirely. In March 1859 he first visited Margaret Bell's school for girls at Winnington Hall, Cheshire, where immediately (Ruskin reported) he fell in love with 35 young ladies at once. Winnington Hall was an unusual and pleasant school, influenced by the 'broad church' vision of men like Coleridge, F. D. Maurice and Frederick Robertson of Brighton, who rejected the 'narrow' doctrine of predestination and literal interpretations of the Old Testament; instead they emphasised 'the cultivation of reverent feeling' in all activities of life. In accordance with these principles, the girls of Winnington Hall spent a good deal of time playing cricket, painting and dancing, led often by the sprightly figures of John Ruskin or Edward Burne-Jones. True education, declared Ruskin at this time, should 'make people not merely *do* the right things, but *enjoy* the right things'.[22]

J. A. Froude, himself once an anguished doubter, was another whose clear, tolerant interpretation of Christianity impressed Ruskin, and it was Froude who invited Ruskin to contribute a further series of articles to *Fraser's Magazine*, of which he was editor. Carlyle, Ruskin and Froude seem to have regarded themselves as a trio of like minds at this time; in 1866 it was even proposed that the three of them co-edit a new periodical, which would surely have been interesting. Ruskin had for some while been moving towards 'broad church' attitudes, and his new contacts accelerated the process. Until recently a fierce anti-Catholic, Ruskin now became almost as savagely hostile to sectarian distinctions. '. . . false, formal Christianity is, I believe of all religions ever invented on this earth, the most abominable – foolish – and in the literal sense of the word – "diabolical" – betraying'.[23] He preached 'deeds not creeds', the spirit rather than the letter. But his disillusion went deeper still. In these middle years of his life Ruskin often referred to himself as a pagan or a heathen, and above all others his confidante was Margaret Bell; only to her could he confess his sense of darkness and desolation at the thought that God took no more interest in him personally than in a midge or a leech.

His relationship with Rose La Touche complicated matters further. Ruskin had first met Rose in the autumn of 1858 when she was aged 9; at her mother's request he had begun to give her drawing lessons. By 1861, when he stayed with the La Touche family in Ireland, she was devoted to him and he was firmly in love with her — not the love he happily professed for the 35 girls at Winnington, but an ever-present, agonising longing for her company. Inevitably the attachment ran into difficulties. Both John James and Mrs La Touche expressed their disapproval, and Rose became ill, her illness compounded with religious fervour. When Ruskin admitted that he had lost his childhood faith, another barrier came between himself and Rose, who remained a strict Calvinist. 'How could I love you if you were a pagan?'[24] she asked him, and she meant it. Ruskin in his turn made a number of public comments (including an entire lecture) plainly intended for Rose, and issued in particular a warning that theology was the one study which was fatally dangerous for women.

He was well aware that in his current state of mind much of what he taught the girls at Winnington was thoroughly hypocritical. Sometimes he refused to talk on the subject of religion, for fear that his views might be damaging to his young audience, but often he simply taught what he did not believe. He explained to Miss Bell 'the necessity and virtue of Hypocrisy in her circumstances, and that it is quite proper to say she believes what she doesn't. I think I've pretty well lectured her out of any foolish honesty'.[25] Ruskin wrote this at a time when 'hypocrisy' in religious questions was widespread and in many cases a condition of employment: Anglican clergymen and university lecturers had to choose between doctrinal orthodoxy and losing their job. Ruskin had no office to forfeit, but he was very conscious of his reputation and his influence, so that his hypocrisy was no trivial matter for him. And yet, reading his correspondence with Margaret Bell, one cannot help feeling that he derived a certain perverse satisfaction from the situation. Through all his despondency a sense of pride can be detected, as if he had joined a secret brotherhood whose mission was nobly to suppress the truth in the interests of society. In his self-indulgent defiance, and his resentment against his father, there is a trace of long-delayed teenage revolt against parental strictness, from which, however, he could never quite shake loose.

He welcomed as a kindred spirit the controversial J.W. Colenso, first Bishop of Natal, who had a daughter at school at Winnington Hall; Colenso's liberal interpretations of Old and New Testaments were predictably denounced by their reviewers for the orgy of heresies they contained. 'But I am so much worse than the Bishop',[26] wrote Ruskin conspiratorially to Margaret Bell.

His parents were desperately concerned at this latest turn in their son's mind, and blamed his association with Carlyle, Froude and Colenso. But in March 1864, at the height of his 'paganism', John James died. Although Ruskin regretted the deep differences that had existed between them, he now felt able to follow his own inclinations more freely, the more so because John James had left him £120,000 in cash, with property and pictures besides. Ruskin embarked on a number of rather random acts of benevolence, and employed as an *aide* the flamboyant, plausible, picaresque Charles Howell ('There's a Portuguese person called Howell, Who lays on his lies with a trowel',[27] as his friend Dante Rossetti observed). In a brief period of engagingly outrageous borrowings and deceits Howell ('There's a Portuguese person called Howell, Who lays on then went to work for Swinburne. Ruskin must have enjoyed his company, as he did Rossetti's – a dramatic contrast to his earnest friends at Winnington.

John James did not live quite long enough to witness his son's first and greatest popular success, *Sesame and Lilies*. This book was composed of two lectures delivered at Manchester in December 1864, entitled 'Of Kings' Treasuries' and 'Of Queens' Gardens'. *Sesame and Lilies* sold well from the start, and after the eighteenth edition in its original form (1898) the publishers stopped numbering their editions and simply counted in thousands – 185,000 by 1908. At last Ruskin reached the large audience that had eluded him: a good proportion, presumably, of the 'young people belonging to the upper, or undistressed middle classes' for whom he had chiefly written the book.[28] 'Of Kings' Treasuries' refers to the value of books and reading, but it is 'Of Queens' Gardens', the classic statement of the doctrine of the Woman's Role, which makes the more fascinating and astonishing reading today. He argues that men and women are intended to fulfil entirely separate and complementary functions in life – a familiar enough thesis; what is supremely artful in Ruskin's presentation is the way in which he manages to suggest that the woman's function is more attractive and certainly more noble than the man's. A startling argument from literature paves the way: 'Shakespeare has no heroes; – he has only heroines.' Moreover the catastrophes in Shakespeare's plays are caused by the follies of men, and if the situation should be retrieved, it is by the wisdom and virtue of a woman. In Scott's great works, he continues, all the wise and resolute characters are again women. If we consider Homer and Dante, we are brought to a similar conclusion, and it is no accident that Chaucer wrote a Legend of Good Women but no Legend of Good Men.

Within this context Ruskin presents the proper functions of each sex:

> The man's power is active, progressive, defensive. He is eminently the doer, the creator, the discoverer, the defender. His intellect is for speculation and invention; his energy for adventure, for war, for conquest, wherever war is just, wherever conquest necessary. But the woman's power is for rule, not for battle, – and her intellect is not for invention or creation, but for sweet ordering and arrangement, and decision. She sees the quality of things, their claims, and their places.[29]

In Ruskin's view, this means that we can reconcile the 'guiding function of the woman' with 'a true wifely subjection', so that there need be no question of superiority on either side. He helps to preserve this illusion by giving most of the phrases suggesting domination to the female side: the woman 'rules the house', she 'guides' and 'directs' her husband. On his part, 'obedience' to the lady is said to be the essence of chivalry.

The ideal lady visualised by Ruskin is to be protected from the dangers, temptations and coarsening experience of the outside world. She is altogether too ethereal a being to be involved in the realities of life, and should be educated accordingly, studying much the same subjects as a man but in a different spirit. She should approach history, for example, not for the mastery of facts but to exercise her feelings and sympathy. On the subjects of science and languages Ruskin puts his case less skilfully:

> speaking broadly, a man ought to know any language or science he learns, thoroughly – while a woman ought to know the

same language, or science, only so far as may enable her to sympathise in her husband's pleasures, and in those of his best friends.[30]

But this does not mean that her education should be more frivolous than a man's – quite the contrary. She should beware of novels, particularly the best novels, which may make everyday life uninteresting by contrast. Her range of literature should be calculated 'to keep her in a lofty and pure element of thought'.[31] The persuasiveness of all this, to which the huge sales of *Sesame and Lilies* testify, is similar to the persuasiveness of 'The Nature of Gothic' and much of his criticism of painting: it depends to a great extent on his skill in basing his arguments on apparently neutral but actually weighted words and phrases, sliding between meanings, and disguising these operations with a cloak of silken eloquence. The techniques of verbal manipulation which he had used to romanticise the crude workmanship of the middle ages came to his aid again as he glorified the role of the housewife. Incidentally, there is a further reminder of his art criticism in his remarks about the female face: every restraint on a girl's natural affection will be 'indelibly written on her features', and 'the perfect loveliness of a woman's countenance' stems only from a peaceful, childlike state of mind.[32]

The success of *Sesame and Lilies* did not help Ruskin make up his mind about his future, for his health remained unreliable and his frustrated love for Rose deepened his gloom and uncertainty. In the mid-sixties Ruskin was prolific but less consistent than ever: in the year 1866 alone he published works as diverse as the obscure *Cestus of Aglaia*, the unreadable *Ethics of the Dust*, and the forthright *Crown of Wild Olive*. But let us, in accordance with the theme of this book, take as final examples two of the lectures which make up the latter publication, lectures in which he did not merely offend his audience, but positively taunted them.

Addressing the cadets at Woolwich Academy, he accused them of being sentimental schoolboys who had joined the army for the sake of excitement and a red coat. Ruskin himself admitted to a consciousness of the glamour of battle, however, and spoke of a predisposition among 'healthy men' for fighting and the sense of danger, which was 'a fixed instinct in the fine race of them'.[33] But he did not like the thought that modern battles were decided by mechanical and chemical equipment, and in fact his attitude to the subject was ambivalent through and through. He recognised that war was unjustified, that it was simply a game played with a multitude of human pawns, and yet he was not opposed in principle to war waged for the sake of dominion, provided that the resulting dominion was benevolent. A race should 'undertake aggressive war, according to their force, wherever they are assured that their authority would be helpful and protective'.[34] The lecture ended uncontroversially with instructions to the cadets to work hard, avoid betting and lead a stainless life; wives and mothers, be patient, support your menfolk and dress plainly.

The bewildered cadets must have felt themselves held back at one moment and egged on the next. Still more must the citizens of Bradford have been affronted when they invited Ruskin up to advise them on the design of a proposed Exchange building. Ruskin told them that they cared nothing for their Exchange, and nor did he; good architecture could not be had merely by asking advice, for it was an expression of national life and character. The Exchange would naturally be built in tribute to the presiding deity, and since his listeners worshipped above all the 'Goddess of Getting-on', they should decorate the frieze of the new building with pendant purses and make its pillars broad at the base, for the sticking of bills.

Here was the scourge of capitalism at his trenchant best. But although he continued to strike out violently for another twenty years, too often he lacked the force of argument, imagination and wit which had formerly driven home his attacks. His unsettled mind and emotions became ever more apparent as his writing fluctuated between the direct and the meandering, and between the harsh and the sentimental.

# 10  Savage Ruskin

Digressions, in the opinion of Tristam Shandy, are the sunshine: 'They are the life, the soul of reading; — take them out of this book, for instance — you might as well take the book along with them.' Much of Ruskin's later work, too, is a mass of digressions, but unlike Laurance Sterne's these are not the sunshine; too often they are the fog, and they spring from Ruskin's growing inability to focus his mind on any single subject. In *Munera Pulveris* (published as a book in 1872) this was already evident. The professed subject-matter of political economy was interrupted by literary or Biblical excursions, sometimes of a most obscure nature. Ambiguous remarks on the subject of slavery led Ruskin on to the differences between Ariel and Caliban in *The Tempest*, and a discussion of currency ran wildly off course into the allegorical significance of Scylla, Charybdis and the Sirens. When the book was published he apologised for his ramblings, but more and more they became his natural means of expression, as he leapt from one topic to another and buried his meaning beneath a heap of allusions.

More than twenty separate publications followed before he was totally incapacitated, including travel-books, works on plants, birds, and rocks, collections of letters, a manual on drawing method, several series of lectures and an autobiography. In all these there are innumerable moments of insight and flashes of brilliance to be found, and (since he was not even consistently inconsistent) there are extended periods of totally lucid presentation. Still, anyone reading these works of the 1870s and 1880s is constantly brought into contact with a tormented mind, plagued by nightmares which could turn into hallucinations, and deep depression which could amount to serious illness. Tranquil, evocative passages alternate with bitter diatribes. It is as if he was haunted by the very 'Gothic spirit' he had described in his prime — 'that restlessness of the dreaming mind, that wanders hither and thither among the niches, and flickers feverishly . . .'

At the root of his troubles lay his hopeless love for Rose La Touche. In October 1863 her first Communion was followed by a more persistent 'brain attack' than any before. Her mother reported that Rose had experienced 'a sort of clairvoyance, both of spiritual and earthly things',[1] but she was left very weak and suffered spells of amnesia. Ruskin missed her desperately. He saw her again in the winter of 1865–6, and on her seventeenth birthday he asked her to marry him; she postponed her reply but did not discourage him entirely. However her parents began to take a stronger line, and stopped her from writing to him.

A painful period ensued of misunderstanding, intrigue and fluctuating hope and despair, until at last she made it clear that they could not be married. For ten years, until she died in 1875, Ruskin remained obsessed with his love, seeing her occasionally but for the most part haunted by her memory, and interpreting every rose — even each rosy sunset — as a mystical symbol. Her death did not remove the cloud from his mind; it had only sealed (as he wrote to a friend) 'a great fountain of sorrow which can never now ebb away: a dark lake in the field of life as one looks back . . .'[2]

From early in his life Ruskin had experienced vivid and often horrifying dreams. His diary records a feverish Christmas spent in Rome when he was 21, with dreams of 'bedcovers and boa-constrictors' and of cold wedges of ice at the corners of his bed.[3] Towards the end of the 1860s nightmares of serpents and clinging leaches became a familiar part of his existence. Often again he dreamt of wading through water, or losing himself in a vast hotel. Once it seemed to him that he was taking out one of his own front teeth, and that part of his jaw came with it; on another occasion he dreamt that he put a little girl in a box, forgot her, and later discovered her dead; another night he seemed to see in a shop window a book entitled *Rose Scenery*, but just as the shopman was handing the book to him, he was woken.

In 1869 Ruskin was elected the first Slade Professor of Fine Art at Oxford University. He took his duties seriously, and to the relief of his friends his opening lectures were methodical, uncontroversial, and even a little dull. As an honorary fellow of Corpus Christi College he was practically licensed to behave in a pleasantly eccentric way, and he fulfilled all expectations in his famous road-digging project, in which a group of undergraduates (including Oscar Wilde, Andrew Lang, and Arnold Toynbee) were set to buy their own spades and pickaxes, and with these to drain and level a muddy track at the nearby village of Hinksey. The result was a poor road, but the project lasted for a good many months and could not be regarded as a failure. On the other hand 'Mr Ruskin's Tea Shop', an experiment in Ruskinian commercial principles at Paddington Street, never prospered at all, partly because Ruskin spent several months deciding whether its sign should be of a Chinese style painted in black and gold, or Japanese in blue on white, or English in rose-colour on green.

Of much more lasting benefit was his active support for Octavia Hill's immensely valuable work in rehabilitating slum houses. When the tea-shop failed, Ruskin was at least able to place its management in her more efficient hands.

But throughout the 1870s he had to contend with bouts of delirium and fevered illness, which interrupted his lecture courses, until he resigned his professorship after a particularly severe manic attack in 1878. He spent most of his remaining 22 years at Brantwood, overlooking Lake Coniston. Until the final decade he continued to travel and to write when he could, and his diaries show how he struggled to publish his work and to fulfil public commitments through spells of deepest depression and intervals of blissful contentment. A few entries taken from the months following Rose's death may serve as a sample.

June 4th   Y[esterday] at lunch with Mr Dodgson . . . Did more Botany; but the days melt away more and more fruitlessly.

June 5th   Y[esterday] with Prince of Wales and Princess at galleries; I entirely uncomfortable.

June 15th   Horrible wet day, and yesterday utterly black all day long, wind tormenting the leaves like a real devil.

June 20th   Y[esterday] the afternoon perfect. At Museum with Westwood and to see final look at diggings. Heavenly clouds above; roses in hedges.

June 27th   Had terrific dreams, last night, after long game of chess, of a house on fire with huge glass windows, which a crowd hanging at, fell back with the shattered glass into the street, blazing ruin falling over them . . . One man in a nightgown, creeping afterwards on the pavement *towards* the fire.

October 31st    Deadly black all yesterday again, and with bitter
    wind; yet I better for going out, and this morning so full of
    useful thoughts that I can't set down one, they push each other
    round in my head.
November 8th    A weary, fighting, yet useful night. No rest
    even in sleep; head full of thoughts . . .
December 5th    I, after good night, horrorstruck more than yet
    at the pallid, dirty, dead, vilely wretched sky. Nature herself
    sick.
December 14th    Heard from Mrs Ackworth, in the drawing-
    room where I was once so happy, the most overwhelming
    evidence of the other state of the world that has ever come to
    me . . .
December 20th    . . . the truth is shown to me, which, though
    blind, I have sought so long.[4]

The last two entries refer to Ruskin's interest in spiritualism:
Mrs Ackworth, a medium, had had a vision of Rose whispering to
him, and although Ruskin could not quite subscribe wholeheartedly to the spirit world, he was receptive to any sign from Rose.
    Dominating all else in his diaries for the 1870s are his constant
notes on air, wind and cloud conditions, which are quite unlike the
observations of sky and cloud in *Modern Painters*; for when in these
later years he wrote of 'pestilent black fog' or 'heavenly sunlight'
he was describing the climate of his own mind as such as any
physical occurrence in the world beyond his window. Sometimes
it was the weather outside which seemed to press on and into his
mind, while at other times his despondency or exaltation coloured
his entire view of external reality. The oppressive clouds far
outweighed the shafts of sunlight: 'South wind, blackest and
wildest, all the sky and air the inside of a manufacturing chimney,
with a chill in it! Utterly dreadful' . . . 'the smoke of hell covers
the sky' . . . 'utterly black ghastly fog, *as fixed as death*' . . .
'wrathful, sulphurous, black smoke cloud' . . . 'the sky one blotch
of filth' . . .[5] Like so many things important to Ruskin, the
weather had taken on human attributes; usually it was a demon
adversary, with its 'fiend-cloud', 'devilry of wind' and 'diseased
motion'.
    While he thus wrestled with the forces of Satan, his religious
outlook was changing again. After a strongly Protestant youth,

and a 'pagan' middle age, he now inclined towards Roman Catholicism. In 1874 he spent the summer at a monastery in Assisi, toying with Catholic doctrine: 'I challenged Fra Antonio [the Abbot] to raise one of his dead friars out of the cemetery, if he wanted me to believe, this morning over our coffee.'[6] Ruskin would never accept the dogma of Roman Catholicism, but he enjoyed the serene atmosphere at Assisi, far removed from the evangelical fanaticism of the dying Rose. Ten years later, when Ruskin had been reappointed to his professorship at Oxford, he mocked Protestantism from his podium. He chose a copy of Carpaccio's 'St Ursula' as typical of Catholicism, but as a type of 'earnest Protestantism' he held up to his audience an enlarged engraving of a pig, and spoke of 'The Protestant and Evangelical art which can draw a pig to perfection, but never a pretty lady'.[7] This lecture was considered too wild to be republished, and Ruskin was finding it difficult to cope with the excitement of speaking in public: although his audiences were large, and the lectures very entertaining, it was suggested that what one newspaper called 'an academic farce' should be brought to a merciful end. The succeeding lectures were planned to attack vivisection and science in general, but he was persuaded to abandon them. The following spring the practice of vivisection in Oxford was officially approved, an event which Ruskin gave as his reason for resigning his post. But he was in no state to teach, and shortly afterwards he gave way to another long spell of delirium.

Throughout his two periods of tenure at Oxford Ruskin had been producing the great *pot-pourri* entitled *Fors Clavigera*, in the form of 'Letters to the Workmen and Labourers of Great Britain', published monthly from 1871 to to 1878 and then irregularly until December 1884. As Ruskin explained, 'Fors' may mean force, fortitude or fortune, and 'Clavigera' may mean club-bearing, key-bearing or nail-bearing; so the reader can pick a translation to suit almost any occasion. A good deal of *Fors Clavigera* consists of readings in Plato, the Bible, Dante, Froissart, Shakespeare and others whom Ruskin admired at the time of writing. Carpaccio and the legend of St Ursula found their way into several of the letters (St Ursula came to represent Rose in Ruskin's mind); political economy was a recurring theme, with discussions of wealth, interest, rent and value. He dwelt also on the duties of government and the State; the dispensability of preaching, lawgiving and fighting as commercial professions (he described lawyers as 'talking broccoli'[8]); Greek and Christian mythology, and snippets of autobiography, some of them later reporoduced in *Praeterita*.

Since *Fors Clavigera* was a monthly publication there were many references to current events. In 1871, for example, the Paris Commune prompted some uncompromising reflections on the leisured classes. Ruskin found the French *communards* misled but not fundamentally at fault: 'the guilty Thieves of Europe, the real sources of all deadly war in it, are the Capitalists – that is to say, people who live by percentages on the labour of others; instead of by fair wages for their own. The *Real* war in Europe, of which this fighting in Paris is the Inauguration, is between these and the workman, such as these have made him'. Three months later these sentiments were balanced by Ruskin's proclaiming himself a 'violent Tory' in his 'most sincere love of kings'.[9]

It was pointed out to Ruskin that the tone of his 'Letters to Workmen and Labourers' was not best suited to his intended audience. Often in *Fors* and in his Oxford lectures he seems once again to be addressing a group of small girls in his most patronising manner. And he would not allow that what he wrote was anything less than incontrovertible . At his most fancifully metaphorical he was liable to declare, 'this is no metaphor!', thereby straining his readers' imagination still further. Much of the polemic of *Fors* is destructive, denouncing modern science, or machinery, or the ideal of liberty, or the economics of competition. But it was also through this medium that Ruskin put forward his most ambitious constructive scheme, the Guild of St George. He set out a code of conduct and Christian belief to which the Companions of the Guild were to pledge themselves; they were then to 'give the tenth of what they have, and of what they earn', towards the creation of a Ruskinian utopia.

We will try to take some small piece of English ground, beautiful, peaceful, and fruitful. We will have no steam-engines upon it, and no railroads; we will have no untended or unthought-of creatures on it; none wretched, but the sick; none idle but the dead. We will have no liberty upon it; but instant obedience to known law, and appointed persons: no equality upon it; but recognition of every betterness that we can find, and reprobation of every worseness. When we want to go anywhere, we will go there quietly and safely, not at forty miles an hour . . .[10]

Some Companions of the Guild would devote their full time to developing this society, and others would support it while pursuing their own professions. Ruskin led the way with his own tithe, which came to £7000; but very few others followed his lead. Having announced the scheme in 1871, he repeated his appeal the year after in greater detail (including a subdivision to be called The Company of Mont Rose), and yet by the end of 1873 there were only seven annual subscribers. Eleven years later, the Trustees' Report showed that 56 individuals had joined the Guild. There were one or two legacies, but Ruskin's own contribution remained much the largest element of the Guild's resources, which were used to buy a little farmland and some cottages, and to promote certain traditional crafts. The only tangible result of any permanence was the Guild Museum, which was organised largely by Ruskin himself – an enthusiastic collector to the last.

The 79th issue of *Fors*, on the other hand, provoked a reaction well beyond his expectations. He had recently seen a series of paintings by Whistler at the newly-opened Grosvenor Gallery, and had taken particular exception to an impression of fireworks over the River Thames, entitled 'Nocturne in Black and Gold: the Falling Rocket'. In *Fors* he wrote of Whistler's 'ill-educated conceit', and added

I have seen, and heard, much of cockney impudence before now: but never expected to hear a coxcomb ask two hundred guineas for flinging a pot of paint in the public's face.[11]

What lay at the root of Ruskin's outburst is debatable. Was it the price of the picture, the exhibitionistic life of its painter, or the work itself? An artist friend of Ruskin believed that his fury stemmed from a lifelong hatred of muted colour schemes; a biographer has given an opposite explanation, that Ruskin had an unconscious fear of light spots surrounded by darkness.[12] We might equally well suggest that he disliked the 'Nocturne' because it offered him no human 'expression'. As Whistler said, the picture was principally an arrangement of light, form and colour, but as such it fell outside the scope of Ruskin's interpretation; if Turner had painted it, Ruskin could no doubt have discovered an underlying significance; but as it was Ruskin had no reason to look beneath the surface. Whistler's was an art which excluded human emotion – or so, I imagine, Ruskin felt.

In any event Whistler sued Ruskin for libel, and Ruskin looked forward to defending himself. But the event proved something of an anticlimax, for when the case came to be heard in November 1878, Ruskin was delirious and quite unable to attend court. Burne-Jones, who took Ruskin's part, was no match for the wit and flair of Whistler. In their different ways both contestants emerged as losers. The judge awarded only a farthing damages to Whistler, and since the artist was already in debt and now had to pay half the costs of the case, the bailiffs were soon in residence at his exquisite White House. Ruskin, on the other hand, gained a reputation which lasts to this day in the minds of many people as a choleric traditionalist, a reactionary against all that was exciting and beautiful in late nineteenth-century art. His casual scorn set him up as the champion of the kind of fossilized conventionality which he had spent much of his life in trying to overcome.

While Whistler was experimenting with delicate harmonies of colour and looking for inspiration to France and Japan, Ruskin was turning back to his tastes of the years before his 'unconversion', to the early Italian masters and Tintoretto, and away from Michelangelo and the High Renaissance. His fresh 'discoveries' fitted into this pattern: Carpaccio and Botticelli from the end of the fifteenth century, Kate Greenaway and Francesca Alexander from the late nineteenth. As in the 1840s the face became a focus of Ruskin's interest. He had probably never lost his fascination with facial expression. He had watched the girls at Winnington Hall listening to Charles Hallé as he played a version of 'Home, Sweet Home', and he had written with rapture of their 'wet eyes, round-open, and the little scarlet upper lips, lifted, and drawn slightly together, in passionate glow of utter wonder' – or, as he related the same event to a correspondent, 'the little coral mouths fixed into little half open gaps'.[13] Later he lavished praise on the expressiveness of the childlike figures drawn by Francesca Alexander, and described their faces as he had once described Fra Angelico's ('. . . the amazement, the sorrow, the judgement, in the Madonna's eyes, all of eternity . . .[14].

His most revealing treatment of expression is to be found in the controversial Oxford lecture on 'The Relation between Michael Angelo and Tintoret', which shocked (among many others) his friend Edward Burne-Jones by its downright condemnation of Michelangelo, Raphael and Titian. Ruskin had returned to the view that a 'deadly catastrophe' took place in the years from 1480 to 1520. He took Giovanni Bellini as an example of one of the last uncorrupted artists, before

> Raphael, Michael Angelo, and Titian, together, bring about the deadly change, playing into each other's hands — Michael Angelo being the chief captain in evil; Titian, in natural force.[15]

Tintoretto nobly resisted the fatal influence for a while, until he too succumbed. The supreme calmness that characterised Giovanni Bellini's art was lost, and worse still, these later artists concentrated on the body; whereas in the highest art, such as Bellini's, the spectator should be compelled to think of the spirit, and this was to be achieved through the *face*. The four essentials of the greatest art, according to Ruskin in 1871, were

1. Faultless and permanent workmanship.
2. Serenity in state or action.
3. The Face principal, not the body.
4. And the Face free from either vice or pain.

Even in subjects which might seem to require violent expression, Ruskin continued, a great artist avoids it: in the hand-to-hand conflict of Bellini's 'The Assassination of St Peter Martyr'[16] there was no bloodstain, and 'in the face of the Saint is only resignation, and faintness of death, not pain — that of the executioner is impassive . . .'

For comparison Ruskin held up a series of Michelangelo drawings from the Oxford University collection, to show that this artist made the human body the subject of interest, leaving the faces unfinished, or else 'entirely foreshortened, backshortened, and despised, among labyrinths of limbs, and mountains of sides and shoulders'. Ruskin mockingly pointed out the expressions of Michelangelo's figures (plate 8a), observing their 'satyric form of countenance', with 'irregular excrescence and decrement of features, especially in flatness of the upper part of the nose, and projection of the end of it into a blunt knob'. Ruskin hinted at the possibility that Michelangelo, whose own nose had reputedly been flattened by a punch when he was young, was simply drawing replicas of his own deformed face.

So Ruskin reverted to the tactics he had learned from Rio twenty-five years before, seeing the artist reflected (or rather distorted) in his art, and relying above all on the expression of the face. No wonder Burne-Jones wanted to drown himself in the Surrey canal when he heard Ruskin dismiss all other artistic criteria and revert to this devastating means of attack. But by now Ruskin hardly needed so elaborate a vehicle for his scorn. *The Cestus of Aglaia* contained a most unsubtle defamation of Rembrandt as a painter of foul and sensual subjects, whose 'inherently evasive' work betrayed his ignorance of natural phenomena. Rembrandt had great technical skill, certainly; but he used it to portray 'the pawnbroker's festering heaps of old clothes'[17]. And Ruskin was capable of violent invective at the most unexpected moments. *Mornings in Florence*, for example, became a standard guide-book for touring gentlefolk, but even in the middle of a calm discussion of Ghirlandaio's frescoes they would be startled by a sudden injection of spleen: the Florentines 'think themselves so civilized . . .yet sell butcher's meat, dripping red, peaches, and anchovies, side by side . . .'[18] It is hard to know whether Ruskin's objections were hygienic or aesthetic.

Sometimes it seems that there was a therapeutic element in the gusts of rage which were claiming such a regular place in his life. There may well be truth in this remark taken from a letter of 1881:

> I don't *anger* my soul nor vex my *own* heart, I relieve it, by all violent language . . . I *live* in chronic fury, only softened by keeping wholly out of the reach of newspapers or men, and only to be at all relieved in its bad fits by studied expression.[19]

One of his last literary efforts was occasioned by Sir John Lubbock's publication of a list of the hundred authors he considered most worth reading. Ruskin must have relished the task of crossing out half of them and of composing acid dismissals of St Augustine, Grote, J. S. Mill, Kingsley, Darwin and Gibbon. In their place Ruskin proposed that his own list of indispensable books should be headed by Edward Lear's *Book of Nonsense*, a choice which gave great satisfaction to Lear in his last years.

The 96th instalment of *Fors Clavigera*, published at Christmas 1884, brought the series to a wistful close. His diary for 6

November that year records that he bought a book at Quaritch's which included a description of a 'Rosy Vale'; later that day he walked over to Kate Greenaway's and 'painted Roses'.[20] The passage was duly reproduced in the final *Fors*, together with accounts of a village called La Rose, of a ceremonial election of 'Rosières' at Nanterre, and of another village which Ruskin also described as a Rosy Vale. The accompanying drawing by Kate Greenaway, of a girl and two children, had the inevitable title of 'Rosy Vale'.

It was a sad conclusion, but the ghost of Rose La Touche was not yet laid to rest. Three years later, at the age of 68, Ruskin fell in love again, with a young girl named Kate Olander whom he saw copying a Turner at the National Gallery. They wrote to each other for a year or so, during which Kate became identified with Rose in Ruskin's mind. But her anxious parents and Ruskin's worsening health prevented the marriage that both he and she had hoped for.

If Ruskin had died from his severe illness of 1885, we might have decided that his over-active imagination had brought him finally to a state of paranoia, and that the imaginary personalities which he had first conceived for literary purposes had in the end taken full possession of his mind. But Ruskin lived on for fifteen years more, spent mostly at Brantwood, before he died on 20 January 1900. And in his last major work he turned his back on the furies of *Fors* and the self-indulgence of his Oxford lectures. Instead he embarked on a quietly-pitched, straightforward autobiography, simply and neatly expressed, omitting (as he disarmingly confessed) whatever he did not care to think about. *Praeterita* is not didactic, combative or rancorous; the reader need not look for the psychological analysis of his personal relationships (in a diary entry Ruskin deplored 'the love of the age for disgusting associations, as a matter of study', in *Middlemarch* and other contemporary novels[21]), for his marriage is not mentioned at all, and his relationship with his father is treated in a detached, mildly ironic fashion. He had to struggle to write the final chapters, which bear signs of the strain. But Ruskin's great literary output closed with a fine description of a glorious evening at Siena, with 'the fireflies everywhere in sky and cloud rising and falling, mixed with the lightning, and more intense than the stars'.[22]

In this last reverie, the savage demons had left him in peace.

# Notes

*Chapter 1*

1.  *The Works of John Ruskin*, ed. E. T. Cook and A. Wedderburn, 39 vols. (1903—12) (referred to hereafter as *Works*) 35, 15—21.
2.  *Works 35*, 25—36.
3.  Quoted in Helen L. Viljoen, *Ruskin's Scottish Heritage* (1956), p. 92.
4.  *Works 35*, 630
5.  Joan Evans *John Ruskin* (1954), p. 59.
6.  *Works 35*, 224.
7.  Sir Nikolaus Pevsner, *The Englishness of English Art* (1956), e.g. pp. 59—60.
8.  *Works 1*, 36—7.
9.  *The Landscape. A Didactic Poem* (1794), pp. 13, 14.
10. *Moral Contrasts* (1798), pp. 43—4.
11. *Three Essays on Picturesque Beauty* (1792), pp. 43—6, 50—6.
12. *An Analytical Inquiry into the Principles of Taste* (1805), p. 142.
13. *Works 14*, 385. In the *Art Journal* of 1849 (pp. 76—7, *Works 12*, 312) Ruskin finds Prout especially sympathetic in his many studies of Venice; Prout may have prepared the ground for Ruskin's enthusiasm for Venetian Gothic architecture.
14. *Works 3*, 202—18.
15. *The Three Tours of Dr Syntax* (1868 ed.), p. 66. The first 'Tour' was published in 1810.
16. *Lectures on Architecture 1809—36*, ed. A. T. Bolton (1829), p. 178.
17. *Builder*, 4 (1846), p. 75.
18. See J. L. Petit, *Remarks on Architectural Character* (Oxford 1846), pp. 5ff; T. L. Donaldson, *Preliminary Discourse on Architecture* (1842), p. 29; W. M. Bucknall, *Builder* (3 July 1852), p. 418
19. *Essays on the Nature and Principles of Taste* (1790), pp. 268—9, 255 ff, 236.
20. *Essays* (1790), p. 283. Similar lists of 'characters' are given in J. C. Loudon, *A Treatise on . . . Country Residences* (1806), pp. 40—3, 78—9.
21. *Essays* (3rd ed., 1812), p. 225
22. *An Encyclopaedia of Cottage, Farm and Village Architecture* (1833), p. 1120.
23. *Works 1*, 125.
24. *Works 1*, 117.
25. *Works 1*, 114.
26. Ibid. Compare Knight, *Inquiry*, p. 223: 'The best style of architecture for irregular and picturesque houses, which now can be adopted, is that mixed style, which characterizes the buildings of Claude and the Poussins.'

27. *Works 1*, 121—4.
28. *Works 1*, 78.
29. *Works 1*, 120—3.
30. *Works 1*, 162ff.
31. *Works 8*, 218.
32. *Works 8*, 108; *1*, 143.
33. G. Wightwick, *The Palace of Architecture* (1840), Preface and pp. 113, 126.
34. *Essays* (1790), e.g. pp. 269—334.
35. *A Treatise on Forming, Improving and Managing Country Residences* (1806), pp. 43, 78—9. Architects used the word as ambiguously as they used the term 'character'. One E. Trotman gave it at least three senses in the course of a single article for the *Architectural Magazine* of March 1834: the first object of architecture, he wrote, is 'the expression of the parts and method of construction', but he also mentioned 'the expression of fitness of purpose' and 'the expression of . . . the support of a horizontal mass' (pp. 33, 30). Loudon's *Encyclopaedia of Cottage Architecture* (1833, pp. 1112ff) distinguished five such senses, and for each design it devoted a paragraph to 'expression', just as other paragraphs were dedicated to 'accommodation' or 'general estimate'. Under the heading of 'expression' came every kind of observation that was not simply practical instruction; and Loudon must himself have found the term rather pretentious, for after page 105 this odds-and-ends paragraph received the more appropriate title of 'Remarks'.
36. *Treatise* (1866), pp. 35—6.

Chapter 2

1. *Works 35*, 195—6.
2. *Works 35*, 205.
3. W. Buckland, *Vindiciae Geologicae* (1820), p.23.
4. W. Buckland, *Reliquiae Deluvianae* (1823), reviewed in the *Quarterly Review* 29 (1823) p. 138 and *Edinburgh Review* 39 (1823) p.196.
5. *Works 1*, 465.
6. *Works 1*, 485.
7. *Works 2*, 193.
8. *Works 2*, 44.
9. Stopford Brooke, *The Life and Letters of F. W. Robertson* (1874) p. 305.
10. *Blackwood's* 40 (October 1836), p. 551.
11. *Works 3*, 571.
12. *Works 3*, 624.
13. *Works 4*, 250—1.
14. *Works 4*, 273—4.
15. *The Works of Sir Joshua Reynolds, Knight*, ed. E. Malone (1798), vol. 1, pp.34, 35;
    *The Complete Writings of William Blake*, ed. G. Keynes (1957), p. 456.
16. J. D. Harding, *The Principles and Practice of Art* (1845), pp. 13, 150.
17. See R. Wittkower, 'Imitation, Eclecticism and Genius', in *Aspects of the Eighteenth Century*, ed. E. R. Wasserman (1965), pp. 143—61.

18. *Works 3*, 100–1. The idea that imitation should not amount to deception was no novelty, having been expounded at unnecessary length by Quatrèmere de Quincy long before. But the reviewer of *Modern Painters* who objected 'we thought this matter had long ago been settled' (*Blackwood's* 70, Sep 1851, p. 331) missed the more interesting point, that Ruskin had rejected *any* interpretation of imitation as a worthy aim for the fully-fledged artist.

19. *Works 1*, 421–2.

20. *Works 35*, 313. Robert Hewison has pointed out that Ruskin's celebrated vision at Fontainebleau may have been imagined in his old age, and that Harding is credited with a similar experience (*The Argument of the Eye*, 1976, pp. 41–2)

21. *Works 6*, 45.

22. *Works 6*, 179.

23. *Works 6*, 232.

## Chapter 3

1. See *The Art Journal, a short history* (Virtue & Co., 1906), pp. 4, 22, 25. There had been previous art periodicals, but all were short-lived.

2. *The Art-Union* (15 Mar. 1839), p. 20. Its editor, S.C. Hall, wrote later that before the time of his journal, the taste of the *nouveaux riches* was for 'old masters' – in fact nearly always fakes. (*Retrospect of a Long Life* (1883), vol. 1, pp. 343–4.)

3. 'The Life of Raphael', *Contributions to the Literature of the Fine Arts*, 1st series (1848), pp. 181–2.

4. T.J. Hogg (?), 'Lanzi's History of Painting', *Edinburgh Review* 48 (Sep. 1828), p. 87.

5. 'An Essay on Modern Architecture' (in *Studies and Examples of the Modern Schools of Architecture* (1839), pp. 12, 8.

6. *The Principles of Beauty* (1857), p. 39.

7. *An Essay*, p. 14.

8. *The Works of Mr Jonathan Richardson*, ed. Jonathan Richardson (the Younger) (1773), pp. 48–51.

9. Roger de Piles, *Cours de Peinture* (Paris, 1708), p. 169

10. A.R. Mengs, *Works* (English translation, 1796), p.76.

11. Ibid., p. 117.

12. *Lectures on Painting by Royal Academicians*, ed. R. Wornum (1848), p. 345.

13. *The Italian Schools of Painting* (1820), pp. 263, 36.

14. *The Works of Sir Joshua Reynolds, Knight*, ed. E. Malone (1798), vol. 1, pp. 117–20; *The Complete Writings of William Blake* (1957), p. 446

15. John Opie et al., *Lectures on Painting by Royal Academicians*, ed. R. Wornum (1848), p. 244.

16. A. R. Mengs, *Works*, p. 64.

17. *The Aesthetic and Miscellaneous Works of Frederick von Schlegel*, trans. E.J. Millington (1849), p. 68.

18. *Art-Union*, May 1839, p. 68.

19. *Art-Union*, May 1841, p. 76.

20. Ibid.

21. *Art-Union*, June 1842, p. 122.

22. *Blackwood's*, 50 (Sep. 1841), p. 349.

23. W. Cosmo Monkhouse, *Pictures by Sir Charles Eastlake* (1875), p. 39.

24. Ibid., p. 161.

25. *Art-Union* (Feb. 1939), p. 1.

26. *Blackwood's* (July 1842), p. 30; *Art-Union* (June 1843), p. 168.

27. *Tour of a German Artist in England* (1836), vol. 2, p. 253.

28. *The Diary of an Ennuyée* (1836 edition), p. 15.

29. See W. Cosmo Monkhouse, *Pictures by Sir Charles Eastlake* (1875).

30. See *Diaries*, vol. 1, p. 126. As late as 1864, Hippolyte Taine followed the pattern of gradual induction: see *Voyage en Italie* (Paris, 1866), pp. 237–41. See also *The Letters of John Keats* ed. H. E. Rollins (1958), vol. II, p. 19 (Letter 137).

31. *Lectures on the History and Principles of Painting* (1833), p. xvii.

32. *The Book of the Cartoons* (1837), p. 182.

33. Rev. W. Gunn, *Cartonensia* (1831), p. 158.

34. *The Diary of a Désennuyée* (1836), p. 45.

35. Benjamin Ralph, *The School of Raphael: Or, the student's Guide to Expression in Historical Painting* (1819), pp. 15–16.

36. B. P. di Figueroa, *An Analysis of the Picture of the Transfiguration of Raphael* (1833), pp. 10–12.

37. *The Artist and Amateur's Magazine,* ed. E. V. Rippingille (the sole author), 1843, pp. 351–2.

38. Tom Taylor, in his edition of *Autobiographical Recollections of the late C. R. Leslie, R. A.* (1860), p. lxxiv.

39. Ibid., p. lxxviii.

40. Ibid., p. xxviii; Ruskin, *Works 14.* 37.

41. Ibid., p. xiii.

42. Thus Flaxman (*Lectures on Sculpture*, 1865, p. 188): The classical Greeks chose 'countenances expressive of the most elevated dispositions of mind and innocence of character'. See also p. 268.

43. *Lectures on Painting and Design* (1844–6), vol. 1, pp. 105, 112, 219–22, 321.

44. Quoted by W. T. Whitley, *Art in England 1821–1837*, p. 232.

45. Sir G. Gordon-Taylor aod E. W. Walls, *Sir Charles Bell* (1958), p. 21. In 1849 it was still a standard prize book of the London Society of Arts – see *Journal of Design and Manufactures* I (May 1849), p. 127.

46. *Essays on the Anatomy and Philosophy of Expression*, 3rd (enlarged) edition (1844), pp. 216, 121–3.

47. J. Landseer, *A Descriptive, Explanatory, and Critical, Catalogue of fifty of the earliest pictures contained in the National Gallery of Great Britain* (1834), p. xxii.

48. *Works 4*, 381.

49. *Essays* (1844), pp. 192–3.

50. *Works 4*, 121n. Ruskin has been likened to Lessing in his antipathy to transient and convulsed features in art (Laridow, p. 141 & n). Ruskin, however, disliked the Laocoon group on these grounds, while Lessing regarded the Laocoon as an example of the restraint he admired.

51. *Works 1*, 522.

52. *The Ruskin Family Letters*, ed. Van Akin Burd (1973), vol. 2, p. 470.
53. *Ruskin in Italy: Letters to his Parents 1845*, ed. Harold I. Shapiro (1972), p. 9.
54. Ibid., p. 65.
55. Bodleian MS Eng. Misc. c213, p. 65. The MS is a typescript made for the use of Cook and Wedderburn (who quote short extracts in vol. 4); the original notes at the Ruskin Galleries, Bembridge, Isle of Wight, are 'in the hand of Ruskin's servant G. Hobbes but noted in places by Ruskin himself'. I have used the (faulty) page numbering subsequently added in pencil.
56. Ibid., p. 48.
57. Ibid., pp. 70, 84, 152, 159.
58. *Works* 4, 147–57.
59. *Works* 4, 158–60.
60. M. A. Shee, *Elements of Art, a Poem* (1809), p. 122n.
61. D. Webb, *An Inquiry into the Beauties of Painting* (1760), p. 16. 'What a perfect knowledge of the human soul must this painter have had, to enter thus feelingly into her inmost workings!' commented Webb (pp. 160–1).
62. Shee, p. 132n. Reynolds (*Works*, vol. I, pp. 118–19) had also disparaged the habit of 'describing with great exactness the expression of a mixed passion'.
63. A. W. Crawford (Lord Lindsay), *Sketches of the History of Christian Art* (1847), vol. 3, pp. 139–41; *Works* 12, 229–31.
64. *Works* 12, 244.
65. *Works* 1, 542.
66. *Works* 35, 422.
67. *Works* 4, 329.

## Chapter 4

1. *Ruskin in Italy*, p. 207.
2. Ibid., p. 220.
3. Ibid., p. 215.
4. *Works* 4, 200–1.
5. *Works* 4, 212–13.
6. *Works* 4, 203, 212.
   In this context it is interesting that A. Paul Oppé, reviewing the lives of the artists who flourished in England in the 1840s (*Early Victorian England*, ed. G. M. Young (1934), vol. 2, pp. 127–30), should have concluded that 'the dominant note of their lives is always that of intense respectability', whereas 'piety is not marked in the men of the earlier generation'.
7. R. P. Knight, 'Northcote's Life of Reynolds', *Edinburgh Review* 23 (Sep 1814), p. 268.
8. *Journals and Correspondence of Lady Eastlake* (née Rigby), ed. C. E. Smith (1895), vol. I, p. 124.
9. A. Gilchrist, *The Life of William Etty, R. A.* (1855), vol. I, pp. 317–19. It should be added that critics of the eighteenth and early nineteenth centuries tended to share the view that good *taste* was linked with personal virtue in a member of the cultivable public; it is only over the question of the character required in an *artist* that clear changes in critical opinion emerge.

10. G. Vasari, *Life of Raphael* (tr Mrs. Jonathan Foster, 1866), p. 1.

11. *A Discourse on the Science of a Connoisseur*, in *Works* (1773), p. 330.

12. *Cartonensia* (1831), p. 62.

13. *A Hand-book for Young Painters* (1855 – a revised edition of his Academy lectures), pp. 104, 62.

14. *Sketches of the History of Christian Art* (1847), vol. 3, p. 50.

15. See especially 'Descriptions of Paintings in Paris and the Netherlands, 1802–4', *The Aesthetic and Miscellaneous Works of Frederick von Schlegel*, trans. E. J. Millington (1849).

16. Ibid., pp. 68–9.

17. Ibid., p. 6.

18. F. W. J. von Schelling, *On the Relationship of the Creative Arts to Nature* (The Catholic Series, 1845), pp. 21–2. See also *The Philosophical Letters and Essays of Schiller*, tr. J. Weiss (The Catholic Series, 1845), p. 267: 'we find scriptural paintings, where the apostles, the Virgin and Christ himself have an expression, as if they had been selected from the commonest rabble. All such productions evince a low taste, which justifies us in inferring a rude and vulgar mind in the artist himself.'

19. J. D. Passavant, *Tour of a German Artist in England* (1836), vol. 2, p. 244.

20. G. F. Waagen, *Works of Art and Artists in England* (1838), vol. 1, pp. 123, 5.

21. *De la Poésie Chrétienne, dans son principe, dans sa matière et dans ses formes* (Paris, 1836), p. 148.

22. *Works 4*, xxiii. Ruskin's own account of the matter is certainly mistaken. In *Praeterita*, written forty years later, Ruskin couples Rio's name with that of Lord Lindsay, saying that these two introduced him to Christian art in the winter of 1844–5; and in the 1883 edition of *Modern Painters*, Lindsay alone is given the credit (*Works 35*, 340; *4*, 348). However, Lindsay's volumes were not published until 1847, whereas Ruskin's diaries (vol. I p. 249) show that he was reading Rio as early as November 1843: and the second volume of *Modern Painters* (1846) refers to Rio, but not – of course – to Lindsay. So Ruskin must have confused the names, rather than the dates, in his old age.

23. Rio, p. 217.

24. *Works 4*, 212. The sitter in this portrait is now identified as Francesco dell' Opere.

25. Rio, p. 194: '. . . c'est à cette sympathie si réelle et si profonde qu'il faut attribuer l'expression si pathétique qu'il a su donner aux divers personnages témoins du crucifiement, ou de la descente de croix, ou de la déposition dans le tombeau.'

26. *Works 12*, 242.

27. *Works 3*, 174.

28. *Works 3*, 178.

29. *Works 3*, 176.

30. *Works 3* 184 & n. 'I retain unqualified this of Domenichino', Ruskin noted in the margin of the copy he kept for revision.

31. *Works 3*, 191.

32. *Works 35*, 305. Ruskin possibly met Turner on a previous occasion – see *35*, 305n.

33. Bodleian MS Eng. Misc. c213, facing p. 73.

34. Ibid., p. 58.
35. Ibid., p. 68.
36. Ibid., pp. 50, 51.
37. Ibid., p. 151.
38. F. G. Townsend, *Ruskin and the Landscape Feeling* (1951), notes three themes common to Rio and Ruskin — hostility to the Renaissance, justification of 'inferior' religious imagery, and the role of art in religious instruction before printing was invented (pp. 27ff).
39. Gerardine Macpherson, *Memoirs of the Life of Anna Jameson* (1878), p.80.
40. Ibid., p. 176.
41. *A Handbook to the Public Galleries of Art in and near London* (1842), p. xiv.
42. Ibid., p. 157.
43. *Sacred and Legendary Art* (1848), vol. 1, pp. 41—2.
44. Ibid., p. 42.
45. *North British Review* 8 (Nov 1847), p. 4.
    The reviewer finds 'this view of the matter' confirmed by Cennini, who in his *Trattato della Pittura* 'lays as much stress on the Christian virtues and moral discipline of the artist as on his technical qualifications' (p. 5).
46. Alexander W. Crawford (Lord Lindsay), *Sketches of the History of Christian Art* (1847), vol. 3, pp. 191, 188—9.
47. *Athenaeum* (22 Apr 1837), pp. 274 ff, and (13 May) pp. 339 ff.
48. See C. C. Abbott, *The Life and Letters of George Darley* (1928), pp. 174—5.
49. *Athenaeum* (1837), p. 341.
50. Ibid. (1846), p. 766.
51. Abbott, *op. cit.*, p. 179.
52. *Blackwood's* 80 (Sep 1856), pp. 352—3.
53. *A Letter to Thomas Phillips, Esq., R.A.* (1840), p. 3.
54. Ibid., pp. 13—14.
55. Mary Lutyens, *The Ruskins and the Grays* (1972), p. 37.


Chapter 5

1. Admiral Sir William James, *The Order of Release* (1948), p. 60
2. Letter of 7 March 1854, quoted in Mary Lutyens, *Millais and the Ruskins* (1967), pp. 154—7.
3. J. H. Whitehouse, *Vindication of Ruskin* (1950), p. 15; also quoted in Lutyens, *Millais and the Ruskins*, p. 191.
4. Mary Lutyens, *The Ruskins and the Grays* (1972), p. 133.
5. Mary Lutyens, *Effie in Venice* (1965), p. 65.
6. Ibid., p. 54.
7. Ibid., p. 131.
8. Ibid., p. 260.
9. *Ruskin's Letters from Venice, 1851—1852*, ed. J. L. Bradley (1955), pp. 59—60.
10. Lutyens, *Millais and the Ruskins*, p. 20.
11. Admiral Sir William James, *The Order of Release* (1948), p. 194.
12. Lutyens, *Millais and the Ruskins*, p. 45.
13. Ibid., p. 71.

14. Ibid., p. 131.
15. Ibid., p. 155.
16. Lutyens, *The Ruskins and the Grays*, p. 71.

*Chapter 6*

1. *North British Review* 21 (May 1854), pp. 172ff.
2. *Letters* (1828), vol. 1, pp. 113–14. This 'letter' is dated 5 August 1817.
3. *Remarks* (1835), pp. 140, 12.
4. *Letters* (1828), vol. 1, p. 255.
5. *Remarks on the Antiquities, Arts and Letters during an Excursion in Italy in the years 1802 and 1803* (1813), pp. 364, 362. The fourth edition was published in 1835.
6. *Architectural Magazine* 2 (1835), pp. 140, 294. In 1843 Joseph Nash's splendid lithographs of *Interiors and Exteriors in Venice* were published, but they were let down by Lake Price's text: St Mark's exterior was said to be strange but picturesque, and the interior 'gloomy to a fault' (vol. 1, facing plates XXX and XXXI). Louisa Costello's *A Tour to and from Venice by the Vaudois and the Tyrol* (1846) enthused over the 'exquisite perfection' and 'harmony and repose' of St Mark's (p. 293), but the book as a whole is a collection of light anecdotes and historical snippets. The first detailed appreciation of Venetian Gothic buildings is to be found in Benjamin Webb's *Sketches of Continental Ecclesiology* (1848).
7. M. Lutyens, *The Ruskins and the Grays* (1972), p. 126.
8. *Works 8*, 15 (Preface to the edition of 1880); 8, xlvii (letter of 15 August 1879).
9. *Athenaeum* (Sep 1849), p. 889; *North British Review*, 12 (Feb 1850), p. 349.
10. E.g. *Works 8*, xxxii–iii.
11. *Works 35*, 350.
12. *British Quarterly Review*, 10 (Aug 1849), p. 49.
13. Edinburgh Review, 95 (Oct 1851), pp. 369–70.
14. Ibid., p. 379.
15. *North British Review*, 12 (Feb 1850), p. 350; *British Quarterly Review*, 10 (Aug 1849), p. 67.
16. *Works 8*, 141.
17. As Whewell observed in *Fraser's Magazine*, 41 (Feb 1850), p. 156; and see *Works 8*, 164.
18. *Works 8*, 168–9.
19. *British Quarterly Review*, 10 (Aug 1849), p. 62.
20. *Works 12*, 492–3n.
21. E. A. Freeman. *A History of Architecture* (1849), pp. xviii, 124, 260; Alexander W. Crawford (Lord Lindsay), *Sketches of the History of Christian Art*, 3 vols. (1847), vol. 2, p. 23.
22. J. Fergusson, *An Historical Inquiry into the True Principles of Beauty in Art, more especially with reference to architecture* (1849), pp. 138–46, 222, 144.
23. Fergusson, p. 78; E. A. Garbett (1850), pp. 19–21.
24. See Fergusson, p. 222, 368, 403.

25. Garbett, p. 21 (italics in original).

26. Freeman, p. 5.

27. 'An Account of the Late Restorations in the Church of Old Shoreham, Sussex', *Transactions of the Cambridge Camden Society* (1841), pp. 29–30.

28. *Architectural Magazine*, 2 (1835), p. 85; 4 (1837), p. 3.

29. G. Durandus, *The Symbolism of Churches and Church Ornaments*, ed. J. M. Neale and B. Webb (1843), pp. 27–8, 22–3.

30. R. Kerr, *The Newleafe Discourses on the Fine Art Architecture* (1846), pp. 156–9.

31. Durandus, p. cxxix.

32. Kerr, p. 127.

33. *Quarterly Papers on Architecture*, ed. J. Weale (1843–5), vol. 3, p. 12.

34. G. P. Landow, *The Aesthetic and Critical Theories of John Ruskin* (1971), pp. 356–70. He adds to the list Carlyle, who is unlikely to have influenced Ruskin at this stage.

35. *Works 8*, 43 (my italics).

36. *Works 8*, 46, 39–40, 42.

37. *Works 8*, 51.

38. Durandus, p.xix.

39. *Ecclesiologist* 15 (1854), p. 3.

40. Durandus, pp. cxxiv–v.

41. The Oxford Society for Promoting the Studies of Gothic Architecture, founded in March 1839, published list of members from 1842 to 1847, in all of which Ruskin's name appears. There is no reference to the Society in Ruskin's *Works*.

42. *Builder*, 18 (1860), p. 294.

43. 'Sources of Expression in Architecture', *Edinburgh Review* 95 (Oct 1851), p. 396.

44. *Christian Remembrancer* 4 (1842), p. 258.

45. *Ecclesiologist* 13 (1852), pp. 352–3.

46. J. F. White, *The Cambridge Movement* (1962), p. 179; see also pp. 115 ff.

47. Sir G. G. Scott, *Personal and Professional Recollections*, ed. G. G. Scott (1879), pp. 88, 104.

48. Philip Freeman, 'On Foliated Wooden Roofs', *Transactions of the C. C. S.* (1841), p. 123.

49. Scott, *Recollections*, pp. 155–6.

50. *Recollections of T. G. Jackson*, ed. B. H. Jackson (1950), p. 56.

51. *Works 8*, 191.

52. *Works 8*, 203.

53. *Works 8*, 214.

54. *Works 8*, 114–5.

55. *Rambler*, 4 (Aug 1849), p. 234 [J. M. Capes?]. Italics in original.

56. Fergusson, p. 504.

57. Garbett, pp. 5–7, developing a remark made by Emerson at the end of his 'Essay on Art'.

58. W. H. Prescott, *History of the Conquest of Peru* (1847), vol. 1, p. 142.

59. Freeman, p. 138.

60. G. A. Poole *A History of Ecclesiastical Architecture in England* (1848), pp. 313–14.

61. *Works 8*, 248 (my italics)


Chapter 7

1. *Works 9*, xxxvi (letter of 18 Feb 1852).

2. *Works 9*, 31 (italics in original).

3. *Works 9*, 32.

4. *Works 9*, 31.

5. *Works 9*, 157.

6. *Works 9*, 371.

7. *Works 9*, 393.

8. *Works 9*, 291.

9. *Works 9*, 302–3.

10. *Works 10*, 241.

11. *Works 10*, 201–2.

12. *Works 10*, 172–3.

13. *Works 10*, 177.

14. *Works 10*, 242. Peter Collins's remark that Ruskin promoted Gothic partly 'because it expressed for him the essence of Protestantism . . . ' does not apply to *The Stones of Venice*, despite this quotation (*Changing Ideals in Modern Architecture, 1750–1950*, 1965, p. 100).

15. 'The Lamps of Greek Art' in *The Legacy of Greece*, ed. R. W. Livingstone (1921), pp. 353–96; reprinted in P. Gardner and Sir R. Blomfield, *Greek Art and Architecture* (1922).

16. *Works 10*, 427. See also *Works 11*, 193–4.

17. *Works 10*, 307–8.

18. *Works 11*, xxxix; *35*, 351.

19. *Works 11*, 6–13, 122–31.

20. *Architectural Principles in the Age of Humanism* (Studies of the Warburg Institute, 1949), p. 1.

21. The first to criticise Ruskin from this point of view was Coventry Patmore, who observed that Ruskin had not given sufficient credit to Renaissance painters and architects for having symbolised 'unity in multeity': 'Character in Architecture', *North British Review* 15 (Aug 1851), pp. 469–70.

22. *Works 11*, 46.

23. *Works 11*, 47–73.

24. Sir Daniel Sandford's article on 'The Rise and Progress of Literature' in the *Popular Encyclopaedia* went a little way towards finding 'the old Greek character' in Greek literature (reprinted in John Potter, *Archaeologia Graeca*, 4th ed. (1844), pp. 721–74).

25. *Recollections of Thomas Graham Jackson*, ed. B. H. Jackson (1950), p. 56, and see p. 58.

26. F. A. Paley, *A Manual of Gothic Architecture* (1846), p. 23n. Frederick Faber was a notable exception.

27. *Works 4*, 329, but see *4*, 119n.

28. *Works 22*, 95.
29. *Works 9*, 68.
30. *Works 12*, 89.
31. *Works 10*, 214.
32. *Daily News* 1 Aug 1853; quoted in *Works 10*, xlv. After the slow sales of volume I, Ruskin had resolved to 'make this record volume as popular as I can, and put a few plates in it and pretty ones. There is no use in writing fine books, if nobody will read them.' *Works 9*. xxxix.
33. See Ernst Gombrich, *In Search of Cultural History* (1969).
34. 'It is usually admitted that Ruskin established the connexion, or at least the coincidence, of the moral and artistic phenomena, at least in the case of Venice.' (Oliver Elton, *A Survey of English Literature 1830–1880* (1920), p. 226). In his *Social History of Art* (1962), vol. 4, p. 107, Arnold Hauser has written that 'there has never been such a clear awareness of the organic relationship between art and life since Ruskin. He was unquestionably the first to interpret the decline of art and taste as the sign of a general cultural crisis'.
35. Arnold Hauser, endorsed by Ernst Fisher, *The Necessity of Art, A Marxist Approach* (1963), p. 149.
36. *Hume's Essays*, ed. T. H. Green and T. H. Grose (1882), vol. I, p. 301.
37. Christian Gottlob Heyne, quoted in H. C. Hatfield, *Winckelmann and his German Critics* (1963), p. 126.
38. *Sacred and Legendary Art* (1848), vol. I, pp. xxi–iv, cf. A. F. Rio, pp. 160–1. Ruskin too remarked on the notable development of 'the critical faculty' in the first half of the nineteenth century, but he observed that it coincided with the 'extinction of the Arts of Design' (*Works 12*, 169).
39. C. R. Leslie, *Memoirs of the Life of John Constable* (1951), p. 169 [reprint of 1845 edition].
40. Rio, p. 527.
41. 'He applies too much epoch sauce. It is tasty and I prefer it to Taine's or J. A. Symond's [sic] . . . ' Letter from Bernard Berenson to Sister Mary Bowe in M. C. Bowe, *François Rio, Sa place dans le renouveau catholique en Europe* (Paris, 1938), pp. 244–5.
42. Eastlake's *Contributions to the Literature of the Fine Arts* do not refer to Rio, although almost every other contemporary source is mentioned in the course of these two volumes. Eastlake presumably read Rio's work (his copy is in the library of the National Gallery) but found the Frenchman's naïve religiosity and unscholarly generalisations too far removed from his own frame of mind.
43. C. R. Leslie, *A Handbook for Young Painters* (1855 edition), p. 78.

## Chapter 8

1. *Works 13*, xxvii.
2. *Works 13*, xxiii.
3. *Works 13*, 597–606.

4. 'Modern Painters, etc.', *Fraser's* 33 (March 1846), p. 368.
5. *Works 3*, 254.
6. *Works 3*, 182.
7. *Works 12*, 359–60.
8. *Works 12*, 370.
9. J. Farington, *Diary*, ed. J. Greig (1922–8), vol. 2, p. 94; *Works 12*. 371.
10. *Works 14*, 107, 108, 109.
11. *Works 14*, 152–7; *Athenaeum* (15 Nov 1857), p. 1406.
12. *Works 14*, 107, 143, 167.
13. Jack Lindsay's biography of Turner (1966) engages in Ruskinian criticism of Turner at both social and personal levels. Turner is said to express the conflicts of the late eighteenth century (p. 88), his personal anguish (p. 95) and his 'deep sense of dialectical opposites' (p. 208). On the other hand A. Paul Oppé (1934, p. 140) aptly remarks of Turner that 'it was his fate to find a prophet who extolled him as the embodiment of precisely those qualities of mind and purpose with which he was least concerned'.
14. *Works 4*, 197.
15. *Works 14*, 47.
16. *Works 14*, 32.
17. *Works 14*, 8.
18. *Works 14*, 37–8.
19. *Works 14*, 31.
20. Henry Brougham [?], 'The History of Painting in Italy', *Edinburgh Review* 32 (Oct 1819), p. 332.
21. *Works 14*, 37–8; *Athenaeum* (12 May 1855), p. 558.
22. *Works 1*, 143–4; *1*, 23; *12*, 44; *14*, 404; *Athenaeum* (11 July 1857), p. 880.
23. *Athenaeum*, ibid.
24. See P. Jullian, *Dreamers of Decadence* (1971), chs. 1 and 2, and T. Hilton, *The Pre-Raphaelites* (1970), pp. 82–3.
25. W. M. Rossetti, *Dante Gabriel Rossetti: his family letters* (1875), vol. I, p. 129.
26. *Household Words* (15 June 1850).
27. *Works 12*, 325.
28. *Works 12*, 339.
29. *Works 12*, 349–54.
30. *Works 12*, 388.
31. *Works 12*, 159, 161, 162–3 (my italics). The latter two references are to the 'Addenda' included in the version published in April 1854.
32. *Works 12*, 385, 359
33. *Athenaeum* (26 May 1855), p. 623.
34. Allen Staley, in his valuable *Pre-Raphaelite Landscape* (1973), seems to me mistaken in saying that 'from 1851 through 1859 Pre-Raphaelitism was seen by most contemporary observers almost solely in terms of the naturalistic orientation proclaimed for the movement by Ruskin' (p. 18).
35. *Athenaeum*, 7 April 1849, p. 362. Stone adds that Rossetti had 'perhaps unknowingly' entered into the feeling of Savonarola.
36. *Athenaeum*, 1 June 1850, p. 590.
37. *British Quarterly Review* 16 (Aug 1852), p. 214.
38. *Les Beaux-Arts en Europe* (Paris, 1855), vol. 1, p. 31.

39. *Works 14*, 66.
40. *Works 14*, 68.
41. *Works 12*, 334.
42. *New Monthly Magazine* 101 (May 1854), p. 49. The discrepancy is noted by G. H. Fleming, *That Ne'er Shall Meet Again* (1971), pp. 2–3.
43. *Athenaeum*, 20 April 1850, p. 424.
44. *Illustrated London News* 16 (11 May 1850), p. 336. The reproduction of the picture printed on the same page exaggerates the morose downward curves of the mouths.
45. *British Quarterly Review* 16 (Aug 1852), p. 218.
46. *Fraser's* 46 (Aug 1852), pp. 235, 234.
47. *Les Beaux-Arts*, p. 39.
48. Tom Taylor, *Punch* 22 (22 May 1852), pp. 216–17. Ruskin, in a dozen published references to these two paintings, only once mentions the face of a figure (34, 167).
49. *Works 14*, 107, 54, 14, 162, 233–4, 9.
50. *Works 12*, 334 (letter to *The Times*, 25 May 1854).
51. *Works 16*, 363–4 Brown, catalogue to his Piccadilly exhibition, p. 9, quoted by A. Staley, p. 35. See also *Works 14*, 153 (1858), '. . . the humblest subjects are pathetic when Pre-Raphaelitically rendered'.
52. *Works 14*, 23.
53. *Works 14*, 236–7.
54. *Works 5*, 52. Compare a letter of Ruskin's (*Sublime & Instructive*, ed. V. Surtees, 1972, p. 239) wishing that he could praise Ford Madox Brown's work, 'seeing that he is an entirely worthy fellow. But pictures are pictures, and things that ar'nt ar'nt [sic].'
55. *Works 5*, 53–4.
56. *La Bible d'Amiens*, translated and introduced by M. Proust (Paris, 1904), p. 80. Although Proust is referring primarily to *The Bible of Amiens*, he adds that 'le péché était commis d'une façon constante . . .'
57. *Quarterly Review* 98 (March 1856), p. 429.
58. *Works 14*, 468.
59. T. Hall Caine, *Recollections of Rossetti* (1928), p. 101.
60. Quoted in W. M. Rossetti, *Dante Gabriel Rossetti, his family-letters, with a memoir* (1895), vol. I, p. 95.
61. Ibid., p. 96.
62. *Letters of Dante Gabriel Rossetti*, ed. O. Doughty and J. R. Wahl (1965), p. 105; partially quoted by W. M. Rossetti (1895), vol. I, p. 180.
63. W. M. Rossetti (ed.), *Ruskin: Rossetti: Preraphaelitism, papers 1854 to 1862* (1899), pp. 110, 107–8, 184.
64. Ibid., pp. 38–9.
65. Ibid., p. 72.
66. The opposite view has been taken by Joan Evans (*John Ruskin*, 1854, p. 208): '. . . Rossetti was a cold-hearted amorist, incapable of simple friendship.'
67. T. Hall Caine, *Recollections of Rossetti* (1928), p. 86.
68. Thomas Sulman, 'A Memorable Art Class', *Good Words* 38 (Aug 1897), pp. 549–50.
69. *Works 7*, 233.

70. *Works 35*, 597.
71. *Journals and Correspondence of Lady Eastlake*, ed. C. E. Smith (1895), vol. 2, p. 276.
72. [Robert Hichens], *The Green Carnation* (1894), pp. 57–9.

*Chapter 9*

1. R. H. Wilenski's study of Ruskin as 'a manic-depressive invalid' (1933) summarises Ruskin's first fifty years under the heading of 'Prologue'; for Wilenski, 'The Play' begins in 1870. J. D. Rosenberg's book *The Darkening Glass* (1961) similarly devotes more attention to the second half of Ruskin's life than to the first.
2. *Works 29*, 89 and *35*, 495–6.
3. *Works 7*, 264.
4. *Works 7*, xl (letter to John James Ruskin).
5. Letter of 3 May 1862 to R. N. Wornum, Keeper of the National Gallery. On the same day, Ruskin sent a second letter to Wornum, informing him that he had just signed a new will leaving some £35,000 to the National Gallery; the interest from this sum was to be used to buy pictures 'by Titian, Paul Veronese, Velasquez, or Sir Joshua Reynolds'. Wornum replied on 7 May, 'I laid your two valuable letters with much pleasure before my Board yesterday, and all were much pleased'. These three letters are in the library of the National Gallery.
6. *Works 16*, 310.
7. Letter of 5 Nov 1860, quoted in *Works 36*, 348.
8. *Works 10*, 194.
9. *Works 12*, lxxx.
10. Ruskin did not smoke, and discouraged others from smoking in his house. However, he often presented boxes of cigars to Carlyle; and the Ruskin Collection at Bembridge, Isle of Wight, includes a packet of American-made 'John Ruskin' cigars, with 'Perfecto Extra' inscribed beneath his full-bearded portrait. See J. Dearden, *Facets of Ruskin* (1970), p. 128.
11. *Works 12*, lxxxii.
12. *Works 5*, 427.
13. *Works 17*, 35.
14. *Works 17*, 44.
15. *Works 17*, 47.
16. For this statistic and the subsequent conclusions, I am indebted to Geoffrey Best, *Mid-Victorian Britain 1851–75* (1971).
17. *Works 16*, 339.
18. *Works 18*, 428 (from *The Crown of Wild Olive*).
19. *Works 27*, 167.
20. *Works 27*, 116.
21. George Bernard Shaw, *Ruskin's Politics* (1921), p. 30.
22. *Works 18*, 435.
23. Letter to Margaret Bell, quoted in *The Winnington Letters*, ed. van Akin Burd (1969), p. 403.

24. *Works 36*, 476.
25. *The Winnington Letters*, p. 391.
26. Ibid., p. 403.
27. W. M. Rossetti, *Rossetti Papers, 1862 to 1870* (1903), p. 495.
28. *Works 18*, 51.
29. *Works 18*, 122−3.
30. *Works 18*, 128.
31. *Works 18*, 129.
32. *Works 18*, 125.
33. *Works 18*, 469.
34. *Works 18*, 480.

*Chapter 10*

1. Quoted in D. Leon, *Ruskin the Great Victorian* (1949), p. 359.
2. *Works 37*, 168.
3. *The Diaries of John Ruskin*, ed. J. Evans and J. H. Whitehouse (1956−9), vol. I, p. 127.
4. These entries are quoted from *The Diaries of John Ruskin*, vol. 3.
5. *Diaries*, vol. 3, pp. 840, 856, 892, 1054, 1056. To avoid repetition, Ruskin even devised a code, using a familiar set of initials: 'Pouring rain with black wind from East' (or West) was to be written 'P.R.B.E.' (or 'P.R.B.W.') − see vol. 3, p. 853.
6. *Diaries*, vol. 3, p. 799.
7. *Works 33*, 509−10.
8. *Works 27*, 283.
9. *Works 27*, 127, 168.
10. *Works 27*, 96.
11. *Works 29*, 160.
12. See *The Diary of Albert Goodwin, R.W.S., 1883−1927* (printed for private circulation, 1934), p. 105, and R. H. Wilenski, *John Ruskin* (1933), p. 138.
13. *Works 19*, 79, and *18*, lxx.
14. *Works 32*, 109, and see *32* plate VIII.
15. For this and the following quotations, see *Works 22*, 82−98.
16. This picture (N.G. no. 812) was given to the National Gallery in 1870 by Ruskin's old enemy, Lady Eastlake. The current National Gallery catalogue ascribes it only tentatively to Giovanni Bellini.
17. *Works 19*, 107−19.
18. *Works 23*, 323.
19. *Works 37*, 371 (letter to Rev. J. P. Faunthorpe, 20 July 1881).
20. *Diaries*, vol. 3, pp. 1085−6.
21. *Diaries*, vol. 3, p. 858.
22. *Works 35*, 562.

# Bibliography

Abbott, C. C., *The Life and Letters of George Darley* (Oxford University Press, 1928).

Aberdeen, George Hamilton Gordon, 4th Earl of Aberdeen, *An Inquiry into the Principles of Beauty in Grecian Architecture* (1822).

Abrams, Meyer H., *The Mirror and the Lamp* (New York, W. W. Norton, 1953).

Aikin, Edmund, 'An Essay on Modern Architecture', *Essays of the London Architectural Society* (1808).

——, *Designs for Villas and other Rural Buildings* (1808).

Alison, Archibald, *Essays on the Nature and Principle of Taste* (1790; 3rd ed. 1812).

Anderson, James, 'Thoughts on the Grecian and Gothic Styles of Architecture', *Recreations in Agriculture, Natural History, Arts and Miscellaneous Literature* 2–4 (1800–1); reprinted in the *Architectural Magazine* 2 (1835).

*The Art Journal, a Short History* (anon., Virtue & Co., 1906).

Barry, James, *The Works of James Barry*, 2 vols. (1809).

Barry, James, Opie, John, and Fuseli, Henry, *Lectures on Painting by Royal Academicians*, ed. R. Wornum (1848).

Bell, Sir Charles, *Essays on the Anatomy and Philosophy of Expression* (1806), 3rd (enlarged) edition 1844.

——, *The Hand: its mechanism and vital endowments as evincing design* (2nd ed. 1833).

Bell, Quentin, *Ruskin* (Oliver and Boyd, 1963; The Hogarth Press, 1978).

Best, Geoffrey, *Mid-Victorian Britain 1851–1875* (Weidenfeld & Nicolson, 1971).

Blake, William, *The Complete Writings of William Blake*, ed. G. Keynes (Nonesuch Press, 1957).

Bowe, Sister Mary C., 'François Rio, Sa place dans le renouveau catholique en Europe', *Etudes de littérature étrangère et comparée*, no. 11 (Paris, 1938).

Britton, John, *Architectural Antiquities of Great Britain*, 5 vols. (1807–26).

Brooke, Stopford, *The Life and Letters of F. W. Robertson* (1874).

Bulwer Lytton, Edward, *England and the English* (Paris, 1833).

Caine, Sir Thomas Hall, *Recollections of Rossetti* (Cassell, 1928).

Camper, Petrus, *The Works of P. Camper* (1794).

Carlyle, Thomas, *Collected Works*, 30 vols. (Centenary Edition, 1896–9).

Cattermole, Rev. Richard, *The Book of the Cartoons* (1837).

Clark, Lord, *The Gothic Revival* (Constable, 1928; John Murray, 1974).

Clarke, Basil F. L., *Church Builders of the Nineteenth Century* (S.P.C.K., 1938; David & Charles, 1969).

Cockerell, C. R., *A Description of the Collection of Ancient Marbles in the British Museum*, part 6 (1830).

Collingwood, R. G., *Ruskin's Philosophy* (Titus Wilson & Son, Kendal, 1922).

Collins, Peter, *Changing Ideals in Modern Architecture, 1750–1950* (Faber & Faber, 1965).

Combe, William, *Dr Syntax's Three Tours* (1868; first 'tour' published in 1810).

Conrad, Peter, *The Victorian Treasure House* (Collins, 1973).

Cook, Sir Edward T., *The Life of John Ruskin*, 2 vols. (George Allen & Co., 1911).

Costello, Louisa, *A Tour to and from Venice by the Vaudois and the Tyrol* (1846).

Crowe, J. A. and Cavalcaselle, G. B., *A History of Painting in North Italy . . .*, 2 vols. (1871).

Cunningham, Allan, *The Cabinet Gallery of Pictures*, 2 vols. (1833, 1834).

Dearden, James S., *Facets of Ruskin* (Charles Skilton, 1970).

De Piles, Roger, *Cours de Peinture* (Paris, 1708).

——, *The Principles of Painting* (1743).

Dickens, Charles, *Barnaby Rudge* (1841).

Donaldson, T. L., *Preliminary Discourse on Architecture* (1842).

Drummond, Henry, *A Letter to Thomas Phillips, Esq., R.A.* (1840).

Du Fresnoy, Charles A., *The Art of Painting*, translated by J. Dryden (1769).

Durandus, William, *The Symbolism of Churches and Church Ornaments*, ed. J. M. Neale and B. Webb (1843).

Early, James, *Romanticism and American Architecture* (New York, A. S. Barnes & Co., 1965).

Eastlake, Sir Charles L., *Contributions to the Literature of the Fine Arts*, 2 series (1848 and 1870).

Eastlake, Charles L. (the younger), *A History of the Gothic Revival* (1872, reprinted by Leicester University Press, 1970).

Eastlake, Lady Elizabeth (née Rigby), *Journals and Correspondence of Lady Eastlake*, ed. C. E. Smith, 2 vols. (1895).

Elmes, James (ed.), *The Magazine of the Fine Arts* (1821 only).

Elton, Lord Oliver, *A survey of English Literature 1830–1880*, 2 vols. (Edward Arnold, 1920).

Evans, Joan, *John Ruskin* (Cape, 1954).

Farington, Joseph, *The Farington Diary*, ed. James Greig, 8 vols. (Hutchinson & Co., 1922–8).

Fergusson, James, *An Historical Inquiry into the True Principles of Beauty in Art, more especially with reference to architecture* (1849).

Fischer, Ernst, *The Necessity of Art: A Marxist Approach*, translated by Anna Bostock (Penguin Books, 1963).

Flaxman, John, *Lectures on Sculpture* (1865).

Fleming, Gordon H., *Rossetti and the Pre-Raphaelite Brotherhood* (Hart-Davis, 1967).

——, *That Ne'er Shall Meet Again* (Michael Joseph, 1971).

Forsyth, Joseph, *Remarks on the Antiquities, Arts, Letters During our Excursion in Italy in the years 1802 and 1803* (1813; 4th ed., 1835).

Frankl, Paul, *Gothic Architecture*, translated by Sir Nikolaus Pevsner (Penguin Books, 1962).

Fredeman, William E., *Pre-Raphaelitism. A bibliocritical study* (Cambridge, Mass., Harvard University Press, 1965).

Freeman, Edward A., *A History of Architecture* (1849).

Fuseli, Henry, et al., *Lectures on Painting by Royal Academicians*, ed. R. Wornum (1848).

——, *The Life and Writings of H. Fuseli*, ed. J. Knowles, 3 vols. (1831).

Garbett, Edward L., *Rudimentary Treatise on the Principles of Design in Architecture* (1850).

Gardner, Percy, 'The Lamps of Greek Art', in *The Legacy of Greece*, ed. R. W. Livingstone (Oxford University Press, 1921); reprinted in P. Gardner and Sir R. Blomfield, *Greek Art and Architecture* (Oxford University Press, 1922).

Gautier, Théophile, *Les Beaux-Arts en Europe* (Paris, 1855).

Gilchrist, Alexander, *The Life of William Etty, R.A.*, 2 vols. (1855).

Gilpin, William, *Three Essays on Picturesque Beauty* (1792).

——, *Moral Contrasts* (1798).

Gombrich, Sir Ernst, *Meditations on a Hobby-Horse and other essays on the theory of art* (Phaidon Press, 1963).

——, *In Search of Cultural History* (Oxford University Press, 1969).

Goodwin, Albert, *The Diary of Albert Goodwin, R.W.S., 1883– 1927* (printed for private circulation, 1934).

Gordon-Taylor, Sir G., and Walls, E. W., *Sir Charles Bell. His Life and Times* (Edinburgh & London, E. & S. Livingstone, 1958).

Gunn, William, *Cartonensia* (1831).

Hall, Samuel C., *Retrospect of a Long Life* (1883).

Harding, J. D., *The Principles and Practice of Art* (1845).

Hatfield, H. C., *Winckelmann and his German Critics* (New York, King's Crown Press, 1963).

Hauser, Arnold, *The Social History of Art*, 4 vols. (Routledge and Kegan Paul, 1962).

Haydon, Benjamin R., *Lectures on Painting and Design*, 2 vols. (1844–6).

——, 'Painting and the Fine Arts', *Encyclopaedia Britannica* (1838).

Hayley, William, *The Life of George Romney, Esq.* (1809).

Hazlitt, William, *The Complete Works of William Hazlitt*, ed. P. P. Howe (J. M. Dent & Sons, 1933).

Herbert, R. L., Introduction to *The Art Criticism of John Ruskin*, ed. R. L. Herbert (Anchor Books, 1964).

Hewison, Robert, *John Ruskin: the Argument of the Eye* (Thames & Hudson, 1976).

Hichens, Robert, *The Green Carnation* (1894).

Hilton, Timothy, *The Pre-Raphaelites* (Thames & Hudson, 1970).

Hitchcock, Henry-Russell, *Early Victorian Architecture in Britain*, 2 vols. (Architectural Press, 1954).

Hogarth, William, *The Analysis of Beauty*, ed. J. Burke (The Clarendon Press, 1955: a facsimile of the 1st ed. of 1753).

Hope, Thomas, *A Historical Essay on Architecture*, 2nd ed. (1835).

Hough, Graham, *The Last Romantics* (Duckworth, 1947; Methuen, 1961).

Huizinga, Johan, 'The Task of Cultural History', in *Men and Ideas*, translated by J. Holmes and H. van Marle (Eyre and Spottiswoode, 1960).

Hussey, Christopher E. C., *The Picturesque* (G. P. Putnam's Sons, London & New York, 1927; Frank Cass, 1967).

Jackson, Sir Thomas Graham, *Recollections of Thomas Graham Jackson*, ed. B. H. Jackson (Oxford University Press, 1950).

James, Rev. John T., *The Italian Schools of Painting* (1820).

James, Admiral Sir William, *The Order of Release* (John Murray, 1948).

Jameson, Anna B., *The Diary of an Ennuyée*, new ed. (Paris, 1836); first published as *A Lady's Diary* (1826).

——, *The Diary of a Désennuyée* (Paris, 1836).

——, *A Handbook to the Public Galleries of Art in and near London* (1842).

——, *Companion to the most celebrated private galleries of art in London . . . With a prefatory essay on Art, Artists, Collectors and Connoisseurs* (1844).

——, *Memoirs of the Early Italian Painters*, 2 vols. (1845).

——, *Sacred and Legendary Art*, 2 vols. (1848).

——, *Legends of the Monastic Orders, as represented in the Fine Arts* (1850; second and enlarged ed. 1852).

——, *Legends of the Madonna, as represented in the Fine Arts* (1852).

Jullian, Philippe, *Dreamers of Decadence* (Pall Mall, 1971).

Kerr, Robert, *The Newleafe Discourses on the Fine Art Architecture* (1846).

Kerrich, Thomas, 'Some Observations on the Gothic Buildings abroad, particularly those in Italy; and on Gothic architecture in general', *Archaeologia*, 16 (1812).

Knight, Richard Payne, *The Landscape, a Didactic Poem* (1794).

——, *An Analytical Inquiry into the Principles of Taste* (1805).

Kugler, Franz T., *A Handbook of the History of Painting from the age of Constantine the Great to the present time* (translated by Mrs M. Hutton), part I: 'The Italian Schools', ed. C. L. Eastlake (1842).

Ladd, Henry, *The Victorian Morality of Art: An Analysis of Ruskin's Esthetic* (New York, R. Long & R. R. Smith, 1932).

Landow, George P., *The Aesthetic and Critical Theories of John Ruskin* (Princeton Univ. Press, 1971).

Landseer, John, *Twenty Engravings of Lions* (1823).

——, *A Descriptive, Explanatory, and Critical Catalogue of fifty of the Earliest pictures contained in the National Gallery of Great Britain* (1834).

Lanzi, Luigi, *Storia pittorica della Italia* (Florence, 1792); translated by Thomas Roscoe as *The History of Painting in Italy* (6 vols., 1828).

Leon, Derrick, *Ruskin, the Great Victorian* (Routledge and Kegan Paul, 1949 and 1977).

Leslie, Charles Robert, *Memoirs of the Life of John Constable* (1st ed. 1843; 2nd and enlarged ed. 1845, reprinted by Phaidon Press 1951).

——, *A Hand-book for Young Painters* (1855).

——, *Autobiographical Recollections of the late C. R. Leslie, R.A.*, ed. Tom Taylor (1860).

Lewis, George Robert, *Illustrations of Kilpeck Church* (1842).

Lindsay, Alexander W. Crawford, 25th Earl of Crawford (Lord Lindsay), *Progression by Antagonism* (1846).

——, *Sketches of the History of Christian Art*, 3 vols. (1847).

Lindsay, Jack, *J. M. W. Turner, his life and work* (Cory, Adams & Mackay, 1966).

Loudon, John Claudius, *A Treatise on Forming, Improving and Managing Country Residences* (1806).

——, *An Encyclopaedia of Cottage, Farm and Village Architecture* (1833).

Lutyens, Mary, *Effie in Venice* (John Murray, 1965).

——, *Millais and the Ruskins* (John Murray, 1967).

——, *The Ruskins and the Grays* (John Murray, 1972).

Macpherson, Gerardine, *Memoirs of the Life of Anna Jameson* (1878).

Matthews, Henry, *The Diary of an Invalid* (1820).

Mengs, Anton R., *The Works of A. R. Mengs* (1796).

Millett, Kate, *Sexual Politics* (Hart Davis, 1971).

Monkhouse, W. Cosmo, *Pictures by Sir Charles Eastlake* (1875).

Morris, William, *The Unpublished Lectures of William Morris*, ed. E. D. Lemire (Detroit, Wayne State University Press, 1969).

Muthesius, Stefan, *The High Victorian Movement in Architecture 1850–1870* (Routledge & Kegan Paul, 1972).

Nicholson, Peter, *Encyclopaedia of Architecture*, ed. E. Lomax and T. Gunyon (1852).

Opie, John, et al., *Lectures on Painting by Royal Academicians*, ed. R. Wornum (1848).

Oppé, A. Paul, 'Art', in *Early Victorian England, 1830–1865*, ed. George M. Young, vol. 2 (Oxford University Press, 1934).

Paley, Frederick A., *A Manual of Gothic Architecture* (1846).

Pardo de Figueroa, Benito, *An Analysis of the Picture of the Transfiguration of Raphael* (1833).

Passavant, Johann D., *The Tour of a German Artist in England, with Notices of Private Galleries and Remarks on the State of Art*, 2 vols. in 1 (1838).

Patmore, Coventry, *Principle in Art*, etc. (1889). (Essays reprinted from the *St James's Gazette*.)

Penrose, Francis C., *An Investigation into the Principles of Athenian Architecture* (1851).

Petit, John L., *Remarks on Architectural Character* (1846).

Pevsner, Sir Nikolaus, 'Reflections on Not Teaching Art History', *Listener* 48 (1952).

——, *The Englishness of English Art* (Architectural Press, 1956).

——, *Studies in Art, Architecture and Design*, 2 vols. (Thames & Hudson, 1968).

——, *Robert Willis* (Smith College, Northampton, U.S.A., Studies in History XLVI, 1970).

——, *Some Architectural Writers of the Nineteenth Century* (Oxford, The Clarendon Press, 1972).

Pilkington, Matthew, *A Dictionary of Painters*, ed. H. Fuseli (1805).

Poole, G. Ayliffe, *The Appropriate Character of Church Architecture* (1842).

——, *A History of Ecclesiastical Architecture in England* (1848).

Prescott, William H., *History of the Conquest of Peru*, 2 vols. (1847).

Price, Lake, *Interiors and Exteriors in Venice* (1843).

Price, Sir Uvedale, *An Essay on the Picturesque as compared with the Sublime and the Beautiful*, 2 vols. (1794–8).

——, *Sir Uvedale Price on the Picturesque, with an enquiry on the origin of taste, and much original matter, by Sir T. P. Lauder* (Edinburgh, 1842).

Proust, Marcel, Introduction to Ruskin, *La Bible d'Amiens*, translated by M. Proust (Paris, 1904).

Pugin, Augustus Welby Northmore, *Contrasts* (1836; 2nd and revised ed. 1841, reprinted by Leicester University Press, 1969).

——, *The True Principles of Pointed or Christian Architecture* (1841, reprinted by Academy Editions, 1973).

Quatremère de Quincy, Antoine C., *An Essay on . . . Imitation in the Fine Arts*, translated by J. C. Kent (1837).

——, *History of the Life and Works of Raffaello*, translated from the third Paris edition by William Hazlitt (1846).

Ralph, Benjamin, *The School of Raphael: Or the student's Guide to Expression in Historical Painting* (1819).

Reynolds, Sir Joshua, *The Works of Sir Joshua Reynolds, Knight*, ed. E. Malone, 3 vols. (1798).

——, *The Characters of the Most Celebrated Painters of Italy* (1816).

Richardson, Jonathan (the elder), *The Works of Mr Jonathan Richardson*, ed. J. Richardson (1773).

Rio, Alexis-François, *De la Poésie Chrétienne, dans son principe, dans sa matière et dans ses formes* (Paris, 1836); translated as *The Poetry of Christian Art* (1854).

Rippingille, Edward V. (ed.), The *Artist and Amateur's Magazine* (1843 only).

Robinson, Peter F., *Designs for Ornamental Villas, the Scenic Views chiefly by J. D. Harding* (1827; 3rd ed., 1836).

Roe, Frederick C., *Taine et l'Angleterre* (Paris, 1923).

Rosenberg, John D., *The Darkening Glass* (Routledge & Kegan Paul, 1963).

Rossetti, Dante Gabriel, *Letters of Dante Gabriel Rossetti*, ed. O. Doughty and J. R. Wahl, 4 vols. (Clarendon Press, Oxford, 1965–7).

——, ed. W. M. Rossetti, *Ruskin: Rossetti: Preraphaelitism, papers 1854 to 1862* (1899).

——, ed. W. M. Rossetti, *Dante Gabriel Rossetti, his family-letters, with a memoir* (1895).

——, ed. W. M. Rossetti, *Rossetti Papers, 1862 to 1870* (1903).

Ruskin, John, *The Works of John Ruskin*, ed. Sir Edward T. Cook and Alexander Wedderburn, 39 vols. (George Allen, 1903–12).

——, *The Diaries of John Ruskin*, ed. Joan Evans and John H. Whitehouse, 3 vols. (Oxford, The Clarendon Press, 1956–9).

——, *Ruskin's Letters from Venice 1851–1852*, ed. J. L. Bradley: Yale Studies in English, vol. CXXIX (New Haven, Yale University Press, 1955).

——, *The Ruskin Family Letters*, ed. van Akin Burd, 2 vols. (Cornell University Press, 1973).

——, *Ruskin in Italy, Letters to his parents 1845*, ed. Harold I. Shapiro (Clarendon Press, Oxford, 1972).

——, *The Winnington Letters of John Ruskin*, ed. van Akin Burd (Allen & Unwin, 1969).

Ruskin, John, *Sublime and Instructive: Letters, 1855–64*, ed. Virginia Surtees (Michael Joseph, 1972).

——, Bodleian Library, Oxford, MS Eng. misc. c. 209–249, and MS Eng. lett. c. 32–52.

Sandford, Sir Daniel K., 'The Rise and Progress of Literature' in the *Penny Cyclopaedia*, vol. 4 (1841), and in John Potter, *Archaeologia Graeca*, new ed. (1844).

Schelling, F. W. J., *On the Relationship of the Creative Arts to Nature* (The Catholic Series, 1845).

Schiller, J. C. F., *The Philosophical Letters and Essays of Schiller*, translated by J. Weiss (The Catholic Series, 1845).

Schlegel, C. W. F., *The Aesthetic and Miscellaneous Works of Frederick von Schlegel*, translated by E. J. Millington (1849).

Scott, Geoffrey, *The Architecture of Humanism* (Constable & Co., 1914).

Scott, Sir George Gilbert, *Remarks on Secular & Domestic Architecture, Present & Future* (1857).

——, *Personal and Professional Recollections*, ed. G. G. Scott (1879).

Seroux d'Agincourt, J. B. L. G., *Histoire de l'art par les Monumens . . .*, 6 vols. (1810–23); translated as *History of Art by its Monuments*, 3 vols. (1847).

Shee, Sir Martin Archer, *Elements of Art*, a Poem (1809).

Soane, Sir John, *Lectures on Architecture 1809–36*, ed. A. T. Bolton (Soane Museum Publications no. 14, 1929).

Staley, Allen, *Pre-Raphaelite Landscape* (Oxford, The Clarendon Press, 1973).

Stephen, Sir Leslie, 'Ruskin', in *Studies of a Biographer*, 2nd series, vol. 3 (Duckworth & Co., 1902).

Symonds, John A., *The Principles of Beauty* (1857).

Taylor, Tom, *The Life of B. R. Haydon*, 3 vols. (1853).

Townsend, F. G., *Ruskin and the Landscape Feeling* (University of Illinois Press, Urbana, 1951).

Varley, John, *A Treatise on Zodiacal Physiognomy* (1828).

Vasari, Giorgio, *Lives of the most Eminent Painters, Sculptors, and Architects*, translated by Mrs J. Foster, 6 vols. (1850–5).

——, *Life of the Florentine Painter and Architect, Raphael Sanzio of Urbino*, translated by Mrs. J. Foster (1866).

Viljoen, Helen G., *Ruskin's Scottish Heritage* (University of Illinois Press, 1956).

Waagen, G. F., *Works of Art and Artists in England*, translated by H. E. Lloyd, 3 vols. (1838).

Walker, Alexander, *Beauty, illustrated chiefly by an analysis and classification of beauty in woman* (1836; 2nd ed., 1846).

Walpole, Horace, *The Yale Edition of Horace Walpole's Correspondence*, ed. W. S. Lewis (Oxford University Press, 1937– ).

Weale, John (ed.), *Quarterly Papers on Architecture* (1843–5).

Webb, Benjamin, *Sketches of Continental Ecclesiology* (1848).

Webb, Daniel, *An Inquiry into the Beauties of Painting* (1760).

——, *Miscellanies* (1802).

Whewell, William, *Architectural Notes on German Churches* (Cambridge, 1830; 2nd ed. 1835).

——, *Notes written during an architectural tour in Picardy and Normandy* (1835).

White, James E., *The Cambridge Movement, the Ecclesiologists and the Gothic Revival* (Cambridge University Press, 1962).

Whitehouse, John H., *Vindication of Ruskin* (Allen & Unwin, 1950).

Whitley, W. T., *Art in England 1821–1837* (Cambridge University Press, 1930).

Whittington, G. D., *A Historical Survey of the Ecclesiastical Antiquities of France* (1809).

Wightwick, George, *The Palace of Architecture* (1840).

Wilenski, Reginald H., *John Ruskin* (Faber & Faber, 1933).

Wilkins, William, *The Antiquities of Magna Graecia* (1807).

Williams, Raymond, *Culture and Society 1780–1950* (Chatto and Windus, 1958; Penguin Books, 1963).

Willis, Robert, *Remarks on the Architecture of the Middle Ages, especially of Italy* (1835).

——, 'On the Characteristic Interpenetrations of the Flamboyant Style', *Transactions of the R.I.B.A.* (1842).

Winckelmann, Joachim, *Reflections on the Painting and Sculpture of the Greeks*, translated by H. Fuseli (1765).

——, *The History of Ancient Art among the Greeks*, translated by H. Lodge (1850); another ed., 2 vols. (1880).

Wittkower, Rudolf, *Architectural Principles in the Age of Humanism* (Studies of the Warburg Institute, 1949).

——, 'Imitation, Eclecticism and Genius', in *Aspects of the Eighteenth Century*, ed. E. R. Wasserman (Johns Hopkins Press, 1965).

Woods, Joseph, *Letters of an Architect from France, Italy, and Greece*, 2 vols. (1828).

Wordsworth, William, *A Guide to the District of the Lakes* (enlarged 5th edition, 1835).

Young, George M. (ed.), *Early Victorian England*, 2 vols. (Oxford University Press, 1934).

# Index